THE PHOTOSHOP ANTHOLOGY

101 WEB DESIGN TIPS, TRICKS & TECHNIQUES

BY CORRIE HAFFLY

Published by SitePoint Pty. Ltd.

424 Smith Street Collingwood

VIC Australia 3066.

Web: www.sitepoint.com

Email: business@sitepoint.com

ISBN 0-9758419-2-0

Printed and bound in Canada

About the Author

Corrie Haffly has been using Photoshop to create web graphics since building her first web page in 1998. After graduating from UC Davis, Corrie worked as a designer for Advantrics LLC, where she brought their PixelMill and John Galt's Templates brands to lead the web site template market. Corrie now works as a freelance web designer in Davis, California.

About the Expert Reviewer

Mark Larmand is a veteran web and graphics designer with over 150 sites to his credit. He's also the author at, and owner of, "The Photoshop Guru's Handbook" tutorials web site, at http://www.photoshopgurus.com, which has been online since 1996. As well, he's been a freelance web and graphics article writer for sites such as sitepoint.com, webdevelopersjournal.com, and Graphics.com.

About the Technical Editor

Before joining the SitePoint team as a technical editor, Matthew Magain worked as a software developer for IBM and also spent several years teaching English in Japan. He is the organizer for Melbourne's Web Standards Group, and enjoys swimming, listening to classical jazz and drinking Coopers Pale Ale, though not all at the same time. Matthew lives with his wife Kimberley and their daughter Sophia.

About the Technical Director

As Technical Director for SitePoint, Kevin Yank oversees all of its technical publications—books, articles, newsletters and blogs. He has written over 50 articles for SitePoint, but is best known for his book, *Build Your Own Database Driven Website using PHP & MySQL*. Kevin lives in Melbourne, Australia, and enjoys performing improvised comedy theatre and flying light aircraft.

About SitePoint

SitePoint specializes in publishing fun, practical, and easy-to-understand content for web professionals. Visit http://www.sitepoint.com to access our books, newsletters, articles, and community forums.

Acknowledgements

Many thanks to Simon, Matt, Priya, and all of the wonderful and cheery SitePoint team for giving me the chance to write this book and for the time and encouragement that they invested in the process.

Thanks also to Jason, Greg, and Eric, first, for believing in the potential of a young mathematics major with a flimsy resume; second, for suggesting that I submit an article to SitePoint (which started all of this); and finally, for their unbelievably flexible and supportive working relationship.

Thanks to Angela, for introducing her kid sister to computer graphics programs, and Leslie, for setting up free travel, room and board, and the summer internship that would introduce me to web design.

I also want to thank the Biggs family (in whose house much of this book was written) for their friendship and generosity, and the Wiekings and Toones for graciously allowing me to use photos of their cute children for some of the examples.

Thanks to my family, especially to my parents, who sacrificed for me and taught me how to work hard, and to Steve, for believing in me, loving me, and giving me an excuse to take breaks.

Finally, I thank the One who has blessed me with every good gift and is my source of inspiration.

Table of Contents

Preface

This book is a resource for web designers who want to use Photoshop to create better-looking web graphics.

Unlike the many other web-related Photoshop books on the market, this book does not encourage you to use Photoshop's generated HTML code, which, as of this writing, does not use semantic markup or conform to W3C guidelines. I view Photoshop as only one of many tools in the web development process; knowledge of how to actually *code* a web site using HTML, CSS, and other web languages is equally important but is not covered in this book, which is strictly about *using Photoshop to create graphics for web sites*. I encourage you to look into the many other resources, both in online and book form, that will teach you the basics of web development if you need to pick up skills in those areas.

Unlike other Photoshop books geared towards web designers, this book comes with downloadable files that you can also create yourself, following my instructions! Many of the glossy, colorful books already on the market have stunning web graphics, but provide them in nearly-complete source files that are designed to help you learn a basic principle in Photoshop, but do not actually show you how to create those graphic effects yourself. This book was written to give you some of *the building blocks and techniques* that will help you to create your own cool web graphics. There's no need to dedicate several hours each week to work through an extensive "project"—the anthology format of this title allows you to quickly look up a task or effect you're curious about, and accomplish it immediately, following clearly outlined instructions.

There are hundreds of online tutorials about creating various web graphic effects in Photoshop. This book shows you how to create many of those same effects, but most solutions include a "Discussion" section that goes beyond the "step-by-step" stage to explain some of *the concepts behind the solution*, enabling you to understand more of how Photoshop works so that you can apply that knowledge in other situations. One of the most valuable solutions in this book, and which can be found at the beginning of Chapter 8, gives you a conceptual "road map" of how to use Photoshop in the web design process and illustrates it with an example that combines many of the techniques explained in earlier chapters (see Chapter 8, *Designing a Web Site*).

Because this book is focused towards web designers, I cover only some of the basic and intermediate tasks related to photo adjustments and retouching. If this area interests you, there are many excellent books, geared towards professional photographers and artists, which provide more advanced instruction than does this title.

My primary hope is that this book will help you to build up the skills and knowledge you need to become comfortable and confident while using Photoshop to create web graphics. Good luck, and have fun!

Who Should Read this Book?

This book is ideal for all web designers working with Photoshop: if you're new to the application, there's enough beginner material here to give you a great grounding in the basics, but if you've got a bit more experience up your sleeve, there's coverage of a multitude of advanced tutorials for you to get your designs looking beautiful.

What Version of Photoshop do I Need?

Most of the techniques in the book will work regardless of the version of Adobe Photoshop that you're using. However, the book is intended for web designers using Photoshop CS2, and there are some solutions that make use of the newer features in this version. Some of the shortcuts differ between versions of Photoshop, so keep this in mind if you're working with an older version.

What's in this Book?

Chapter 1: Getting Started with Photoshop

If you're brand new to Photoshop, come here to learn about how to get around. If you're not brand new, you may still enjoy the time-saving tips included in these pages.

Chapter 2: Basic Skills

Build a good foundation for your use of Photoshop with these basic skills, including resizing, rotating, and hiding parts of your picture.

Chapter 3: Creating Buttons

Make buttons of every shape and style by following the solutions in this chapter.

Chapter 4: Creating Backgrounds

Create tiling backgrounds that you can use in design elements such as headings and menu bars, or even the page background itself!

Chapter 5: Working with Text

Learn to adjust type settings and make cool text effects for your next logo or web graphic.

Chapter 6: Adjusting Images

Fix, salvage, and adjust photographs that are over-exposed, under-exposed, or just dull-looking. Or, take a good photograph and make it look even better!

Chapter 7: Manipulating Images

Start with a photograph or image and add your own effects such as scanlines, reflections, and more!

Chapter 8: Designing a Web Site

Bringing all the skills from previous chapters together, this chapter shows you how to create web design mockups in Photoshop, then generate web-optimized images.

Chapter 9: Advanced Photoshop Techniques

Automate and animate! This chapter shows you how to save time when performing similar tasks on many different files, then shows you how to use Photoshop and ImageReady to create animations.

The Book's Web Site

Located at http://www.sitepoint.com/books/photoshop1/, the web site supporting this book will give you access to the following facilities.

The File Archive

The file archive is a downloadable ZIP archive that contains all of the examples presented in the book as PSD files. It contains a file for every example covered, including original photos used and final versions. You can get it from http://www.sitepoint.com/books/photoshop1/archive.php.

Updates and Errata

The Corrections and Typos page on the book's web site will always have the latest information about known typographical and code errors, and necessary updates. Visit it at http://www.sitepoint.com/books/photoshop1/errata.php.

The SitePoint Forums

While we've made every attempt to anticipate any questions you may have, and answer them in this book, there's no way that *any* book could teach you everything you'll ever need to know about using Photoshop. So, if you have a question about anything in this book, or about the implementation of the techniques you've learned here in other projects, the best place to go for a quick, helpful and friendly answer is http://www.sitepoint.com/forums/—SitePoint's vibrant and knowledgeable community.

The SitePoint Newsletters

In addition to books like this one, SitePoint offers free email newsletters.

The SitePoint Tech Times covers the latest news, product releases, trends, tips, and techniques for all technical aspects of web development. The long-running SitePoint Tribune is a biweekly digest of the business and moneymaking aspects of the Web. Whether you're a freelance developer looking for tips to score that dream contract, or a marketer striving to keep abreast of changes to the major search engines, this is the newsletter for you. The SitePoint Design View is a monthly compilation of the best in web design. Covering everything from new CSS layout methods to subtle Photoshop techniques, the newsletter delivers a wealth of practical information compiled by SitePoint's chief designer.

Browse the archives or sign up to any of SitePoint's free newsletters at http://www.sitepoint.com/newsletter/.

Your Feedback

If you can't find an answer through the forums, or you wish to contact us for any other reason, the best place to write is books@sitepoint.com. We have a friendly and helpful email support team available to help you with your inquiries, and if our staff are unable to answer your question, they send it straight to the author. Suggestions for improvement, as well as notices of any mistakes you may find, are especially welcome.

Getting Started with Photoshop

You've heard of Photoshop, right? Of course you have—you wouldn't be reading this book otherwise! You've probably heard of Photoshop's sidekick, ImageReady, too, but you might not be quite sure of what it does or where it fits in.

Photoshop and ImageReady are two of the most commonly used tools in the web designer's arsenal. From the preparation of initial design comps to generating optimized graphics for a web page, most web designers rely heavily on these two programs.

In this introductory chapter, I'll cover some of the basic tools and tasks that we'll draw on in the later chapters. I'll also share some of the shortcuts and time-savers that I use frequently. This chapter won't give you an exhaustive review of the many things that Photoshop can do (where would it end!), but it should provide the bare bones that will help get beginners started. If you're already familiar with the interface and can perform tasks like making selections, applying gradients, and working with layers, you might want to skip ahead to the next chapter.

So what are you waiting for? Open up Photoshop and let's go!

rushes

rush Presets

rush Tip Shape

] Shape Dynamics
] Scattering
] Texture
] Dual Brush
] Color Dynamics
] Other Dynamics
] Noise
] Wet Edges
] Airbrush
] Smoothing
] Protect Texture

1	2	3	4	5
7	8	9	10	11
14	16	18	20	22
164	85	40	45	90

Diameter   Use Sample Size

☐ Flip X ☐ Flip Y

Angle: 0°

Roundness: 100%

Hardness

☑ Spacing   165%

100%   Doc: 398.4K/1.36M

The Photoshop Workspace

Photoshop's "out of the box" workspace consists of the following components:

- **options bar**

  You will probably already be familiar with the **menu bar** from other programs. This runs across the top of your Photoshop window, and contains various menu options for Photoshop's tools.

- **options bar**

  The **options bar** sits beneath the menu bar and holds contextualized options for different tools. It also contains the **palette well**, where you can "dock" palettes.

- **toolbox**

  By default, the **toolbox** sits to the left of your Photoshop window, and contains shortcuts to Photoshop tools.

- **palettes**

  Individual "panes" that hold information or options for working with your file, known as **palettes**, float on the right-hand side. Each palette is labeled with a tab, and can be minimized, closed, grouped with other palettes, or dragged to the palette well. In the example at the top of the next page, the Navigator palette contains a thumbnail of the image that allows you to zoom in or out of the image quickly, and to change the part of the image displayed on the screen.

- **document windows**

  Each open document has its own **document window** with a **status bar** along the bottom. The status bar sits to the right of the zoom percentage displayed in the bottom left-hand corner, and displays information that's specific to the document.

> **TIP Comps and Turtlenecks: Designer Lingo**
>
> Now that you're going to be working in Photoshop, you might want to start talking like a designer. Designers, like professionals in most specialist fields, have their own terminology and words for things. A comp (short for "composite") refers to a mockup of the final solution that a designer has in mind. Traditionally, "comp" is used in the print world to refer to page layouts, but for web designers it usually refers to a static interface prepared entirely in Photoshop for the client to look over before he or she decides to proceed. You might even hear it being used as a verb: "comping" is the process of creating that mockup site.

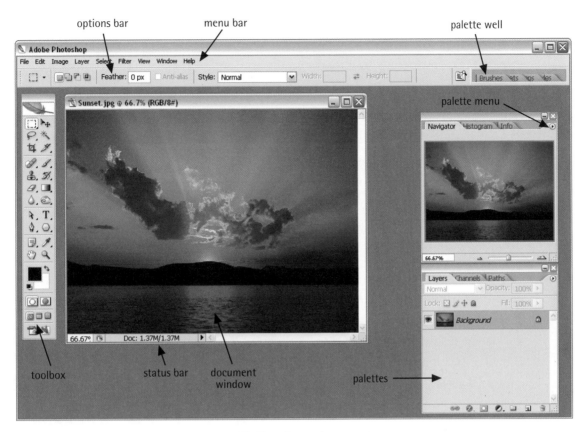

The Photoshop workspace

Customizing your Workspace

You can customize your Photoshop workspace to suit you or your project—almost everything within your workspace can be repositioned and reconfigured! You might choose to customize your workspace by:

■ **changing the look of the menu bar**

You can change which menu items are visible in your menu bar, and even add color to your menu items. If you wanted, you could also assign new or different keyboard shortcuts to menu commands (which I don't recommend until you feel *very* comfortable with Photoshop or have a compelling reason to do so!). Go to **Edit > Menus** and use the dialog box to modify the menu bar and palette menus.

■ **moving the options bar**

If you want to move the options bar, you can do so by clicking on the handle on its left side and moving it around. The options bar will "dock" to the top or bottom of the screen automatically if moved near those areas.

■ **moving the toolbox**

The toolbox is extremely portable, and can be moved to any location on your screen. Move the toolbox by clicking on the gray area at the top of it and dragging it around.

■ **rearranging palettes**

There are many ways to rearrange your palettes. You might want to separate a palette from its palette group, and move it into another group. You can do this by dragging the palette tab out of its original group and into the new group. You might also decide to drag some of your palette tabs into the palette well, and close the rest. To display a palette that has been closed, go to **Window** and select the palette you want to show.

■ **displaying different information in the document window status bar**

The status bar displays the document file size by default. The file size is shown as two numbers separated by a forward slash: the first number is an approximation of the image file size with all layers merged (known as "flattening" the image), and the second number is an approximation of the total file size of the image with layers intact. If all this sounds new to you, don't worry—we'll be discussing layers shortly. You can set the status bar to display different information, such as the document dimension in pixels, or the version number of the file. To do this, click on the arrow icon next to the status bar, select **Show** and choose the information you'd like to see.

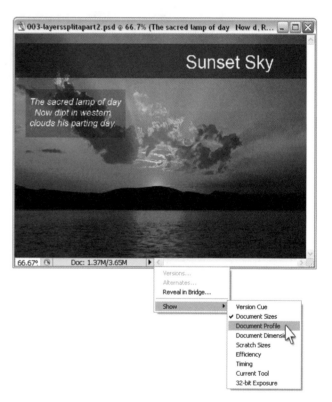

Changing the status bar

Saving your Customized Workspace

As you become more proficient with Photoshop, you may discover that you use certain sets of palettes for different types of projects, and that there are some palettes that you don't use at all. Photoshop allows you to save and load different

workspaces—different arrangements of palettes, menus, and even different keyboard shortcuts—to help you work more efficiently.

After you've customized your workspace to your satisfaction, select **Window > Workspace > Save Workspace** from the menu bar and enter a name for your workspace, such as *Creating Thumbnails* or *My Default Workspace*. You can then load your different workspaces by opening **Window > Workspace** and selecting your custom workspace from the menu list.

Working in Photoshop

Now that you've been introduced to the Photoshop workspace and have a basic idea of where everything is, let's start getting our hands dirty.

Creating New Documents

You can create a new document by selecting **File > New** from the menu bar, or pressing the keyboard shortcut *Ctrl-N* on a PC or *Command-N* on a Mac. The **New** dialog box will appear, where you can specify the document size and other settings.

The **New** dialog box

Opening Files

Open files by selecting **File > Open** from the menu bar, or pressing *Ctrl-O* (*Command-O* on a Mac). You can select and open multiple files by holding down *Ctrl* (*Command* on a Mac) and clicking on all the files you require in the file dialog box.

Saving Files

Save a file by selecting **File > Save**, or pressing *Ctrl-S* (*Command-S* on a Mac). For a newly-created document, this will save your work in *Photoshop Document* (PSD)

> **TIP   Snappy Presets**
>
> If you're designing for a web site with a minimum screen size of 800×600 pixels, I'd recommend you start with a 750×550 pixel document. The smaller dimensions give you a better estimate of your actual screen area after you take into account scroll bars and menu bars. Also, be sure to set the resolution at 72dpi to reflect the actual screen resolution.
>
> If you want easy access to these dimensions for other new documents, it's probably a good idea to click **Save Preset** and give the settings a name like *Web Page*. The next time you create a new document, you will be able to load your *Web Page* settings from the Preset list.

format. If you would prefer to save a copy of the document, you can use **File** > **Save As** or pressing *Ctrl-Shift-S* (*Command-Shift-S* on a Mac) instead.

Saving Files for the Web

Photoshop files themselves can't be embedded into a web page. You will need to export your file and save it in a web-friendly format. There are three formats for web graphics: GIFs, JPEGs, and PNGs.

- **GIF**

  The **GIF** format (pronounced "jiff" or "giff" depending on which side of the tracks you grew up) can have a maximum of 256 colors. GIF files support transparency and animation, and work best with graphics that have large areas of the same color, as shown in the logo below.

- **JPEG**

  The **JPEG** format (pronounced "jay-peg"), works best with photographic images or images that have more than 256 colors and gradients, such as the flower on the opposite page. Images saved in JPEG format are compressed, which means that image information will actually be lost, causing the image to degrade in quality.

- **PNG**

  The **PNG** format (pronounced "ping") is similar to the GIF format in that it supports transparency and works best with solid-color images like the logo

Example of an image that should be saved as GIF or PNG

shown to the right, but it's superior to the GIF format as it has the ability to

---

TIP   Double-clicking Power

As if keyboard shortcuts weren't quick enough, Windows users have even more ways to open and save files, such as:

- holding down *Ctrl* and double-clicking the work area to create new documents
- double-clicking the work area to pull up the **Open** dialog box to open files
- holding down *Alt* and double-clicking the work area to open existing files as new documents
- holding down *Ctrl-Shift* and double-clicking the work area to save documents
- holding down *Shift* and double-clicking the work area to access *Adobe Bridge*—Adobe's "control center" and file browser

The **work area** is the gray area behind the document windows. If your shortcuts aren't working, check that you are clicking on an empty spot on the work area, and not in one of the document windows or Photoshop tools! Alas, Photoshop on a Mac does not have a work area, so Mac users won't get to enjoy the goodness of double-click shortcuts.

support true levels of transparency for colored areas. Transparent PNGs are currently not in widespread use on the Web because older versions of Microsoft Internet Explorer do not support them; however, they're often used in Macromedia Flash movies. PNGs can produce a better quality image at a smaller file size than can GIFs. Photoshop allows you to save an image as a PNG-8 file (which works the same way as a GIF would with 256 colors) or a PNG-24 file (which allows for millions of colors as well as variable transparency).

To save for the Web in Photoshop, select **File > Save for Web...** or press *Ctrl-Alt-Shift-S* (*Command-Option-Shift-S* on a Mac). This will bring up the **Save For Web** dialog box shown overleaf, which will show you a preview of the image that will be exported, with its optimized size in the bottom left-hand corner. You can adjust the settings for the image using the options in the pane on the right. Choose whether you want to save the file as a GIF, JPEG, PNG-8, or PNG-24, and have a play

Example of an image that should be saved as JPEG

with the other settings, keeping an eye on the optimized file size. Try to strike a balance between the quality and file size of the image. When you're happy with your result, click **Save** and give your image a filename.

If you tried the above exercise, you're probably quite pleased with yourself for saving an image of reasonable quality at a file size significantly smaller than the original. You managed this by altering the settings in the right-hand pane, but what do these settings actually *do*?

GIF/PNG-8

■ **colors**

Adjusting this setting reduces the number of colors used in the image. This will usually make the biggest difference in the final image.

■ **dither amount and type (No Dither, Diffusion, Pattern, Noise)**

This setting has nothing to do with being nervous or agitated (although it's quite possible that you may have been a few moments ago!). Dither refers to a compression technique in which the pattern of dots is varied to give the illusion of a color gradient. Changing the dither will result in a more noticeable degradation for images that involve a large number of colors blended together.

■ **transparency**

If you want transparent areas in your graphic, check this box. We'll look more closely at transparency in Chapter 2.

■ **matte color**

For transparent images, the matte color is used to help blend the edges of your image into the background of the web page. For non-transparent images, the matte color defines the background color of the image. Using matte color with transparent images is covered in more detail in Chapter 2.

JPEG

■ **quality**

Changing the value in the **Quality** drop-down box alters the level of compression for the image. Reducing the quality may result in blurring or pixelation, but too high a setting will produce a large file that will take users too long to download. A good approach is to decrease the quality value gradually until you notice the degradation of your image becoming unacceptable. A reasonable compromise will be somewhere around this point.

Save For Web dialog box

Saving Files for the Web in ImageReady

You can optimize images for the Web in ImageReady using the **Optimize** palette, shown at right. Set the file type and options in the **Optimize** palette in advance, and when you're ready to export your web image, select **File > Save Optimized** or press *Ctrl-Alt-S* (*Command-Option-S* on a Mac). ImageReady will save the image based on the settings that you've defined.

> ### TIP   Why Two Tools?
>
> Considering that it's possible to save files for the Web in Photoshop, it's perfectly reasonable for you to wonder why ImageReady even exists! While it's true that both programs can perform many of the same tasks, there are certain things that ImageReady can do that Photoshop can't, for example, creating animated GIFs. ImageReady also makes web-specific tasks easier, and since it's a smaller program that doesn't contain the full suite of Photoshop effects, it loads more quickly than Photoshop. As you work through this book you'll come to learn which tool is more suitable for particular tasks.

Optimize palette in ImageReady

Photoshop Layers

Layers are a powerful feature of Photoshop that allow you to work on one part of an image without disturbing the rest of it. While the concept of layers may seem intimidating at first, once you get the hang of using layers you'll wonder how you ever survived without them! The examples on the next page show how the layers in the Photoshop document to the right stack together.

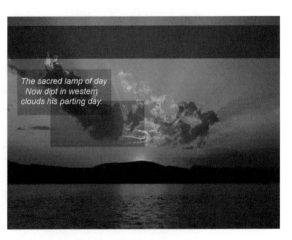

Layered Photoshop document

The transparent parts of any layer, shown by the checkered grid, allow the layers beneath that layer to show through.

You can show and hide each layer in an image by clicking on its corresponding eye icon in the **Layers** palette, as shown at the bottom of the following page.

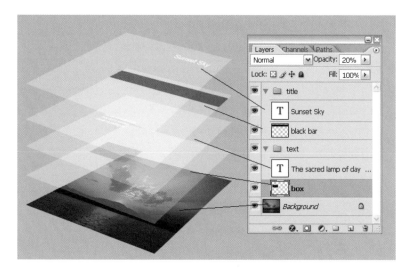

The layers in a layered Photoshop document

To organize your layers, you can arrange them into **layer groups** by going to **Layer >
New > Group....** Each layer group displays in the same way as any ungrouped layers
on the **Layers** palette. A layer group is signified by a folder icon. You can collapse or
expand layer groups by clicking on the triangle to the left of the folder icon, and nest
layer groups within each other by dragging one folder icon into another.

Hiding a layer

Layer Shortcuts and Tasks

- Rename layers by double-clicking on the layer name.
- Change the transparency of a layer by changing its opacity with the **Opacity**
  slider, or typing a value into the **Opacity** box (which is visible when you have the
  Selection, Move, or Crop tools selected).

- Duplicate a selected layer by pressing *Ctrl-J* (*Command-J* on a Mac). You can also duplicate a layer by dragging it while pressing the *Alt* (*Option*) key.

- Select multiple layers by holding down *Ctrl* (*Command* on a Mac) and clicking the layer names. This forms a temporary link between the selected layers that allows you to move them as one unit, delete them all, and so on.

- You can also link layers together. Select layers by clicking on them while holding down *Shift* or *Ctrl* (*Command* on a Mac). Once you have selected all the layers you wish to link, click the **Link Layers** button at the bottom-left of the **Layers** palette (signified by the chain). Linking layers allows the link relationship to remain even after you select a different layer (unlike the process of simply selecting multiple layers).
  To unlink all the layers, select one of the linked layers and go to **Layer > Unlink Layers**. To unlink a single layer, select the layer you wish to remove from the link and click its corresponding link icon; the other layers will stay linked. To temporarily unlink a layer, hold down *Shift* and click on its link icon (a red "X" will appear over the link icon). Reactivate the link by holding down *Shift* and clicking the link icon again.

- Rearrange layers by dragging the layer above or below other layers. Use the "move down" shortcut *Ctrl-[* (*Command-[* on a Mac) and the "move up" shortcut *Ctrl-]* (*Command-]*) to move selected layers up and down. *Shift-Ctrl-[* and *Shift-Ctrl-]* (*Shift-Command-[* and *Shift-Command-]* on a Mac) will bring layers to the very top or the very bottom of the stack.

- Select a layer by using the keyboard shortcuts *Alt-[* and *Alt-]* (*Option-[* and *Option-]* on a Mac). These keystrokes let you move up and down through the layers in the **Layers** palette.

- Create a new layer by pressing *Shift-Ctrl-N* (*Shift-Command-N* on a Mac). This will bring up the **New Layer** dialog box. Want to create new layers quickly without having to deal with the dialogue box? Simply press *Shift-Ctrl-Alt-N* (*Shift-Command-Option-N*).

- Merge a layer into the one beneath it by pressing *Ctrl-E* (*Command-E*). If you have selected layers, this shortcut will merge those selected layers together.

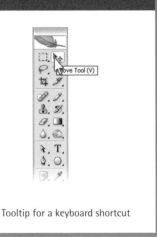
Photoshop Toolbox

You've probably been hanging out to get stuck into the very nifty Photoshop toolbox. In this section, I'll introduce some of the most frequently used tools found in the toolbox. I'll discuss some of the other tools in later chapters as we apply them to solutions.

You'll notice that some of the tool icons have small black triangles in their bottom right-hand corners. These icons contain hidden treasures! The triangle indicates that there are more related tools available; if you click on the tool icon and hold it down, a "flyout" menu will appear, displaying the additional tools.

Finding the "hidden" tools

Selection Tools

You can use the selection tools to select certain areas of your document for editing. If you use a selection tool, only the area that's selected will be affected by any changes you make. You can "feather" selections (specify a fuzzy radius for them) using the **Feather** field in the options bar. The example at the top of the next page shows two rectangles: one created by filling in a selection with a feather of zero pixels, and one that's created by filling in the same selection with a feather of five pixels.

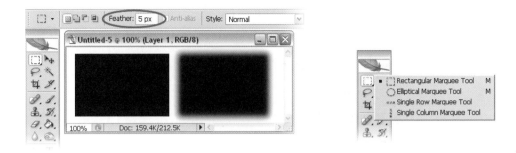

"Fuzzy" edges with feathered selections   Marquee tools

Marquee tools (**M**) are used to create rectangular or elliptical selections, including selections that are "single row" (one pixel tall, stretching across the entire width of the document) and "single column" (one pixel wide, stretching through the entire height of the document). To make single-row or single-column selections, click with the appropriate tool on the image area where you want to select a row or column.

You can use the Lasso tools (**L**) to create freeform selections. The Lasso Tool comes in three different forms:

Lasso tools

- **Lasso Tool (*L*)**
  Click and drag the Lasso Tool to draw a selection area. Releasing the mouse button will close the selection by joining the start and end points with a straight line.

- **Polygonal Lasso Tool (*L*)**
  Click at different points to create vertices of a polygonal shape. Close the selection by moving your cursor to the beginning and clicking once, or pressing the ***Enter*** key.

> **NOTE** *No Selection Sometimes Equals All Selected*
>
> If you've made a selection, only the pixels within the selection are active and can be worked on. Some tools can be used without making a selection at all. However, be aware that if you have not made a specific selection, Photoshop will assume that you are working on the entire layer and any changes you make will affect all pixels in the layer.

- **Magnetic Lasso Tool (*L*)**
  If you think you need help with making your selection, try the Magnetic Lasso Tool. Photoshop will attempt to make a "smart" selection by following the edges of contrast and color difference. Click once near the "edge" of an object and follow around it—Photoshop will automatically lay down a path. You can also click as you follow the line to force points to be created on the path. Close the selection by pressing the ***Enter*** key or clicking at a point near the beginning of the selection. The Magnetic Lasso Tool is not available in ImageReady.

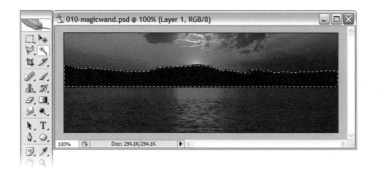

Using the Magic Wand to create a selection

Magic Wand

The Magic Wand Tool (**W**) selects areas of similar color. You can change the **tolerance** (how close the color values should be to the sampled color in order to be selected) of a Magic Wand selection, and choose whether you want the selection to be **contiguous** (pixels that are touching) or not (in which case, matching colors across the entire document will be selected).

TIP Selection Shortcuts and Tasks

- Hold the *Shift* key to add another selection to the first.
- Hold the *Alt* key (*Option* key on a Mac) to subtract your new selection from the first.
- Hold *Shift-Alt* (*Shift-Option*) to select the intersection of your first and second selections.
- Use the arrow keys to move the selection pixel by pixel. If you feel that this doesn't move your selection quickly enough, hold down *Shift* and use the arrow keys to move the selection ten pixels at a time.
- Press *Ctrl-J* (*Command-J* on a Mac) to *copy* the selection into its own layer.
- To *cut* the selection into its own layer, press *Shift-Ctrl-J* (*Shift-Command-J*). If this seems familiar to you, it's because I mentioned earlier how to copy a layer using the same keyboard shortcut. Now that you know that not selecting anything sometimes means that everything is selected, it makes sense that simply by selecting a layer in the **Layers** palette, you can copy the entire layer by pressing *Ctrl-J* (*Command-J*).
- To deselect a selected area, click outside of it with one of the Marquee tools, or press *Ctrl-D* (*Command-D* on a Mac).
- To reactivate your last selection, press *Shift-Ctrl-D* (*Shift-Command-D*).

The Move Tool

The Move Tool (**V**) moves a selected area or an entire layer. You can invoke the Move Tool temporarily when using most other tools by holding down the *Ctrl* key (*Command* key on a Mac).

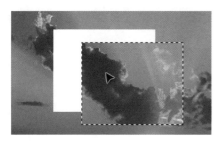

The Move Tool in action

> **TIP** *Move and Copy Shortcut*
>
> For most tools, holding *Ctrl-Alt* (*Command-Option* on a Mac) and dragging a selected area will temporarily invoke the Move Tool, allowing you to move and duplicate the selected layer quickly.

You can also duplicate a layer by holding down the *Alt* key (*Option* key on a Mac) while using the Move Tool, as shown in the image below.

Copying a layer with the Move Tool

The Crop Tool

The Crop Tool (*C*) is used to trim images. Create a selection using the Crop Tool, then double-click the center of the selection, or press *Enter*, to crop the image to the size of the selection.

To cancel without cropping, select another tool or press the *Esc* key.

Creating a selection using the Crop Tool

Cropped image

> **TIP   Crop Outside the Box**
>
> You can use the Crop Tool to resize your canvas. Expand your document window so that it's larger than the image area, and create a crop selection that includes the image and extends onto the gray areas "outside" the image. Applying this crop will resize your canvas to include those extended boundaries, making your canvas larger.

Drawing and Painting Tools

Apart from its extraordinary photo editing abilities, the multi-talented Photoshop also provides drawing and painting tools that allow you to create your own shapes and backgrounds.

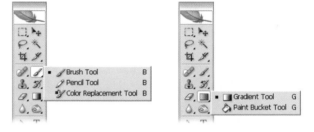

Drawing and painting tools

Brush

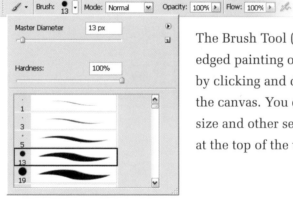

Brush options

The Brush Tool (**B**) is suitable for soft-edged painting or drawing. Draw strokes by clicking and dragging the mouse over the canvas. You can change the brush size and other settings in the options bar at the top of the window.

Pencil

The Pencil Tool (**B**) is suitable for hard-edged drawing or painting and has similar options to the Brush Tool for setting its size, opacity, and more. The Pencil Tool is often used for drawing on, and editing individual pixels in, zoomed-in images.

Eraser

The Eraser Tool (**E**) removes pixels from the canvas. You can choose between **Pencil**, **Brush**, or **Block** mode from the **Mode** drop-down menu in the options bar.

> **NOTE   *Aliased vs Anti-aliased***
>
> Unlike the Brush Tool, the Pencil Tool's edges are **aliased**. The term *aliased* refers to the edges of an object being "jagged," in contrast to an anti-aliased object, in which the edges are "smooth." In the two examples shown here, the top shape in each example was created using the Pencil Tool, while the bottom shape was created using the Brush Tool. Notice the difference in the "jaggedness" of the edges of these curves. We'll look more closely at anti-aliasing when we discuss the Text Tool.
>
> Aliased vs anti-aliased lines

Paint Bucket

The Paint Bucket Tool (**G**) fills a selection with a flat color. To use the Paint Bucket Tool, click once in the area that you wish to fill. If the chosen area is not within a selection, the Paint Bucket Tool will fill all similarly-colored pixels within the vicinity of the clicked area.

Gradient

Gradient options

The Gradient Tool (**G**) fills a selection with a blend of two or more colors, known as a **gradient**. You can easily create your own gradient, or use any of the preset gradients available in Photoshop.

Display the gradient presets and tools by clicking on the small triangle on the right-hand side of the Gradient Tool. Apply a gradient by setting your desired colors, choosing your gradient style, then clicking and dragging the cursor over the area to be filled.

The Gradient Tool is not available in ImageReady.

I find that I use the first two gradients—the foreground-to-background gradient, and the foreground-to-transparent gradient—most often. The former will blend your foreground color into your background color, while the latter will blend your foreground color into a transparent background, giving it a "fading out" effect.

Text Tool

The Text Tool (*T*), true to its name, creates text layers. This one's easy to use—just select the Text Tool, click on the canvas, and start typing! You can also click and drag to create a rectangular text area that will force text to wrap within its boundaries. You can change the font size, color, and other text properties using the options bar along the top of the window.

When the Text Tool is active, you can move the cursor outside of the text area. The cursor will change from the "text insert" cursor to the "move" cursor, and you'll be able to move the text layer around.

It's worth noting that when the Text Tool is active, you can't use keyboard shortcuts to access other tools. This may seem like an obvious thing to point out now, but it won't always be so apparent—especially when your text mysteriously starts spurting strange characters because you've been trying to use the shortcut keys!

To finish using the Text Tool, press ***Ctrl-Enter*** (***Command-Return*** on a Mac). You can then resume your regular keyboard shortcutting!

Shape Tools

You can create shapes simply by clicking and dragging Photoshop's Rectangle, Rounded Rectangle, Ellipse, Polygon, Line, and Custom Shape tools (*U*).

The specific options for each shape tool are displayed in the options bar, and you can access additional options by clicking on the arrow to the right of the Custom Shape button. For example, the Line Tool has options for displaying arrowheads, and for controlling the shapes and sizes of those arrowheads, as shown in the example below.

If you look at the options for each shape, you'll notice that there are three different methods you can use to create a shape:

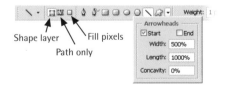

Shape options

■ **as a shape layer (default)**

Your shape will be created
as a solid-colored layer
covered with a vector shape
mask. Confused? Think of
the mask as a sheet of dark

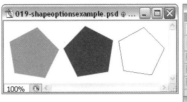

paper that has a hole (your shape) cut out of it so that the
color shines through the hole. To change the color,
double-click on the color block in the **Layers** palette
as shown in this example. To change the vector shape
mask, use the vector editing tools.

Different ways to create shapes

■ **as a path**

Your shape will be created as a path in the **Paths** palette, as shown in the example
above (in which the path has been named *Work Path*).

■ **as filled pixels**

Your shape will be created on whichever layer is currently selected. I created a
new layer, then created a shape using the **Fill pixels** option on *Layer 1* in the above
example.

Selecting Colors

Set foreground and background colors by clicking on the appropriate tile and
choosing a color from the **Color Picker**, as demonstrated in the example below.

Selecting foreground and background colors using the Color Picker

TIP   Color Picker Shortcuts

Press *X* if you want to switch the foreground and background colors. Press *D* if you want to revert to a black foreground and white background.

Eyedropper

The Eyedropper Tool (*I*) lets you sample another color from your image, and set this as the foreground color. In fact, it's actually possible to sample colors from anywhere in your display and even from other applications outside of Photoshop. Simply click inside the document window, then drag the cursor to the color you wish to sample. Click to select that color.

The Eyedropper Tool also allows you to set the background color. To do so, hold down the *Alt* key (*Option* key on a Mac) as you select colors using the eyedropper. If your **Swatch** palette is open, use the *Ctrl* key instead (*Command* key for Mac users).

The Paint Brush, Pencil, Paint Bucket and any of the other painting or drawing tools can temporarily be turned into the Eyedropper Tool by holding down *Alt* (*Option*).

The Hand Tool

The Hand Tool (*H*) moves your canvas, which is handy (pardon the pun!) when you're zoomed in to an image, or have a very large document open.

What's even handier is the fact that you can invoke the Hand Tool while you're using any other tool (except the Text Tool) by holding down the spacebar. This is a neat way to position your image exactly where you want it without having to chop and change between tools to do so.

Other Useful Tasks and Shortcuts

Zooming

Zooming right into your image is the only way to make subtle changes at the pixel level. Use *Ctrl +* to zoom in and *Ctrl –* to zoom out. You can also zoom using the slider on the **Navigator** palette.

Making a Selection Using the Layers Palette

To select the pixels on a particular layer, press *Ctrl* (*Command* on a Mac) and click the thumbnail of the layer. This selection will also take into account the transparency of any pixels, so painting in the selection will recreate the transparency settings of the original layer. The example at the top of the next page shows a selection I made based on one of the text layers in my sunset document.

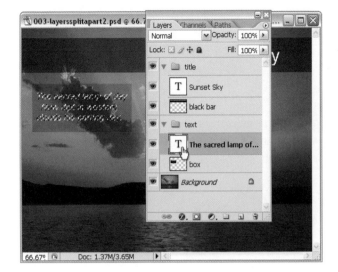

Creating a selection based on a layer

Making a Selection Using a Quick Mask

Quick Masks are one of those closely guarded trade secrets that professional designers use all the time, but beginners often are wary of trying because they seem complicated at first. Well, they're not!

A Quick Mask is an alternative way of making a selection. The usual way to use a Quick Mask is to go into Quick Mask Mode (**Q**) and, using a tool such as the Brush Tool, painting the things you *don't* want to select. This is called painting a "mask," and the resulting reverse-selection will display as the transparent red color that you can see in the example overleaf. You can edit this red layer—honing the mask shape, for instance—using the drawing and painting tools. Those alterations won't affect your image, though: they impact only on your final selection. Switching back to Standard Mode (**Q**) will complete your selection.

Why would we use this technique instead of those trusty selection tools that we've all come to depend on so heavily? Well, Quick Masks have a couple of advantages over the standard selection tools:

1 They allow you to control the level of transparency of your selection.
2 It's easier to color an object in, than it is to carefully draw a line around it.

Initially, it can be difficult to get your head around the fact that you aren't painting on your image: you're just painting the selection. But once you master that concept, you'll feel confident to be able to make a selection quickly on any shape, no matter how difficult it seems!

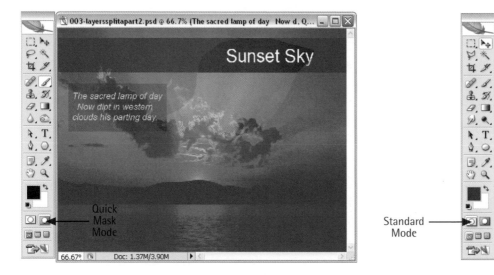

Painting a reverse selection in Quick Mask Mode   Returning to Standard Mode

TIP   Quick Mask Options

I prefer to set Quick Mask Mode so that it lets me paint in the *selected* areas rather than the *non-selected* areas, as shown in this example. To alter your settings to do the same thing, double-click on the Quick Mask Mode icon and change the **Color Indicates:** option to **Selected Areas**.

The **Quick Mask Options** dialog

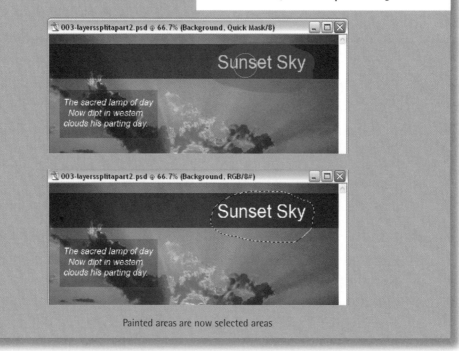

Painted areas are now selected areas

Alpha Channels and Selections

You can use alpha channels to create selections and save them for later use. If you open the **Channels** palette, you'll see several channels, displayed in a similar way to layers in the **Layers** palette. By default, you'll see the color channels, which represent how much of each color is represented in the document. You can click the **Create New Channel** icon at the bottom of the palette to create your own alpha channel.

Creating a new alpha channel

You can then use any of Photoshop's painting or drawing tools to create a grayscale image that will represent your selection—white areas represent selected areas, black areas represent deselected areas, and grays represent the levels of transparency in the selection.

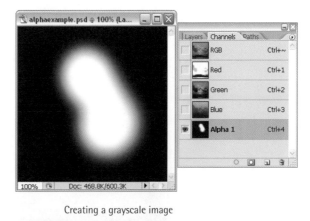

Creating a grayscale image

To turn your alpha channel masterpiece into a selection, simply hold down *Ctrl* and click the channel's thumbnail (hold *Command* and click if you're on a Mac).

Creating a channel-based selection

To return to the normal image view, click on the **Layers** palette tab, and select any layer. Your selection will still be visible.

Returning to the **Layers** palette

You can also create your own alpha channels from existing selections—a capability that can be very useful! For example, let's say you've created a selection of an island silhouette like the one shown in the example below. You have a feeling that you'll be reselecting this island pretty often, but you'd rather not recreate the selection each time. No problem! Once the selection has been made, use **Select > Save Selection**. Name your selection (in this example, *Land*), and click *OK*.

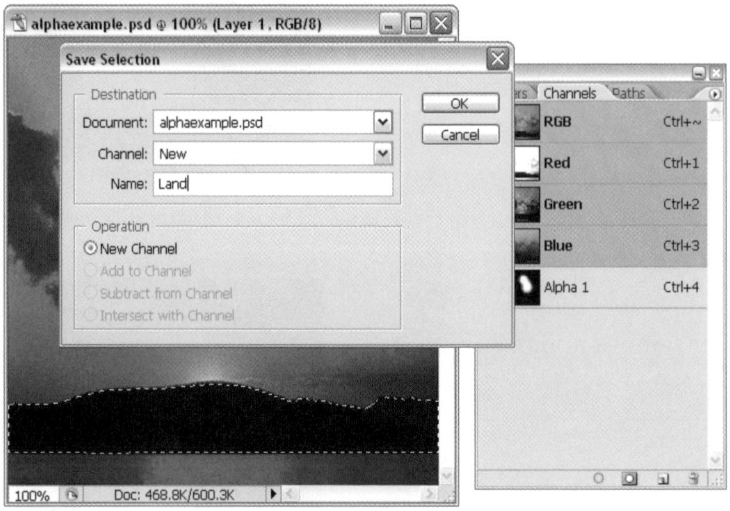

Saving the selection to a channel

If you go to the **Channels** palette, you'll see a new selection at the bottom of the list, named *Land* in the following image—that's your saved selection. Now you can reload your *Land* selection as many times as you need to!

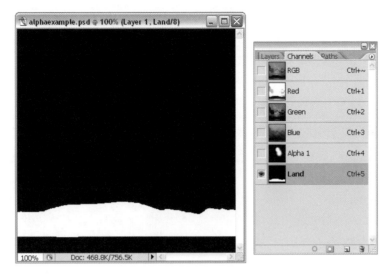

New channel in **Channels** palette

The History Palette

The **History** palette is your key to time travel (in Photoshop, anyway). It lists the most recent steps that you've made, and allows you to undo your actions by rolling your image back to a previous state. You can set the number of steps that are stored in the memory by selecting **Edit** > **Preferences** > **General** (**Photoshop** > **Preferences** > **General** on a Mac) and changing the value in the **History States** text box.

Like most of Photoshop's other tools, the **History** palette has a set of useful keyboard shortcuts for quick access:

- *Ctrl-Z* (*Command-Z* on a Mac) lets you undo and redo the previous step.
- *Ctrl-Alt-Z* (*Command-Option-Z*) steps back through the **History** palette.
- *Shift-Alt-Z* (*Shift-Option-Z*) steps forward through the **History** palette.

As only a limited number of history states are available, there may be cases in which you want to save a "snapshot" of your document so that you can revert back to it later if required. To do so, click on the small triangle on the top-right of the **History** palette and choose **New Snapshot...**. You can save a snapshot of the whole document, the current layer, or merged layers.

Creating a history snapshot

When Photoshop Stops Working

Woah! Photoshop stops working? That certainly doesn't sound too promising! Before you panic, let me explain. Given the multitude of powerful features and fantastic tools it offers, it's no wonder that, on occasion, Photoshop can exhaust itself. It may start behaving a bit erratically, and might even freeze, crash, or automatically exit during startup. If you find yourself in this situation, the first thing to do is reset the preferences file. The preferences file (which you can customize by going to **Edit > Preferences** on a PC, or **Photoshop > Preferences** on a Mac) holds Photoshop settings and can often become corrupted.

The location of the preferences file depends on the operating system and version of Photoshop you are using. For Photoshop CS2, the preferences file is named *Adobe Photoshop CS2 Prefs.psp*. The preference file for other versions of Photoshop will have a similar name.

> **TIP   Backing Up Your Preferences File**
>
> It's a good idea to back up your preferences file by copying and pasting it into a location *outside* of the Photoshop settings folder. Then, if the preferences file Photoshop is using becomes corrupted, you can copy your backup back into the settings folder to replace the corrupted file, without losing any of your settings.

To reset the preferences file, locate the current preferences file, delete it (while Photoshop is closed), and restart Photoshop—it will recreate the preferences file using default settings. Creativepro.com provides a detailed tutorial[1] that explains how to find and replace your preferences file, and includes preference filenames for different versions of Photoshop.

If Photoshop continues to act up, restart it while holding down the *Shift-Ctrl-Alt* keys (*Shift-Command-Option* on a Mac), and click **OK** when asked if you wish to delete the Photoshop settings file. Unfortunately, this will also delete your custom actions, tools, and other settings, but the good news is that it should fix your Photoshop problems.

Summary

This chapter provided an overview of the Photoshop and ImageReady interfaces and common tools, and also explained a few basic tasks such as creating new documents and saving files for the Web. You also took a quick tour of handy keyboard shortcuts and other time-saving tips. Even if you haven't used Photoshop before, you now have the tools that you'll need to work with the examples we'll discuss throughout the rest of this book.

---

[1] http://www.creativepro.com/story/feature/17478.html

2 Basic Skills

Now that you're familiar with Photoshop, you're probably eager to get right into it! This chapter covers some of the basic tasks that Photoshop users should master, such as resizing and rotating documents and layers, working with masks, creating curves and custom shapes, working with transparent images, and more!

This chapter covers fundamental solutions that we'll call upon throughout the remainder of this book. And as an added bonus, I'll show you how to create a coupon box with dotted borders—no doubt you've always wanted to make your very own one of these!

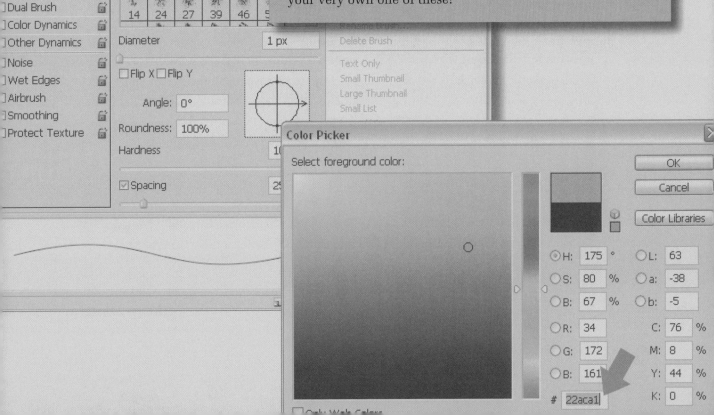

Placing a Graphic in your File

Often you'll want to import existing graphics and artwork into your Photoshop document. A problem for Photoshop? Not at all—in fact, there are several ways you can do this!

External graphics can be placed in Photoshop as raster layers or Smart Objects. First, I'll show you how to place these graphics, then we'll talk about the difference between raster layers and Smart Objects.

Solution

- **placing artwork from a web page**

  Copy the artwork from the web page, then select **Edit > Paste** or press *Ctrl-V* (*Command-V* on a Mac) to paste it into your Photoshop document. Photoshop will create a new layer containing the artwork, or place it into a selected empty layer. The artwork will be on a raster layer.

- **placing artwork from flattened image files**

  A flattened image file—such as a GIF, JPEG or PNG—contains artwork on a single layer. Open the file in Photoshop and use **Select > All** or press *Ctrl-A* (*Command-A*) to create a selection of the entire document. Click on your Photoshop document then select **Edit > Paste** or press *Ctrl-V* (*Command-V*) to paste it. Photoshop will paste the document into a new or selected empty layer as it does when pasting artwork from a web page. The artwork will be on a raster layer.

- **placing layers from a different Photoshop document**

  Position the document windows so that both are visible. Select the window of the document you wish to import from, to bring up its **Layers** palette. Select and drag the necessary layers over to the new window and release the mouse button when you see a thick, black outline around the window. This will copy the layers across as shown in the example at the top of the next page. The copied layers will retain their original properties.

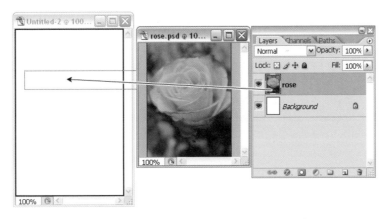

Copying a layer from one Photoshop document to another

■ placing artwork from Illustrator

Open Illustrator and select the artwork you wish to export to Photoshop. Copy the artwork using *Ctrl-C* (*Command-C* on a Mac). Switch to Photoshop while Illustrator is still open and paste your copied artwork using *Ctrl-V* (*Command-V*).

A dialog box will appear, asking you whether you wish to paste the artwork as a **Smart Object**, **Pixels**, **Path** or a **Shape Layer**.

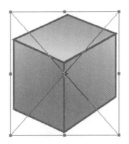

Paste dialog box

■ placing artwork as a Smart Object

Select **File** > **Place** and choose the file you wish to import. Click **Place** to import the file into your Photoshop document as a Smart Object. For PDF and Illustrator files, Photoshop will display a dialog box that asks you to select the pages you wish to place. Choose the pages you want and click **OK**.

The Smart Object will initially be placed with a bounding box surrounding it, as shown here. You can use this bounding box to move, rotate, scale, or make other transformations to the object. When you're done, double-click inside the bounding box to commit the Smart Object to its layer.

The bounding box for an image pasted as a Smart Object

Discussion

Smart Objects

A Smart Object is an embedded file that appears in its own layer in Photoshop. A Smart Object layer is distinguished by an icon that overlays the thumbnail image displayed in the **Layers** palette, as shown in the example below.

Smart Objects are different from other layers because they are linked to a source file (e.g., an Illustrator file, JPEG, GIF or other Photoshop file). If you make changes to the source file, the Smart Object layer will also be updated with those changes.

Raster layer vs Smart Object layer

In contrast, **raster layers** (or regular layers) are fully editable, so you can draw and paint on them, fill them with colors, or erase pixels. Unlike Smart Objects, where you retain image quality, if you resize a raster layer smaller, you will lose information.

This is demonstrated in the example on the next page, which shows the result of a Smart Object that has been decreased in size, then resized back to its original dimensions. The same steps, when applied to a raster layer, produce an image that is blurred and of lower quality.

Smart Object resized to 50% *raster layer resized to 50%*

Smart Object resized to 25% *raster layer resized to 25%*

Smart Object resized back to 100% *raster layer resized back to 100%*

The difference in image quality when resizing a Smart Object compared to a raster layer

Because Smart Objects are linked to an outside document, you can resize them without losing the original image data. While you can apply layer effects and some transformations to Smart Object layers, you cannot actually manipulate (paint, draw, erase) their pixels because they are not editable from external documents. You can open the original source file for editing by double-clicking on the Smart Object icon.

Rasterizing

You can **rasterize** Smart Objects by right-clicking on the name of the Smart Object layer and choosing **Rasterize Layer**. This will break the link to the original source file and treat the layer as an ordinary raster layer.

Resizing a Document

Solution

Bring up the **Image Size** dialog box by selecting **Image > Image Size** or pressing *Ctrl-Alt-I* (*Command-Option-I* on a mac). You can resize the document by altering either the **Pixel Dimensions** or the **Document Size**. Use the former when resizing images that will be used on screen (such as images that will be used on a web page), and the latter when resizing images that will be printed. You can maintain the original document proportions as you resize the image by checking the **Constrain Proportions** checkbox. To scale layer styles (drop shadows, strokes, etc.), check the **Scale Styles** checkbox.

Image Size dialog box

Resizing a Layer or Selection

Photoshop also lets you resize layers or particular portions of a document without affecting the overall size of the document.

Solution

From the **Layers** palette, select the layer that contains the element you wish to resize. If the layer contains other elements that you don't wish to resize, select your element using one of the selection tools.

After making your selection, use **Edit > Free Transform** or press *Ctrl-T* (*Command-T* on a Mac). A bounding box with handles will appear around your selection. Click and drag these handles to resize the element, as shown in this example. To keep the transformation in proportion so that the image does not appear squashed or stretched, hold down the *Shift* key and resize it using the corner handles.

Resizing an element using corner handles

You can also resize the element to a specific width or height using the options bar. In the example below, I clicked the **Maintain Aspect Ratio** button (signified by chain links), then specified the width—this changed the height of my element automatically. If I had not maintained the aspect ratio, only the width of my rose would have changed.

Press *Enter* or double-click inside the bounding box to apply the transformation.

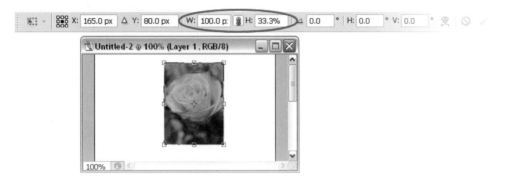

Using the **Free Transform** options

Discussion

When you resize different layer types, you get different results.

- Vector shape layers, such as text or shape layers, can be resized larger or smaller without loss of quality.
- Smart Objects can also be resized larger or smaller without loss of quality, depending on the original file. If the original file is a vector graphic, the Smart Object can be resized without ever losing quality. If the original file is a GIF or similar, the Smart Object can be resized up to the size of the image dimensions, above which it will start to lose quality.
- Raster layers or selections can only be resized smaller. Resizing them larger will usually result in loss of quality.

Rotating a Layer or Selection

Earlier, you may have used the **Free Transform** command to resize layers and selections, and thought it was pretty swell. What you probably weren't aware of at the time is that the very same command can also be used to *rotate* layers and selections!

Solution

Make a selection or choose the layer you'd like to rotate. Select **Edit > Free Transform** or press *Ctrl-T* (*Command T*), and move your cursor outside the bounding box. You'll see that it turns into a curved, two-headed arrow as shown in this example. You can click and drag this cursor to rotate the elements within the bounding box.

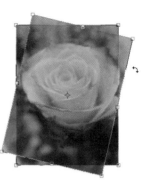

Hold down the *Shift* key to constrain the angle movement to 15-degree increments. You can also set a specific angle of rotation (between −180° and 180°) in the **Angle** text box in the options bar.

Rotating a selection

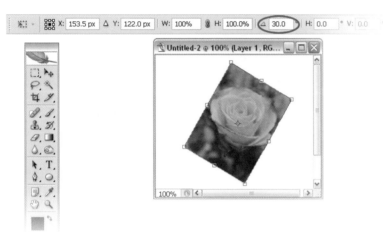

Setting the angle of rotation in the options bar

> **TIP Rotation Alternatives**
>
> For 90- or 180-degree rotations, you can select **Edit > Transform** and choose from **Rotate 180°, Rotate 90° CW,** or **Rotate 90° CCW.**

Press *Enter* or double-click inside the bounding box to complete the transformation.

Using Drawing Tools to Create Lines

Solution

Vertical and Horizontal Lines

Using the Brush or Pencil Tool (**B**), move the cursor to the position from which you'd like the line to start on your document. Click and hold down the mouse button. Hold down the *Shift* key to constrain mouse movement to straight lines, then drag the cursor to draw your line. Release the mouse button to complete the line.

Diagonal Lines

Using the Brush or Pencil Tool (**B**), position the cursor at the point from which you'd like the line to start and click once (release the mouse button this time). Hold down **Shift** and click on the spot where you'd like your line to end. Photoshop will connect the dots with a straight line.

Perfect Squares and Circles

Solution

If you've been a bit adventurous and tried your hand at drawing a few shapes in Photoshop, you've probably found that it can be difficult to draw a perfect square or circle "freehand."

The solution is simple—if you hold down the **Shift** key while creating a rectangle or ellipse, Photoshop will ensure that the shape is a perfect square or circle. This works for both the selection and the shape tools.

Straightening the Edges of a Rounded Rectangle

It's pretty straightforward to create rectangles and rounded rectangles using their respective shape tools. But what if you want a rectangle on which only some corners are rounded?

Solution

1   Create a rounded rectangle using the Rounded Rectangle Tool (**U**) highlighted in this example. Be sure to use the **Shape layers** option in the option bar, not the **Fill pixels** option.

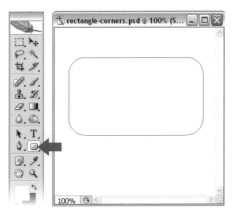

Creating a rounded rectangle

2   Choose the Convert Point Tool (**P**),
     which you'll find in the Pen Tool
     flyout menu. Click on the path to
     show the **anchor points** of the
     vector shape. These are represented
     by small white squares, as shown at
     right.

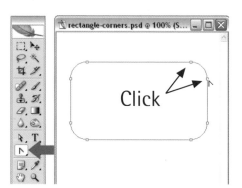

3   Click on each of the anchor points
     that make up the rounded corner
     you want to "straighten."

Clicking on the anchor points with the Convert Point Tool

This will change the curve into a "cut" corner, as shown in the example below.

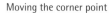

The result of using the Convert Point Tool

4   Select the Direct Selection Tool (**A**) and
     click on the top angled point (zoom in if
     necessary). Holding the **Shift** key to
     constrain the movement to a horizontal
     path, drag the point laterally until it
     aligns vertically with the bottom point,
     as shown in this example. You can move
     the point using the arrow keys for more
     precision if you prefer.

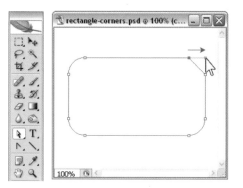

Moving the corner point

5   To tidy it up, select the Delete Anchor
     Point Tool (found in the Pen Tool flyout
     menu), and click on the bottom point
     to delete it (as shown in this example)
     as it's now become redundant. *Voila*!
     You've got a straight edge on a rounded
     rectangle!

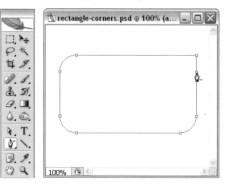

Deleting the anchor point

Curved Design Elements

There may come a time when you find yourself wanting to create curved design elements such as those shown here. You've probably noticed that Photoshop doesn't have a "curve" tool. Where does the curvy goodness come from?

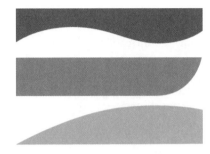

Curved design elements

Solution

The answer, in a nutshell, is the Pen Tool (*P*).

Creating curves involves learning how to draw your own vector shapes—it's exciting stuff! If you've never used vector drawing tools before, you're in for a treat!

Think back to your adventures with the pencil and brush drawing tools, where you clicked and dragged the mouse to create a shape. The Pen Tool is distinctly different, because instead of creating a shape, you are clicking and dragging to set anchor points and curve directions. It takes some practice, but mastering the Pen Tool is your key to creating delightful curves.

Let's start with the basics. Before I explain how to make curved shapes, I'll quickly go over how to draw polygon shapes with the Pen Tool—it's quite easy, and sets a good foundation for drawing trickier curves.

Let's draw a triangle. Each click with the Pen Tool will create a corner point. Click once to create the first point, then again to create the second point. A line segment will automatically connect these points to form a path. Click again to create the third point—a line segment will connect this to the second point, extending the path. Any subsequent points created hereafter will be connected with line segments, but since we're creating a triangle, we only need three points. To make the triangle shape, simply close the path by clicking on the first point we created. You'll notice that the cursor changes into a pen with a little circle when you move it over the original point—this means that you can close the path by clicking on that point. Alternatively, you could close the path simply by pressing *Enter*. The example below shows the four clicks described to create a triangle.

Using the Pen Tool to create a polygon

Let's have a go at creating some curves. This time, when you click to place a point, drag the mouse. You'll see two lines extending from the point you've made. These are known as Bezier control handles, or "handlebars." The length and direction of these handlebars will determine the curvature of the path that we are about to

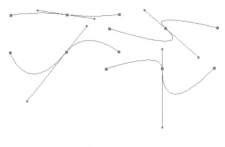

Curved paths

make. Release the mouse button and move your cursor to another position. Click and hold down the mouse button again. You'll see that a path has been created between your first and second points, and that one of your handlebars has disappeared. If you drag your mouse, new handlebars will extend from the second point.

Choose the Direct Selection Tool (**A**) and adjust the curve by dragging the end points of the handlebars, as shown in this example.

Adjusting the curve with handlebars

Let's try making the curved shapes I showed you on the previous page using these techniques.

Curved Shape 1

Follow along with the diagram opposite.

1   Using the Pen Tool (**P**), click once to create a point.
2   Hold down the **Shift** key and click above the first point to create a straight, vertical line.
3   Keeping the **Shift** key down, click to the right of the top point to create a straight, horizontal line.
4   Still holding the **Shift** key, click below the point on the right-hand side to create a vertical line segment a bit shorter than the first one we created.
5   Position your cursor as shown. Press **Shift** and click and drag to create a point with horizontal handlebars.

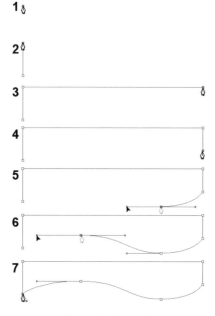

Step by step for Curved Shape 1

6   Position the cursor as shown in step 6 in the diagram. Hold down *Shift*, click and then drag to create another point with horizontal handlebars.

7   Click once on the original point to close the shape.

Curved Shape 2

1   Using the Pen Tool (*P*), click once to create a point.

2   Hold down the *Shift* key and click above the first point to create a straight, vertical line as shown.

3   Keeping the *Shift* key down, click to the right of the top point to create a straight, horizontal line.

4   Position the cursor as shown. Click and drag to create a point with handlebars, then hold down *Shift* and drag to the left to create the curved section.

5   Click once on the original point to close the shape.

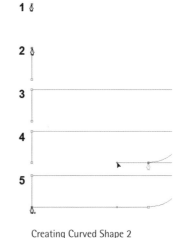

Creating Curved Shape 2

Curved Shape 3

1   Using the Pen Tool (*P*), click once to create a point.

2   Hold down the *Shift* key and click to the right of the first point to create a straight, horizontal line.

3   Keeping the *Shift* key down, click above the point on the right-hand side to create a straight, vertical line.

4   Hold down the *Alt* key (*Option* on a Mac). Click on the point you just created and drag the mouse up and to the left to create a handlebar.

5   Click on the original point to complete the shape, but do not release the mouse button. Drag the mouse downwards and to the left, as shown in step 5 in the diagram, to create a handlebar. Use the Direct Selection Tool (*A*) to adjust your curve with the handlebars.

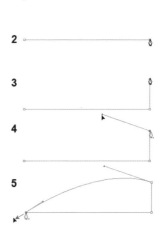

Creating Curved Shape 3

Reusing Vector Shapes

As you work more with shapes, you may find that you're often recreating the same vector shape. If it's a simple shape—one that doesn't involve outlines or layers—you can save it as a **custom shape** and access it later using the Custom Shape Tool (*U*).

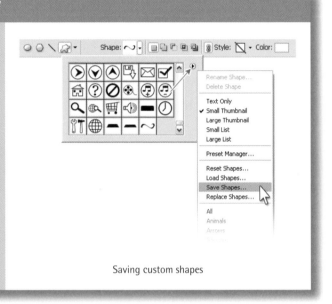

WARNING Save your Shapes!

After you create and add your custom shape, I recommend that you click on the small arrow in the custom shape flyout box and select **Save Shapes...**. This will save all of the custom shapes that are currently visible into a *.csh* file. This way, if you ever need to reinstall Photoshop or reset the preferences, you'll be able to reload your shapes.

You'll find that most customizable elements, such as layer styles, patterns, and brushes, provide menu options that allow you to save the custom settings you've created for them.

Saving custom shapes

Solution

1   Select your vector shape by clicking on it with the Path Selection Tool (the black arrow).

2   Select **Edit > Define Custom Shape...**.

3   Type a name in the **Shape Name** dialog box and click **OK**.

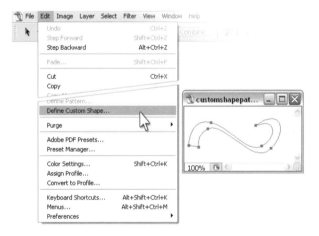

Defining a custom shape

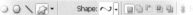

New custom shape

4   To use your shape, select the Custom Shape Tool (*U*) and scroll down the list of available shapes—you'll see that your shape's been added!

Sampling Colors from Image Files

Solution

Open the image file in Photoshop. If you're not able to open it in Photoshop (the image might be embedded in a document, for example), open it in an appropriate program that lets you view the file on your computer (such as a web browser, or Microsoft Word if the image is in a Word document).

■ If the image is open in Photoshop, select the Eyedropper Tool (*I*) and click on the image to grab the color. Your foreground color will be set to the color you selected.

■ If you've opened the image in another program, resize and move the Photoshop window so that you can see both the Photoshop window and the image simultaneously (this example shows the SitePoint web site next to the Photoshop window). Select the Eyedropper Tool (*I*). Click anywhere in the Photoshop window, and then drag the eyedropper out to the image you're sampling color from. In the example shown here, I sampled the orange color from the SitePoint logo. You can see that this color has been set to the foreground color in the Color Picker.

Sampling a color from outside the Photoshop interface

Finding the Hexadecimal Code for a Color

Solution

When you're working on the HTML and CSS for a web site design, you'll need the six-digit hexadecimal codes for the colors that you use. Photoshop makes these available to you in two ways.

TIP   Time-saving Tip

Some icons in the **Info** palette have a little arrow icon next to them. You can change the **Info** palette display options by clicking on these icons—this way, you won't need to go through the **Palette Options** dialog, which saves you two clicks!

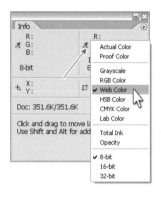

Choosing the color display option

Using the Info Palette

As you move the cursor around a document, the **Info** palette will show you the value for the color over which the cursor is positioned. By default, the palette is set to display the RGB and CMYK values for colors. You can configure the information displayed in the palette by clicking on the small arrow on the top right-hand side of the palette

and selecting **Palette Options**.... A dialog box will appear, displaying the options you can change. Among other things, you'll see two drop-down menus to change the **Color Readout** —change one of these to **Web Color**.

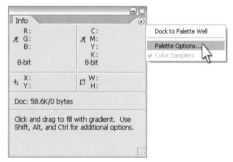

Selecting **Palette Options...** for the **Info** palette

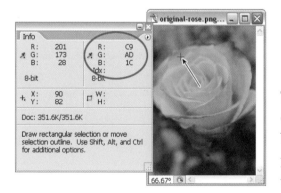

The **Info** palette displays the hexadecimal color codes

This will display the hexadecimal codes for the color's red, green, and blue values. String these together to get your six-digital hexadecimal code. In this example, the hexadecimal code is *c9ad1c*.

Using the Color Picker

The hexadecimal codes for colors are also displayed in a text field at the bottom of the **Color Picker** dialog box, as shown here. You can highlight the color code, copy it using *Ctrl-C* (*Command-C* on a Mac), and paste it into a style sheet or HTML file. Note that the hash sign (#) isn't copied, so don't forget to add that when you're pasting the code!

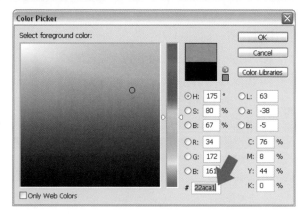

The hexadecimal color code displays in the **Color Picker**

Adjusting Layer Transparency

Solution

We talked about this task briefly in "Layer Shortcuts and Tasks" in Chapter 1. To adjust the transparency of a layer, change its opacity using the **Opacity** field in the **Layers** palette.

If you have the selection, move, or crop tools selected, you can change the transparency simply by typing a number—the opacity level will magically change to reflect that percentage!

Changing the opacity of a layer

Fading an Image into the Background

An effect that's commonly used in web design is to fade a whole image, or part of an image—its edges, for example—into the background on which it sits. You can easily produce this funky effect using gradients and layer masks in Photoshop.

Solution

Initial document

1 Arrange your Photoshop document so that the image you wish to fade is on one layer, and the background color is on another layer.

2 Select the image layer and click on the Add Layer Mask icon (signified by a white circle on a dark gray background) at the bottom of the **Layers** palette, as shown in this example. A blank rectangular thumbnail will appear next to the layer thumbnail, representing the layer mask. Make sure this thumbnail is selected.

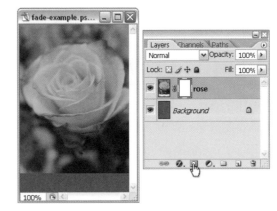

Creating a layer mask

Selecting the Foreground to Transparent gradient

3 Set your foreground color to black. Select the Gradient Tool (**G**) and choose the Foreground to Transparent gradient.

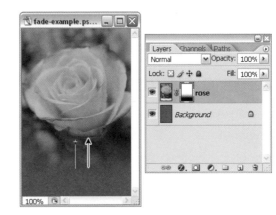

Adding the fade effect

4 Apply the gradient by clicking at the bottom edge of the image and dragging the mouse upwards. Hold down *Shift* to constrain the gradient path to a straight line. Release the mouse button, and the gradient will be applied. Your fade effect is complete!

Discussion

Layer masks are grayscale images that show or hide areas of the layers to which they have been applied. The gray tones on the mask reflect the transparency of corresponding areas on the layer: black areas are completely transparent and, therefore, invisible; white areas are not transparent at all, so they're completely visible; and shades of gray have varying degrees of transparency, depending on how dark the gray is (the closer it is to black, the more transparent the corresponding section on the image layer will be).

You can edit a layer mask using any of the drawing or painting tools, including the pencil and brush tools (**B**), the Gradient Tool (**G**), and the Paint Bucket Tool (**G**). Drawing on a mask affects the mask only, and does not touch the pixels that make up the image. Draw or paint on the mask in black, white, or gray.

In this solution, I used a black-to-transparent gradient to create a gradient on the layer mask. This allowed the upper part of the image to remain visible, but let the lower part fade away so that the background color could show through.

We could also created a fade effect with the Brush Tool (**B**). In the example shown, I've selected a soft-edged brush, set my foreground color to black, and painted along the bottom of the image on the layer mask to paint out the areas I want to fade.

Creating a layer mask using the Brush Tool

You're probably wondering why you wouldn't just paint a green gradient on the bottom of the picture layer, or on its own layer, to achieve the same effect. Why use a layer mask?

The beauty of layer masks is that they are **non-destructive**. They don't actually modify any of the pixels on the image layer itself—a benefit that, ultimately, gives you greater flexibility. If you decided that you didn't want the effects you'd created using your layer mask, you could get rid of the mask and the original image would remain intact. Or, if you decided you didn't like the green color, you could change the background color and the fade effect would still work.

Blending Two Images Together

Solution

Blending two images together is very similar to fading an image into its background: you'll apply a layer mask to at least one of your images. If you haven't created layer masks before, read the solution titled "Fading an Image into the Background, in Chapter 2."

Arrange your Photoshop document so that one of the images overlaps the other, as shown in the example below. I've usually found that the effect works best if the image backgrounds have similar colors or textures, although this is not mandatory by any means!

Initial document with two image layers

Create a layer mask for the top layer and use the Gradient Tool (**G**) or the Brush Tool (**B**) to create a fade effect as I described in "Fading an Image into the Background." If you've hidden too much of the layer with the layer mask, you can make these areas visible again by painting them back with white on the layer mask.

Creating a layer mask

Personally, I'm pretty happy with that effect so I'll leave it there. You can see the final result here.

Beautiful flowers

Rounding the Corners of a Photo

Solution

1   Select the Rounded Rectangle Tool (**U**) and choose the **Paths** option, as shown here.

Choosing the Paths option

2   Use this to create a rounded rectangle path over the image. You can view the path in the **Paths** palette.

Creating a rounded rectangle

3   Select **Layer > Vector Mask > Current Path**. Photoshop will create a vector mask using the rounded rectangle path you just created. The example here shows the new vector mask in the **Layers** palette. You can use the Direct Selection Tool (**A**) to modify the path and change its shape.

Creating the vector mask

Masking Multiple Layers with the Same Shape

Let's say that you have multiple layers and you want them to be masked with the same shape. You could create a layer mask for one and then duplicate the mask for each layer, but what if you want to change the shape layer later? If you were motivated enough, you could go through each layer and modify the shape mask … but why would you bother when you could easily halve the time that job would take using the clipping mask?

Solution

In this solution, I'll start with an interface design for a simple web site. It has a header bar, a menu bar, and a content area as shown in the example here.

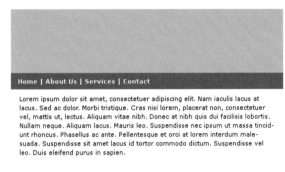

Web site design

I'll paste in the flower images that I blended together earlier in this chapter. As you can see in the example below, the images are bigger than the header area. I want them to be contained within the header region, but I still want to be able to move them around. The solution may seem simple at first—a layer mask on each layer will do the trick. But what if I decide to change the header height later? I'll have to modify all the masks.

Images for header area

Enter the clipping mask. First, your document must have a shape layer that contains the shape of the "masking" area. Put the layers you need to mask directly on top of this shape layer.

In the **Layers** palette, move the cursor to the boundary between the shape layer and the layer above it. Hold down the *Alt* key (*Option* on a Mac). The cursor will change into two overlapping circles, as shown in this example.

Holding the *Alt* (*Option*) key changes the cursor

Click once. The top layer will be **clipped** by the bottom layer. If you examine the **Layers** palette, you'll notice that the thumbnail for the top layer now has a black arrow next to it, and our shape layer's name is underlined.

Clipping one of the layers with another

Now let's do the same with our second image. Move your mouse up to the edge of the next layer in the **Layers** palette, hold down *Alt* and click.

Clipping another layer

Both layers have now been clipped by the base layer, as shown in the example below.

Creating a clipping mask for multiple layers

You can move the individual layers around, and they will remain clipped by the shape of the base layer. The image below illustrates this point.

Moving a layer with a clipping mask

As a final flourish, I'm going to use the solution from "Fading an Image into the Background" to fade the right edge of the second flower into the background. Our final result is shown below.

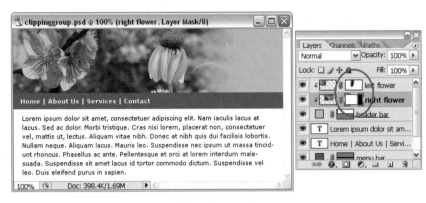

Adding a layer mask

Discussion

A clipping mask allows you to mask multiple layers using a single, editable mask that sits on its own layer. This mask will clip all the layers that sit above it, which saves you from needing to create multiple layer masks based on the same shape.

The clipped layers inherit the base layer's properties. So, for example, if the base layer has a 50% opacity, the clipped layers will also have 50% opacity.

To unclip layers, hold the *Alt* (*Option*) key and click below the layer you wish to unclip. All the layers above it will be unclipped.

Making a Dotted Coupon Box

You've probably seen dotted coupon boxes before, and saved a good dollar or two by using them! This solution shows you how to create a coupon-style box with dotted borders using customized brush strokes.

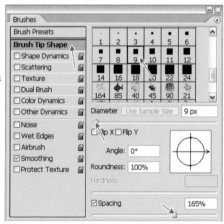

Loading square brushes

Solution

1 Select the Brush Tool (**B**).

2 Open the **Brushes** palette. Click on the small arrow in the top right-hand corner and select **Square Brushes**. A dialog box will appear, asking you whether you want to replace or append to the list of brushes you currently have displayed. You can always restore your original brush settings by selecting **Reset Brushes...** (click **Append** if you'd rather add the default brushes to your current list, otherwise click **OK**.)

3 Choose **Brush Tip Shape** and select a square brush whose diameter matches the length you want each dotted stroke to have. If the size is not quite right, you can adjust it with the **Diameter** slider as shown in the image on the right.

4 Increase the **Spacing** slider until the spacing between brush strokes works for you.

Modifying brush tip shape options

Changing the height of the stroke

5 You might want to squash your brush so that it's more of a rectangle. Click on the top or bottom point of the circle in the dialog box and drag it towards the horizontal axis until the stroke looks similar to that in the image at left.

6   Check the **Scattering** checkbox and change the scattering amount to 0%.

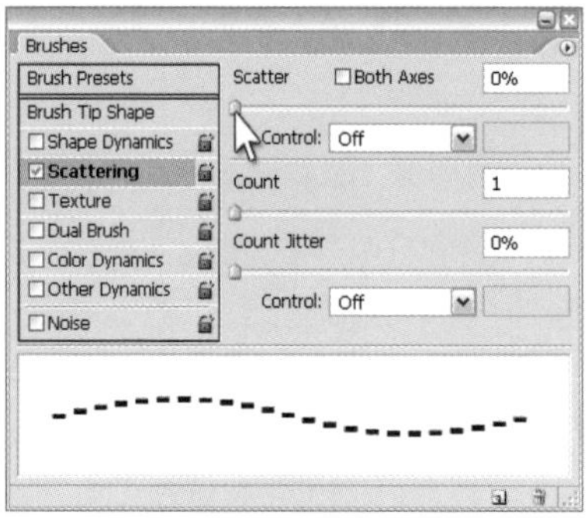

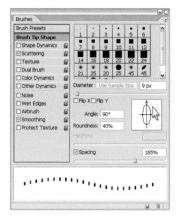

Changing the scattering amount

7   Right. Now you're ready to draw your box! Choose a foreground color for your dotted line. Create a new layer, hold down the **Shift** key, and drag across your document to draw a horizontal line.

Drawing a dotted line

8   Next, return to the **Brushes** palette and drag on the horizontal axis arrow to rotate the brush by 90 degrees (or type **90** in the **Angle** textbox). This will allow you to draw vertical strokes.

9   Hold down **Shift** and drag the mouse down to draw a vertical line.

10 Rotate your brush back to zero, and draw your second horizontal line.

11 Complete your box by rotating the brush to 90 degrees once more and drawing the last vertical line.

Rotating the brush

Finished coupon box

Applying a Drop Shadow

Solution

Choose the layer to which you wish to apply the drop shadow, and select **Layer >
Layer Style > Drop Shadow**. Play with the opacity, angle, distance, and other settings in
the **Layer Style** dialog box until you're happy with the effect.

Note that the value for **Angle** will affect all drop shadows in your document, so that
the light source is consistent across your entire image.

TIP   Dragging your Shadow

You can also click directly in the document window and drag the drop shadow around, as
shown here. Make sure **Drop Shadow** is highlighted in the **Layer Style** dialog box, otherwise
this won't work!

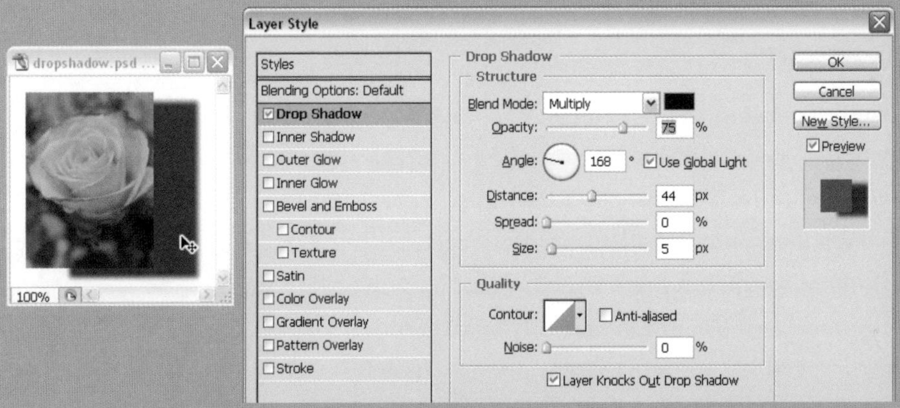

Moving the drop shadow

Images with Transparent Backgrounds

Solution

Open a Photoshop document that
contains transparent areas.
You'll see that Photoshop marks the
transparent areas with a gray,
checkered pattern.

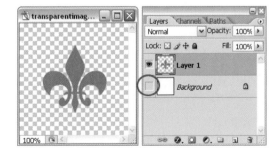

Document with background layer turned off

Select **File** > **Save For Web…**, or press *Shift-Alt-Ctrl-S* (*Shift-Option-Command-S* on a Mac). In the dialog box that appears, choose **GIF** and check the **Transparency** option, as shown in the image to the right. While both GIFs and PNGs support transparency, some browsers (including Internet Explorer 6) do not support PNG transparency. For this reason, I'd recommend that you use GIFs to meet your transparent image needs.

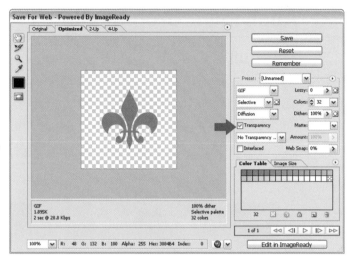

Saving as a transparent GIF

Click **Save** and name your file.

Discussion

Images with curved, smooth edges, like the one in this example, maintain the illusion of crisp edges as a result of **anti-aliasing**—partially transparent pixels are added onto the edges of the image to smooth them, as shown here. However, when you save an image as a GIF, these partially transparent pixels are saved as non-transparent pixels where white is the default "background" color.

Close-up of anti-aliased shape

If you're not placing this image on a white background, it might be wise to define a custom matte color by clicking on the **Matte** arrow, as shown here. Otherwise, you'll end up with a white "color halo" around the image.

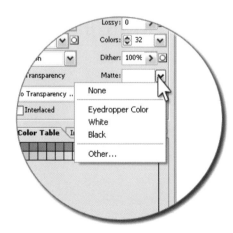

Choosing alternate matte color

Let's say that we're going to place this graphic against a bright red background. Click on the **Matte** arrow, choose **Other...**, and select a bright red.

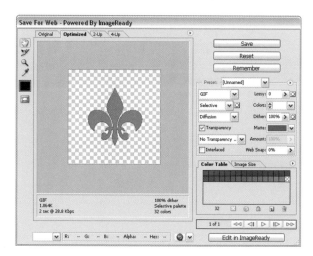

Setting a bright red matte color

Now you'll be able to see a red color halo around the graphic. If you zoom in, you'll see that those anti-aliased pixels behave as though they're sitting on a red background.

Click the **Save** button to save your image.

No matte vs red matte

Close-up of color halo

Summary

In this chapter, we looked at solutions to some of the basic functions that Photoshop users should master. We learned how to import graphics into a Photoshop document, how to resize and rotate images and selections, how to use the *Shift* key to constrain movements, and how to use masks and basic layer styles to create effects. We also looked at the basics of creating vector shapes and saving transparent GIFs. These skills form a great foundation for using Photoshop, and we'll definitely turn to them in the coming chapters!

3 Creating Buttons

Now, onto the good stuff!

In this chapter, we'll be making navigation buttons. The solutions I'll describe are for creating button effects. Don't worry about making a complete navigation interface in Photoshop yet; I'll help you design layout comps later in the book.

The techniques you'll learn here can be applied to any "button-like" object, including icons, bullets, title and navigation bars, and other page accents.

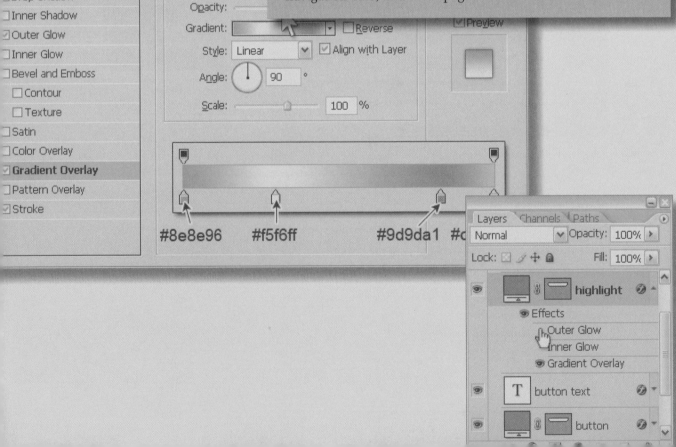

Making a Simple, Flat Button

Solution

Rectangular Flat Button

We're going to draw a basic, rectangular button. Set the foreground color to a color of your choice, then draw a rectangle with the Rectangle Tool (**U**).

I told you it was basic! I've made mine more interesting by drawing another rectangle in a lighter color to give my button a thick border on its left-hand side, as shown at right.

A rectangular button with a thick border

Rounded Flat Button

You can also create basic, rectangular buttons with rounded corners using— you guessed it—the Rounded Rectangle Tool (**U**). Alter the "roundness" of your corners using the **Radius** field in the options bar, as shown here.

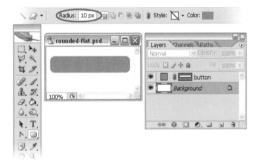

Rounded rectangular button with a ten-pixel radius

> **NOTE Photoshop Doesn't Replace CSS**
>
> On a web page, you'd probably use CSS instead of images to achieve this rectangular button effect. However, this technique is handy when it comes to drawing simple buttons for web comps in Photoshop.

Rounded rectangular button with 20-pixel radius

Adding an Outline to a Button

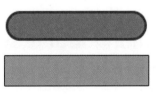

In this solution, we're going to be adding outlines to our basic buttons to make them look like the ones shown here.

Buttons with outlines

> ### NOTE Adding Layer Styles
>
> In this chapter and beyond, we'll be making heavy use of layer styles, which are applied by launching the **Layer Style** window. There are a few different ways to launch this window, but the one I use most often is to click on the little **f** button at the bottom of the layer palette, as shown here.
>
> Clicking this button will display a dialog box listing all of the different layer styles available. Simply choose the one you want and the **Layer Style** window will launch, with the specific effect selected. It's also possible to select the same styles from the menu bar (**Layer > Layer Style**), but using the icon saves you one mouse click!

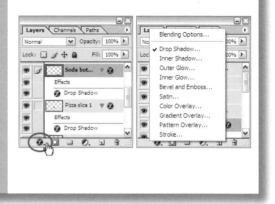

Solution

Let's add outlines to the basic buttons we created earlier. Select the layer that contains your button. Open the **Layer Style** dialog box by clicking on the **Add a layer style** button at the bottom of the **Layers** palette and selecting **Stroke…** from the menu that appears. You'll see that the **Stroke** style is checked and highlighted—

Adding an outline to a button by changing its stroke options

this adds the outline to your button. Change the look of your stroke by adjusting the settings. You can see from the dialog shown above that I gave mine a black outline by clicking on the color patch and setting the color to black, and gave it a thickness of one pixel by typing *1* into the **Size** field (you could also use the slider to adjust the size of the stroke).

Making a Smooth, Beveled Button

They're getting fancier! Let's have a go at creating the beveled buttons shown here.

Smooth, beveled buttons

Solution

By now, you should be an expert in creating basic, rectangular buttons. Just as well, because you'll need one for this solution! Create or select your basic button. Open the **Layer Style** dialog box by clicking on the **Add a layer style** button at the bottom of the **Layers** palette and selecting **Bevel and Emboss...** from the menu that appears. You've just added a bevel to your button. You can give the bevel a more rounded appearance by increasing the **Size** and **Soften** levels. I'm using *7px* for **Size** and *8px* for **Soften**, as shown in the image below.

Make the effect more subtle by changing the **Shadow Mode** color. Since my button is blue, I've changed the **Shadow Mode** color from black to blue (a slightly darker shade than my button color).

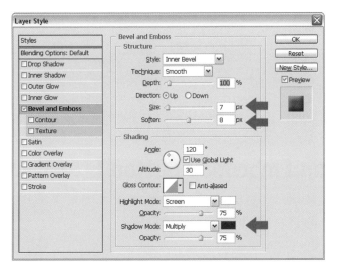

Bevel and Emboss options for smooth bevel

Creating a Chiseled Button Effect

The **Bevel and Emboss** layer style is a versatile tool that can be used to create many different button effects. In this solution, we'll use it to create hard-edged, chiseled buttons like the ones shown here.

Chiseled buttons

Solution

Create or select a basic button. Then, open the **Layer Style** dialog box by clicking on the **Add a layer style** button at the bottom of the **Layers** palette and selecting **Bevel and**

Emboss... from the menu that appears. From the **Technique** drop-down menu, select **Chisel Hard** and set the **Soften** field to *0px*. Increase the **Depth** of the bevel to chisel "deeper" into the button.

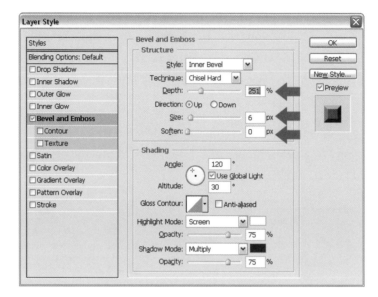

Bevel and Emboss options for chiseled bevel

Creating an Embedded Button Effect

In this solution, I'll show you a button effect that makes your buttons look like they're embedded into the page, as shown here.

Embedded buttons

Solution

Select or create a basic button. Open the **Layer Style** dialog box by clicking on the **Add a layer style** button at the bottom of the **Layers** palette and selecting **Bevel and Emboss...** from the menu that appears. From the **Style** drop-down menu, select **Pillow Emboss**—this will give your button an "embedded" effect.

Experiment with the settings to change the look of your effect. Both the buttons in the example shown above are pillow embossed, but they look different because I've set the **Technique** to **Smooth** for the top one, the settings for which are shown on the next page, and **Chisel Hard** for the bottom one.

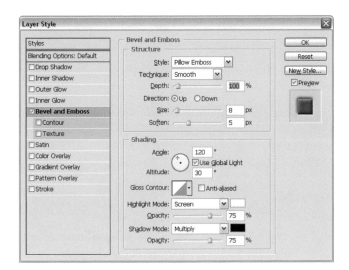

Pillow Emboss options for the smooth embedded button

Making a Gradient Button

Two-toned gradient buttons like the ones shown here are the "new black" of graphic design. This effect has become increasingly popular—no doubt you'll have seen it used on the buttons, menu rows, and heading backgrounds of trendy web sites. In this solution, I'll show you how easy it is to create your very own gradient buttons.

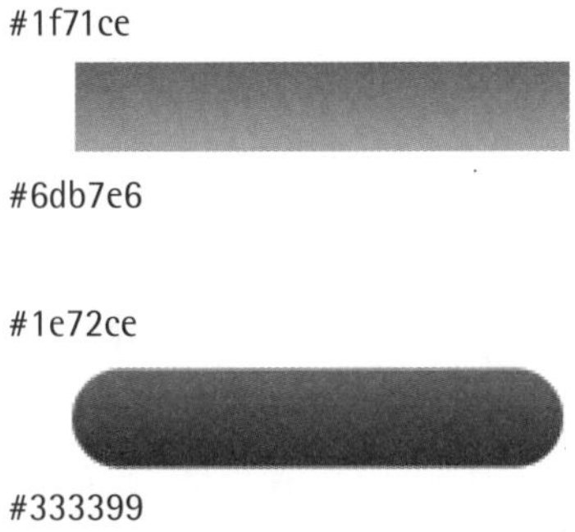

#1f71ce

#6db7e6

#1e72ce

#333399

Examples of gradient buttons

Solution

Raster Buttons

Using a selection tool, such as the Marquee Tool (**M**), create a rectangular selection for your button. Set the foreground and background colors to the two tones you want in your gradient, and create a new layer. With the

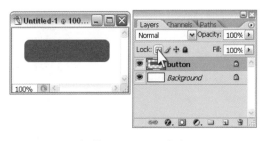

Locking transparent pixels

Gradient Tool (**G**) selected, choose the Foreground to Background gradient option and click and drag the mouse to fill in your selection. (Holding down *Shift* will constrain the gradient direction to a horizontal or vertical line.)

WARNING   Useful, but not Terribly Usable!

For all its power, the **Layer Style** dialog is amazingly unintuitive. What I find most confusing is the fact that you can apply a style without selecting it!

That's right—once you've launched the **Layer Style** dialog, you can apply a style (with Photoshop's default settings) by checking its checkbox. If you have the **Preview** checkbox ticked, you'll see the effect this style has on your image. Fairly straightforward, right? But what's confusing is that this doesn't actually *select* the style, so you can't change its settings! You need to *highlight* the name of the style to bring these up—simply checking the checkbox won't do!

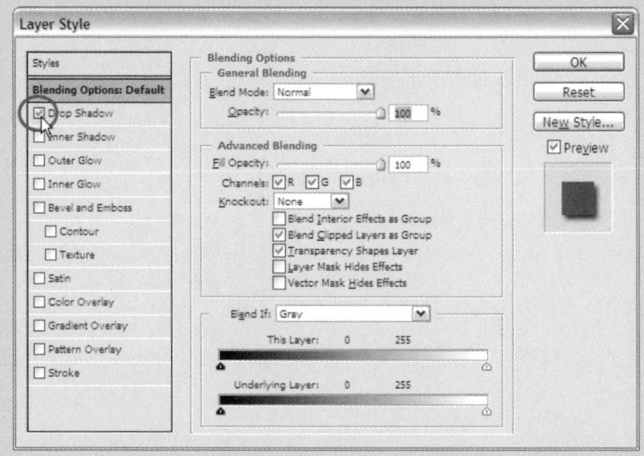

The example shown here demonstrates this: In the top image I've checked the **Drop Shadow** style, which has been applied, but the settings in the dialog box are for the layer's **Blending Options**. This means I can't make any changes to my drop shadow!

If I click on the *name* of the layer style instead, my drop shadow is applied *and* its settings are displayed (as shown in the second image). Because of this, you might think that if I click on the name of another style that I've applied, it will be turned off in the document. That's not the case—you'll have to uncheck the checkbox for that!

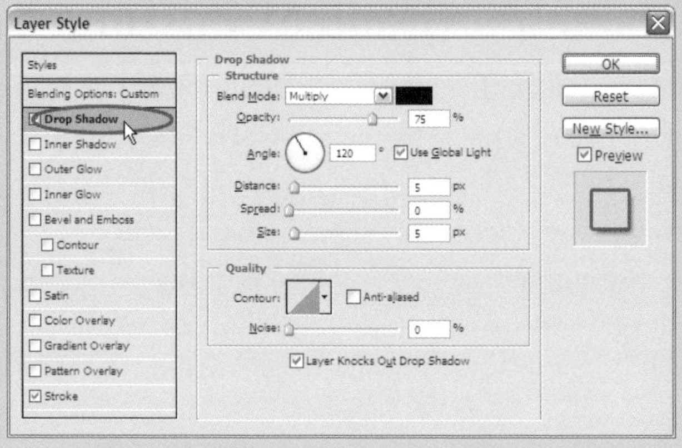

Applying a Layer Style

Selecting (and applying) a layer style

I'd suggest you spend a minute selecting and applying a few different layer styles until you get the hang of how it all works—it'll save you from confusion later on!

We can achieve the same gradient button effect using the **Lock Transparent Pixels** option that's provided for layers. This option is useful for rounded rectangles or other shapes for which we're not provided with automatic selection tools.

Let's use it to make a rounded rectangle button. Using the Rounded Rectangle Tool (*U*) with the **Fill Pixels** option selected, create a sold-colored, raster button on a new layer. Click the **Lock Transparent Pixels** icon in the **Layers** palette, as shown in the example above. Then, set the foreground and background colors to your gradient tones and apply the gradient. Since you've locked the transparent pixels, the gradient will be applied only to non-transparent elements in the layer: your button, in this case.

Vector Buttons

If you're not happy
making raster buttons,
you can create vector
shapes and apply the
gradient effect to them.
Open the **Layer Style**
dialog box by clicking
on the **Add a layer style**
button at the bottom
of the **Layers** palette and
selecting **Gradient Overlay...**
from the menu that appears.
The gradient overlay options will be displayed.

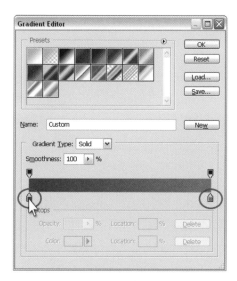

Gradient Overlay options

Adjust your gradient by clicking on the
Gradient patch in the **Layer Style** dialog
box. This will bring up another dialog box,
the **Gradient Editor**, shown here, which you
can use to set your gradient options. The
colors of your gradient are represented
in tiny color patches underneath the
gradient bar. Double-click on them to
bring up the **Color Picker**—you can use this
to change the color of the patch (and
consequently, your gradient). Add more
colors by clicking anywhere along the
bottom of the gradient bar—a new color
patch will be placed there.

The **Gradient Editor** dialog

Click **OK** in both dialog boxes, and *voila*!
You've got your two-toned gradient button.
And because we've "overlaid" our gradient
onto our button, the original color of the
button is inconsequential!

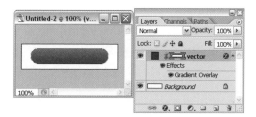

Vector button with **Gradient Overlay**

Making a Round Push-button

In this solution, we'll call on the trusty gradient button-creating skills we learned in the solution "Making a Gradient Button" to make a round push-button like the one shown here.

Round push-button

Solution

1   Create a circular gradient button on a new layer.

2   On another layer, create a circular gradient button that's a bit smaller than the first. The direction of the gradient on this button should be the opposite to that of the first button—in this example, my big circle has a white-to-gray diagonal gradient and my small circle has a dark-to-light diagonal gradient.

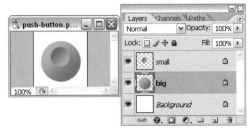

Creating two circular gradient buttons

(Don't be too concerned about lining the shapes up just yet.)

3   Select the layer for the smaller circle from the **Layers** palette. Hold down *Ctrl* (*Command* on a Mac) and click on the layer thumbnail for the larger circle to create a selection based on the pixels of that layer, as I've done here. (We talked about this in Chapter 1, remember?)

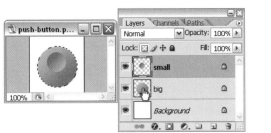

Creating a selection

4   After you've created the selection, select **Layer** > **Align Layers To Selection** > **Vertical Centers** as shown here. This will vertically align the center of the small circle with the center of the larger one.

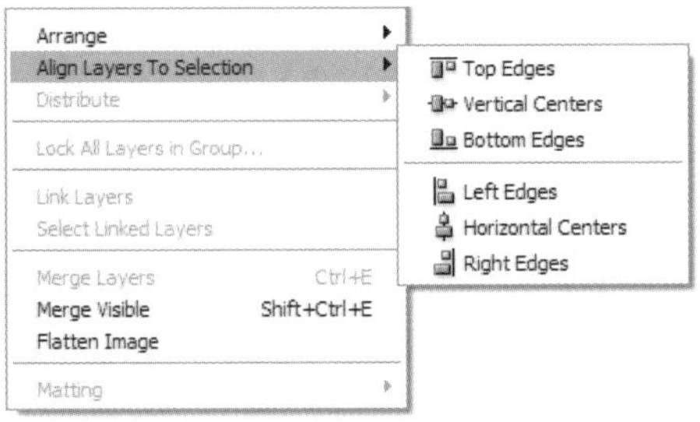

5   Finally, select **Layer** > **Align Layers To Selection** > **Horizontal Centers**, and just as you suspected, the centers of both circles will align horizontally.

Aligning vertical centers

Your push-button is complete!

Making a Metallic Button with a Matte Finish

More buttons that use gradients! Just as well we brushed up on our gradient button-making skills in "Making a Gradient Button". We're going to make matte-finish metallic buttons like the ones shown here.

Matte-finish metallic buttons

Solution

Rectangular, Matte-finish, Metallic Button

1   First, create a simple raster gradient button. I'm going to use two different shades of gray for mine.

#a7acaf

#707578

Creating a grayscale gradient button

2   Lock the layer by clicking on the **Lock Transparent Pixels** icon at the top of the **Layers** palette. Select a light gray (I've used #ebeef0) and use the Pencil Tool (**B**) to draw left-hand and top borders on the rectangle button layer.

3   Select a dark gray (I've used #515a60) and draw bottom and right-hand borders onto the button layer, as shown in the example below. Remember to keep your lines straight by holding down *Shift* as you're drawing them.

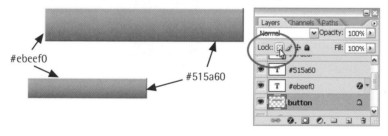

#ebeef0

#515a60

Drawing borders

4   Sure, we could use the button as is, but I'd like to do a few more things to it. First, we're going to apply a noise filter to our button. Before we do this, make sure that you're happy with the size, shape, and color of the button, as it's hard to make changes to these properties after the filter has been applied. To add the matte finish, select **Filter > Noise > Add Noise**. This will give the button a grainy look and display the **Add Noise** dialog box. Be sure to check the **Monochromatic** checkbox, and adjust the amount of noise that you want to introduce. I've set mine to 2%.

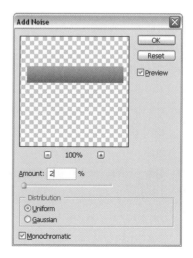

Adding noise

5   If you feel that the grainy effect is too pronounced, select **Edit** > **Fade Add Noise** to drop it back a bit. Change the opacity of the fade (in the example below, I set mine to 50%) and click **OK**.

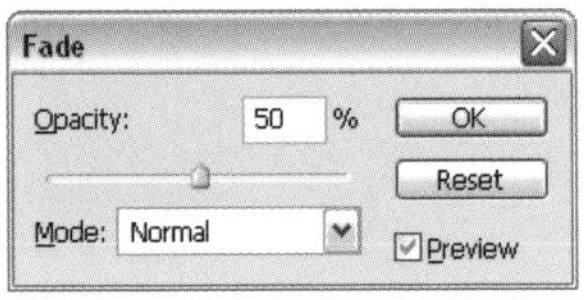

Fading the noise effect

NOTE   Use Fade Promptly!

To use the **Fade** command on a filter, you'll need to do so immediately after the filter has been applied—otherwise it won't be available.

6   Let's look at our button now. It's certainly something we could use, but while we're on a roll, let's jazz it up a bit more with some lighting effects. Select **Filter** > **Render** > **Lighting Effects** to bring up the **Lighting Effects** dialog box, shown to the right. Select **Spotlight** from the **Light type** drop-down menu.

Rectangular matte metallic button

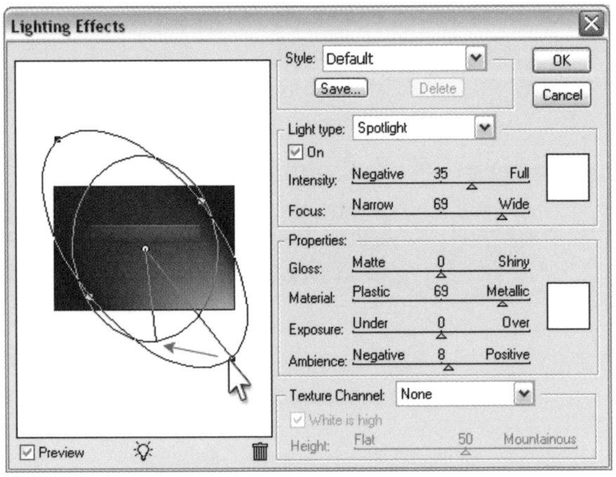

Changing the direction of the spotlight

7   In the preview graphic, you'll see an ellipse with a line through it—this line indicates the direction of the light. Click on the direction handle at the end of the line and drag it to the upper left-hand corner of the preview window. You can then click and drag the handles on the ellipse outwards to increase the "spotlight" area, as shown to the right.

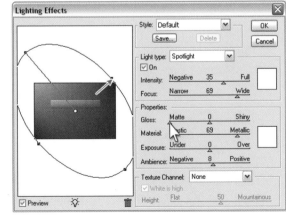

Applying the lighting effect

8   Finally, drag the **Gloss** property slider towards its **Matte** side (shown at the bottom of the previous page). When you're satisfied with your button preview, click **OK**.

Now we're happy! Our finished button is shown below.

Our pride and joy

Rounded, Matte-finish Metallic Button

Creating a rounded matte-finish button is pretty much the same as creating a rectangular one. The main difference is that we're going to use a stroke layer effect to add the borders, since it's going to be difficult for us to draw the borders accurately by hand.

1   Create a rounded gradient button. I used the same shades of gray I used for the rectangular button in the previous solution.

#a7acaf

#707578

Rounded gradient button

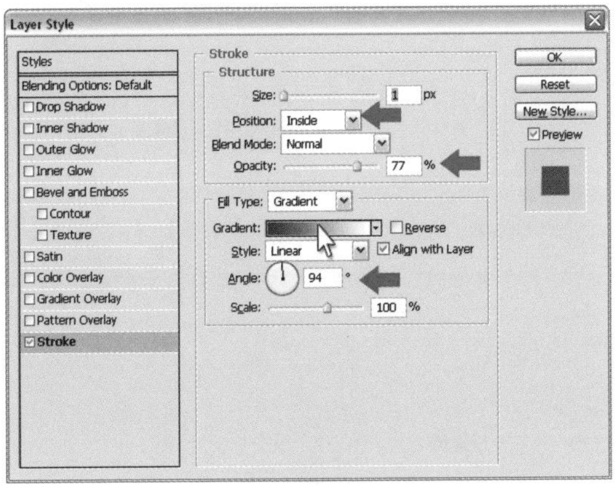

Stroke layer style settings

2   Now, instead of drawing a border as we did for the rectangular button, open the **Layer Style** dialog box for **Stroke** and give your border the settings shown here:
   ■ **Size:** *1px*
   ■ **Position:** *Inside*
   ■ **Opacity:** *75%*

3   Change the **Fill Type** to **Gradient**. Click on the **Gradient** swatch and set the gradient colors to white (#ffffff) and a darker gray (#384046). As the opacity of the stroke is lowered, you'll want more contrast between the light and dark colors. (If you're wondering why you need to lower the opacity, it's so that the noise and lighting effects will show through.)

4   Adjust the **Angle** so that most of the gradient stroke is at a slight angle in relation to the button.

5   Click **OK** to apply the stroke effect. The example at right shows the result of our stroke.

#ffffff

#384046

Applying the stroke effect to the button

6   Now, add noise and apply a lighting effect
    (steps 4–8 in the Rectangular, Matte-finish
    Metallic Button solution), and your rounded
    button is complete!

Completed rounded matte-finish metallic button

Making a Shiny Metallic Button

Here, I'm going to show you how to create shiny,
metallic buttons like the ones shown to the right.
I'll also show you how you can vary their
appearance using different settings.

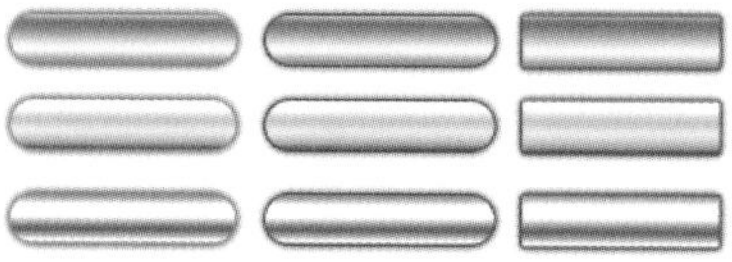

Shiny metallic buttons

Solution

1   Create a raster or vector button. I've created both
    a rounded and rectangular button in this example.
    The color of the button is unimportant, as it won't
    affect the final result.

Basic buttons

2   The fun begins! Open the **Layer Style** dialog box by clicking on the **Add a layer style**
    button at the bottom of the **Layers** palette and selecting **Outer Glow** from the menu
    that appears. In the dialog box, change the **Blend Mode** to **Normal**, and click on the
    color swatch (light yellow by default) and change it to gray, as shown here.

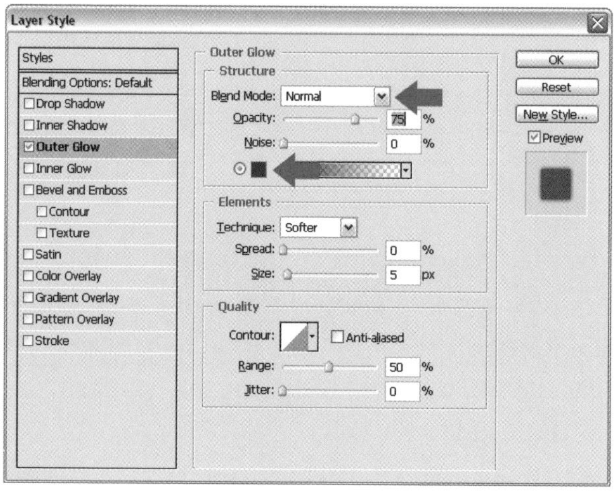

Applying outer glow

3   Now, select **Stroke** from the styles list in the dialog box to add a stroke layer effect. I used a dark gray, 1px stroke, as shown here.

4   We're ready to add the gradient overlay (there go those gradients again!). Select **Gradient Overlay** from the **Styles** list in the dialog box, and double-click on the **gradient** color swatch to open the **Gradient Editor** dialog box. Set the colors of the gradient as I've done overleaf.

Applying a stroke to the button

Add more color patches to the gradient bar by clicking anywhere along the bottom of it. Edit the color of a patch by double-clicking on it to bring up the **Color Picker**. You can also click and slide color patches to adjust the appearance of your gradient.

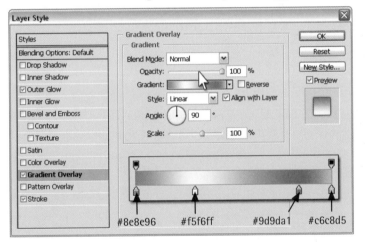

Adding the gradient overlay

5   Click **OK** to apply all the layer styles. Your shiny, metallic button is complete! Turn off the **Stroke** style for a more subtle effect (uncheck its checkbox to do so)—I did this for the left button in the examples shown here.

Completed shiny, metallic buttons

Variations

You can vary the appearance of your shiny button by playing with the gradient editor settings. The examples below show how the look of our shiny button changed when different gradient configurations were applied.

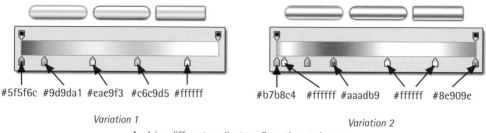

#5f5f6c #9d9da1 #eae9f3 #c6c9d5 #ffffff   #b7b8c4 #ffffff #aaadb9 #ffffff #8e909e

Variation 1   *Variation 2*

Applying different gradient configurations to buttons

Making an Aqua Button

In this solution, I'll show you how to make the brightly colored, glassy buttons that originated from Apple's Aqua interface many years ago, and since then have come to be affectionately known as "aqua buttons."

Examples of aqua buttons

As we're talking about buttons in this chapter, I'll show you how to create the button effect here, but if you've taken a particular liking to the brushed metal background I've used in this chapter, don't worry—we'll learn how to create that in the next chapter!

Solution

1   Start with a rounded vector button. We're going to be adding a gradient overlay to it, so its color's unimportant—use any color you like! The first step is to apply a gradient overlay to our button. Open the **Layer Style** dialog box by clicking on the **Add a layer style** button at the bottom of the **Layers** palette and selecting **Gradient Overlay** from the menu that appears.

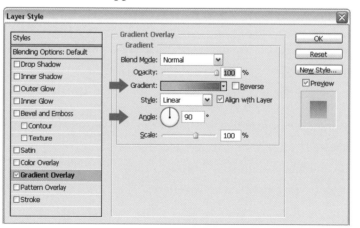

Applying a gradient overlay to the button

2   In the dialog box, set the angle to 90° (shown above) and click on the **Gradient** patch to display another dialog box for the **Gradient Editor**, shown opposite.

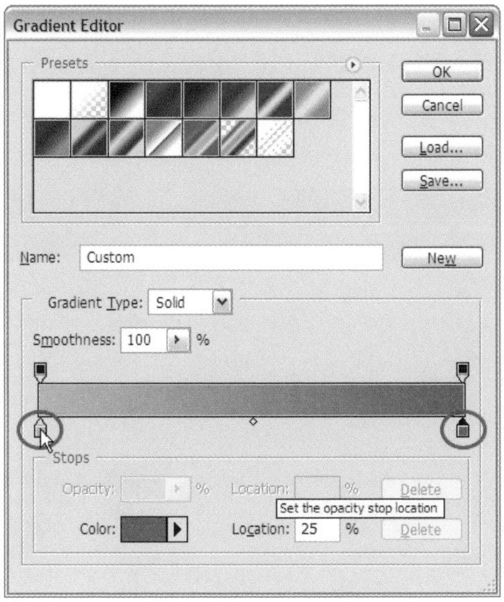

Changing the gradient settings

3   Let's change our gradient settings using the **Gradient Editor**. Double-click on each of the tiny color patches below the gradient bar to change its color. Create an aqua-to-blue gradient by setting the color of the patch on the left to aqua (#3cc9e2), and the color of the patch on the right to blue (#1160c2). Set the **Location** of the aqua patch to *25%*, and click **OK** to apply the gradient.

4   Back in the **Layer Style** dialog box, click on **Inner Glow**. Set the **Blend Mode** to **Normal**, the **Opacity** to *50%*, and the **Size** to about *10px*, depending on the size of your button. Click on the color patch and change the color to a dark blue, as shown in the example below—I've used #003298.

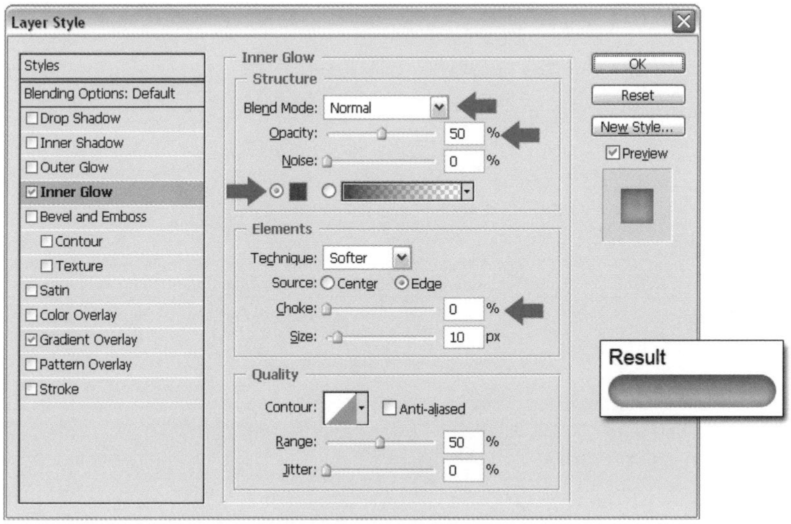

Applying an **Inner Glow** layer style

5   Next, we'll apply a slight glowing effect. Click on **Outer Glow**. Change the **Blend Mode** to **Normal**, the **Opacity** to *50%*, the **Spread** to *4%*, and the **Size** to *5px* (you might need to tweak these settings to suit the size of your button). Change the color patch to a bright aqua color, as shown below—I've used #00bae8.

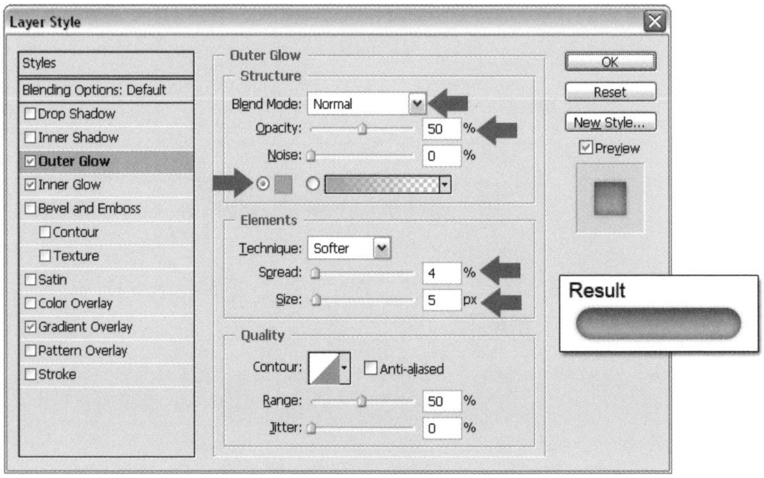

Applying the **Outer Glow** layer style

6   Click **OK** to apply all the styles.

7   To create the button highlight, duplicate the button layer by pressing *Ctrl-J* in the **Layers** palette (*Command-J* on a Mac). Turn off the **Outer Glow** and **Inner Glow** styles for this layer by clicking on their corresponding eye icons, as shown at right.

8   Double-click on the **Gradient Overlay** style name in the **Layers** palette. The **Layer Style** dialog box will appear, with **Gradient Overlay** selected. Click on the **Gradient** patch to bring up the **Gradient Editor**.

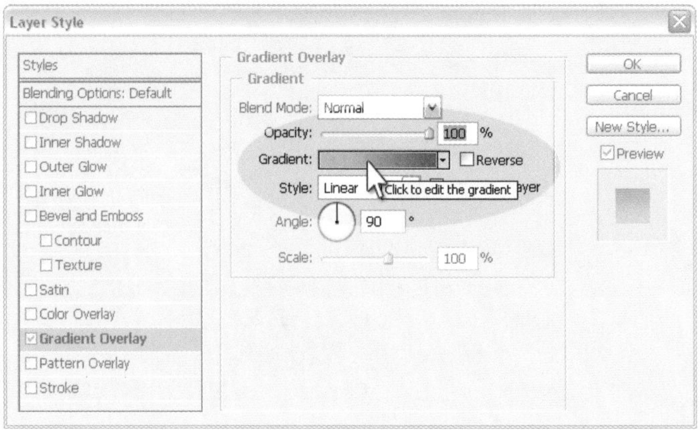

Turning off the layer styles of the highlight

Editing the gradient

9 Double-click on the color patches underneath the gradient bar in the **Gradient Editor** and set them both to white.

10 Click on the patch *above* and on the left-hand side of the gradient bar— this is the left opacity stop. Set its **Opacity** field to *0%*, as shown at right.

11 Click **OK** to exit the **Gradient Editor**, and again to apply the new style.

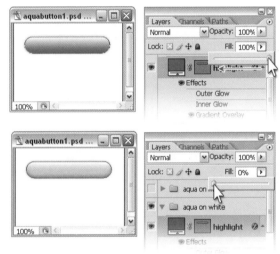

Step 10: Creating a white-to-transparent gradient

12 In the **Layers** palette, change the fill for the shape to *0%*. This will allow the button on the bottom layer to show through, as shown at right.

13 With the highlight layer selected, open **Edit > Free Transform** or press *Ctrl-T* (*Command-T* on a Mac). A bounding box will appear around the highlight. Click on the bottom edge of the bounding box, and drag it upwards to squash the highlight a little bit.

Step 12: Changing the fill of the highlight layer

14 Next, click on the right- and left-hand sides of the bounding box, and drag the edges of the highlight until they are just inside the button layer. Your highlight layer should look something like the one shown in the graphic at right. Apply the transformation by double-clicking inside the box, or pressing *Enter* (*Return* on a Mac.)

Step 13: Transforming the highlight layer

15 Switch to the Direct Selection Tool (**A**). Click and drag the bottom edge of the highlight path upwards to flatten it, as shown below. Use **Ctrl-+** (**Command-+** on a Mac) to zoom in if you need to.

Changing the shape of the highlight

16 We're finally ready to add the text! Create a text layer in between the highlight and button layer and type in your text. I've used a dark blue color for mine. I've also added a subtle drop-shadow style to my text using the settings shown in the example below.

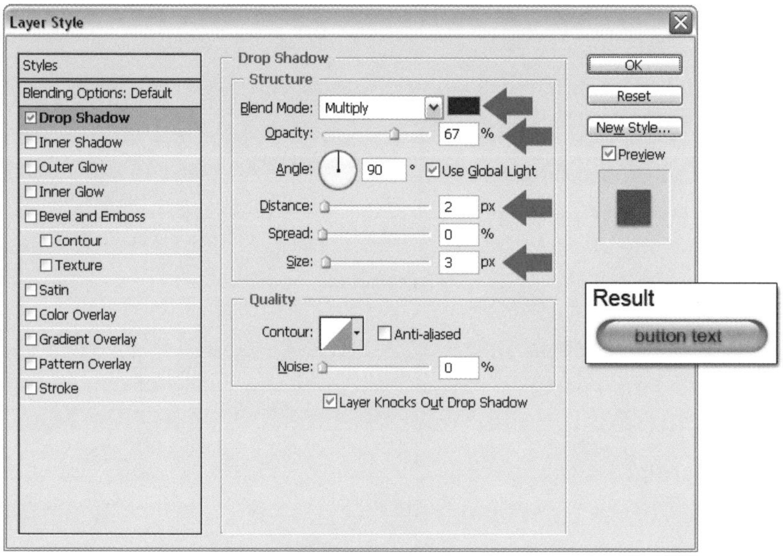

Applying a drop shadow to text

17 At this point, we've got a snazzy aqua button that will work well on most web sites, but since we've made a habit of taking things those few steps further, why stop now? Let's make our button look like it's been embedded into the page. Duplicate the button layer and drag it to the top, above the other layers. Let's call this top layer *emboss*; your **Layers** palette should now look like the image shown at right.

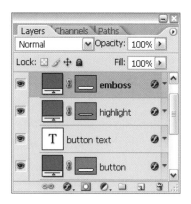

Duplicating the button layer

18 Hide all the layer styles on our *emboss* layer by clicking their respective eye icons in the **Layers** palette. Open the **Layer Style** dialog box by clicking on the **Add a layer style** button at the bottom of the **Layers** palette and selecting **Bevel and Emboss...** from the menu that appears. Select **Pillow Emboss** from the **Style** drop-down menu and change the technique to **Chisel Hard**. Set the **Size** to *2px* and the **Angle** to *90°*.

Applying the **Bevel and Emboss** style

19 Towards the bottom of the dialog box you'll see opacity fields for **Highlight Mode** and **Shadow Mode**. Set these both to *93%*.

20 Finally, apply a stroke to the edge of the button. You should be familiar with this by now! Select **Stroke** from the **Layer Style** dialog box and give your button a *1px* black stroke with *60%* opacity, as shown in the dialog at right.

21 Click **OK** to apply the layer styles.

Adding a **Stroke** layer effect

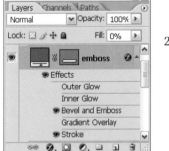

Changing the fill of the emboss layer

22 Let's change the **Fill** of the *emboss* layer to *0%*, as shown at left, so that the button layer beneath it can show through.

Our embedded aqua button is complete! The image at right shows our normal and embedded aqua buttons.

Completed aqua buttons

Discussion

Since we created this aqua button using vector shapes and layer styles, we have a scalable button that's easy to edit. If we want to change its colors, all we have to do is change the colors of the gradients and effects in our layer styles. If we want our button to be slightly longer, we can use the Direct Selection Tool (*A*) to modify the vector path.

This solution has demonstrated an important concept about layers: even when the fill of a layer is set to 0%, the layer styles still show up! You may find this useful when you're creating your own effects.

Another cool thing about this technique is the fact that once you've created your first aqua button, it's very easy to create other buttons— you just have to copy the layer effects. I'll quickly show you how you can make a rectangular aqua button in a few simple steps.

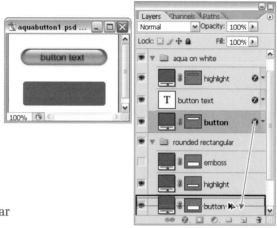

Copying styles to another layer

1   In the **Layers** palette, create the layers you'll need for the rectangular button: the base *button* layer, the *highlight* layer, and, if you're planning on using the embedding effect, an *emboss* layer, as shown above.

2   To copy the layer effects from the original aqua button to the rectangular button, hold down *Alt* (*Option* on a Mac) and drag the **layer style** icon from the original *button* layer over to its corresponding rectangular *button* layer, as shown in the image above.

3   Change the fill of the *highlight* layer to 0%.

4   Add the button text and repeat step 2 to copy the drop shadow style we used for the original text.

That's it! Your rectangular aqua button is ready to be used, and should look like the one on the page opposite.

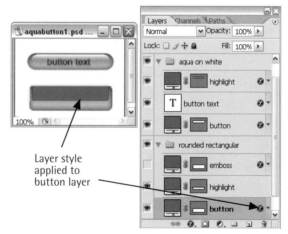

Layer style applied to button layer

Button layer with styles applied

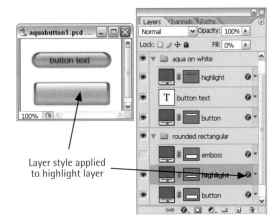

Layer style applied
to highlight layer

Highlight layer with styles applied

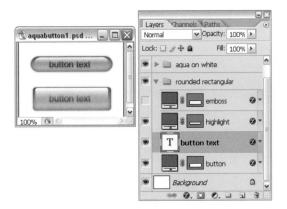

The final rectangular button, and the rounded button on which it was based

Making a Transparent Aqua Button

We can also make our aqua buttons see-through, like the one shown here. In this solution we're going to begin with a basic aqua button. If you don't already have one (and everyone should!), you can make one by following steps 1–16 of the "Making an Aqua Button" solution.

Transparent aqua button

Solution

1   Place your basic aqua button on top of a faint, patterned background, as shown here.

Basic aqua button on top of faint, striped background

2   Double-click on the **f** icon for the layer—
    this will bring up the **Layer Style** dialog
    box. Select the **Gradient Overlay** style
    and click on the **Gradient** swatch to
    bring up the **Gradient Editor**.

3   Click once above the gradient bar, in the
    position shown in this image,
    to create a new opacity stop.
    Change its opacity to *50%*.

4   Click **OK** to exit the **Gradient Editor**,
    and **OK** again in the **Layer Style** dialog
    box to apply the style.

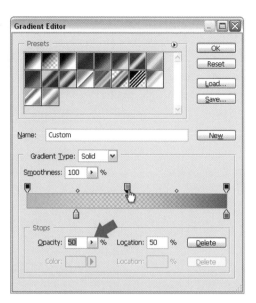

Adding new opacity stop

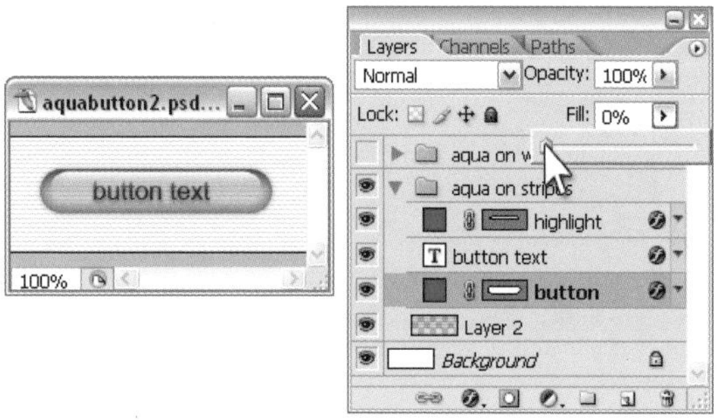

5   Set the fill of the button layer
    to 0%, as shown at left. The
    background will show through.
    That's looking pretty good! But,
    as always, there are a couple of
    things we can do to make it look
    even more polished.

Changing the fill of the button layer

6   Double-click the
    f icon to open the
    Layer Style dialog box,
    and select the **Drop
    Shadow** style. Choose
    a bright aqua color for
    the shadow (#90c9e7)
    and increase the
    Distance and **Size**
    slightly. Change the
    Opacity to *40%*, as
    illustrated at right.

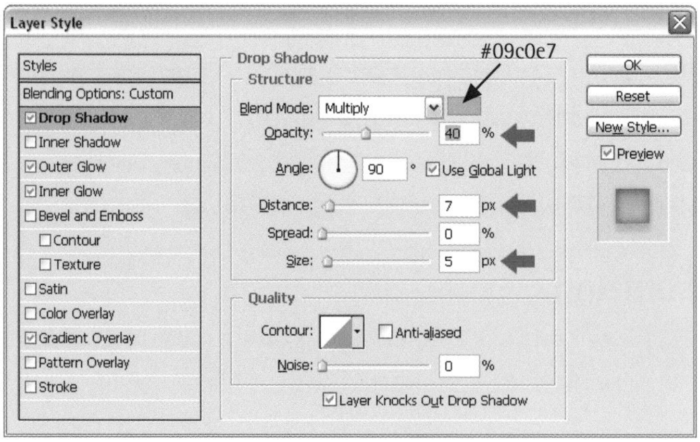

Adding a drop shadow

7 Next, select the **Stroke** style. Add a dark blue (#0d487b) 1px stroke, with about 75% opacity, as shown below.

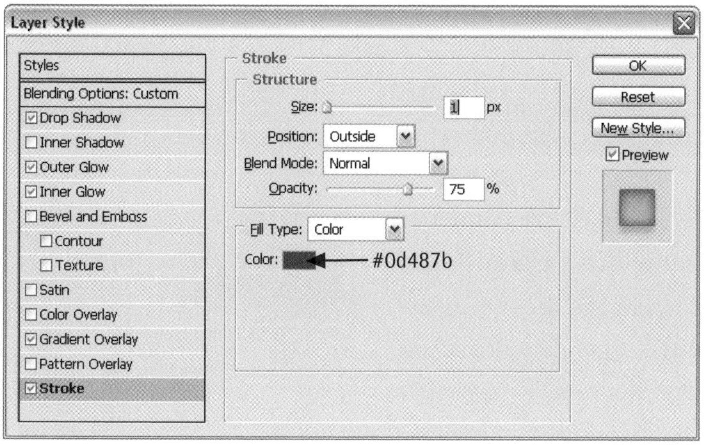

Adding a stroke

8 Finally, select the **Inner Shadow** style. Change the shadow color to a blue that's slightly darker than the one we used in the original gradient button. Lower the **Opacity** to *50%*, and change the **Distance** to about *10px* (or whatever suits the size of your button), as shown below.

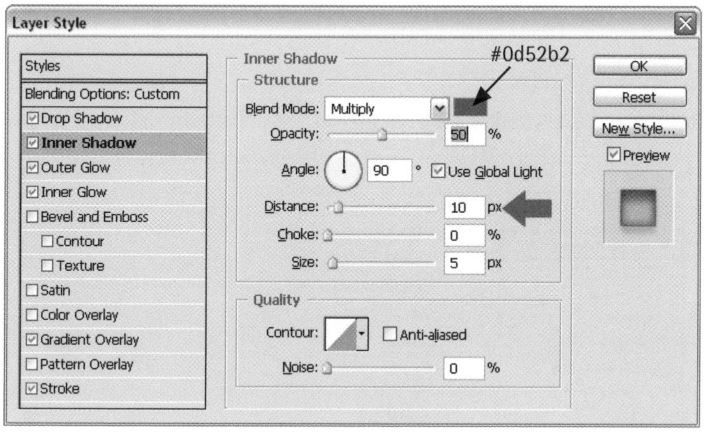

Adding an inner shadow

9 Click **OK** to apply these new styles. And—as you can see below—we've got our final transparent aqua button! Swish, *very* swish!

See-through aqua button

Making a Plastic Button

In this solution, we'll be using Photoshop magic to turn our friend, the basic gradient button, into a plastic button like the one shown here.

Plastic button

Solution

1. Start with a rounded rectangle gradient button that has a radius of 5px. You can change the radius in the Rounded Rectangle options bar. Use the color stops shown here in your gradient overlay layer style. If you're unsure of how to do this, look at the solution for "Making a Gradient Button." I've made my button green, but you can use different colors for yours if you like.

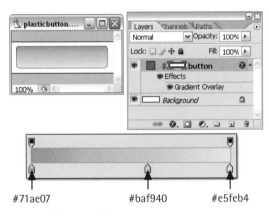

#71ae07   #baf940   #e5feb4

Green rounded rectangle gradient button

Just choose a darker shade of your color for the color patch on the far right, a very light shade for the color patch on the far left, and a bright shade for the patch in between, as shown above.

2   Add a dark green, 1px stroke layer style to your button, as shown below.

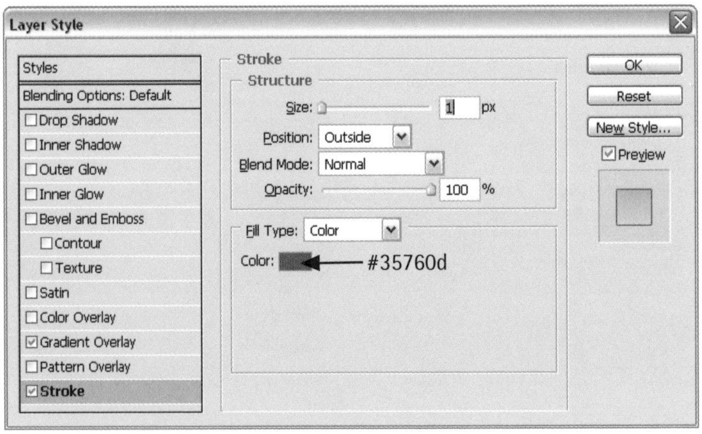

Adding a stroke to the button

3   Add an outer glow using a bright version of the button color, as shown below.

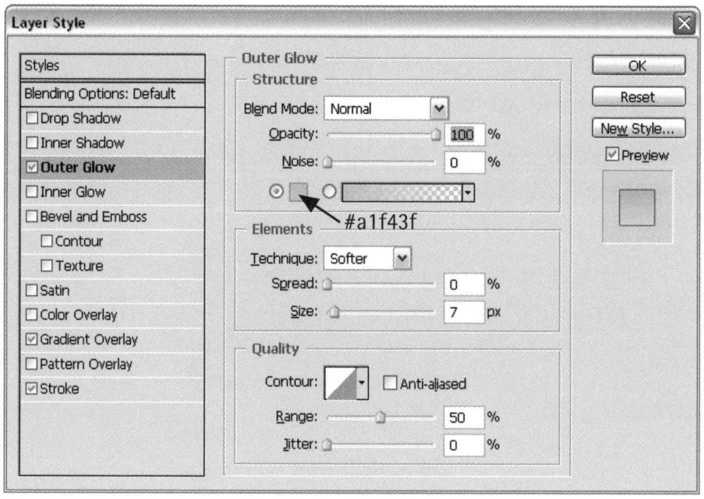

Adding an outer glow

4   Select the *button* layer in the
    Layers palette and duplicate it
    using *Control-J* (*Command-J* on
    a Mac). Right-click (hold *Control*
    and click) on the new layer and
    select **Clear Layer Style** from the
    menu that appears, as shown at right.

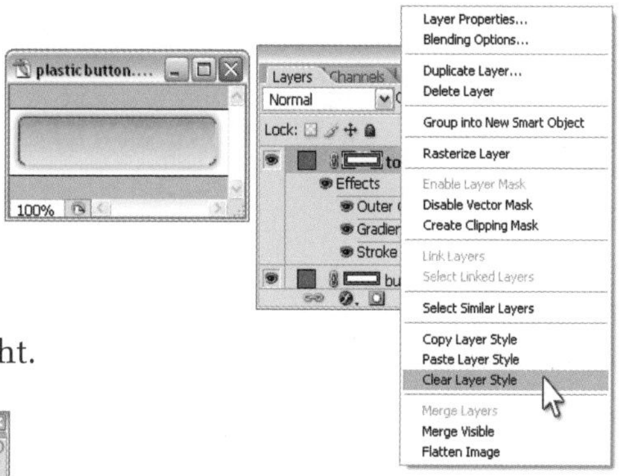

Clearing the layer style

Changing the color of the shape layer

5   Change the **Opacity** of this layer to 50%, and double-click on its color patch to
    open the **Color Picker**. Set the color of the shape to white, as shown above.

6   Now, click on the vector shape for the
    same layer in the **Layers** palette. Using
    the Direct Selection Tool (**A**), click on the
    bottom line of the rounded rectangle and
    drag it up a little bit, as shown at right.
    You might need to zoom in for this.

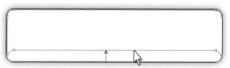

Editing the vector shape

7   Still using the Direct Selection Tool (**A**), click on the bottom-left anchor point so that you can see the handlebars of the point (zoom in if you need to). Click on the bottom handlebar, hold down **Shift**, and drag the handle up to curve the corner.

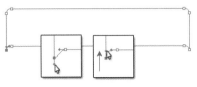

Curving the corner

8   Repeat step 7 with the bottom-right point. The sides of your shape should now look like those shown at right.

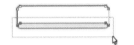

Selecting multiple points for editing.

Shape after modifications

9   With the Direct Selection Tool (**A**), click and drag the mouse to make a selection that captures all of the bottom points, as shown in the image to the left.

10   Hold down **Shift** and drag the selected points up to make a thin strip, as shown at right—this is our highlight. Fine-tune the movement using the up and down arrow keys if you need to.

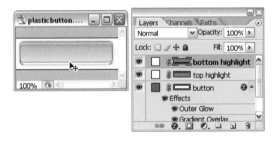

Making the highlight strip

11   Select the highlight layer in the **Layers** palette and duplicate it using **Ctrl-J** (**Command-J**). Select **Edit > Transform > Flip Vertical** to flip the duplicated layer.

12   Use the Move Tool (**V**) to move the flipped highlight to the bottom of the rectangular button, as shown at right.

13   We're almost there! Now duplicate the button shape layer and name it **middle highlight**. Change the color of the shape to white.

Adding bottom highlight

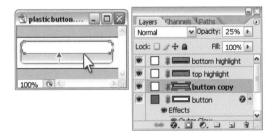

Modifying the third highlight shape

14   Select the bottom anchor points of the **middle highlight** shape and move them up to the center of the original button shape. Change the opacity of this layer to **25%**, as illustrated in the image on the left.

15 Add a text layer immediately on top of the original button shape (beneath the three highlight layers) and type your text. If you like, add a drop shadow for an added three-dimensional effect, as I've done for the completed button at right.

The completed plastic button

Making a Glass Button

In this solution, we're going to create an eye-popping glass button that's particularly effective when it's overlaid on photographs and non-solid backgrounds.

Example of glassy button

Solution

1 Start with a vector button of any shape in a color that blends in with your background. Here, I'm using a pink that I color-picked from the sunset image onto which I'm going to place my button. Set the fill for the button layer to 0%. Open the **Layer Style** dialog box by clicking on the **Add a layer style** button at the bottom of the **Layers** palette and selecting **Bevel and Emboss...** from the menu that appears. Apply the settings used here, which are illustrated in the dialog below:

- **Style: Inner Bevel**
- **Technique: Chisel Hard**
- **Depth:** *800%* or larger (depending on the size of your button)
- **Direction: Up**
- **Size:** *13px* (You may need to adjust this later.)
- **Soften:** *7px*
- **Angle:** *-65°*
- **Altitude:** *65°*

Bevel and Emboss settings for the glass button

- **Gloss Contour:** Rolling slope-descending (Set this by clicking on the drop-down arrow next to the contour shape and choosing the Rolling slope-descending option, as depicted overleaf.)
- **Highlight Mode:** White, *75%*
- **Shadow Mode:** Dark gray, *75%*

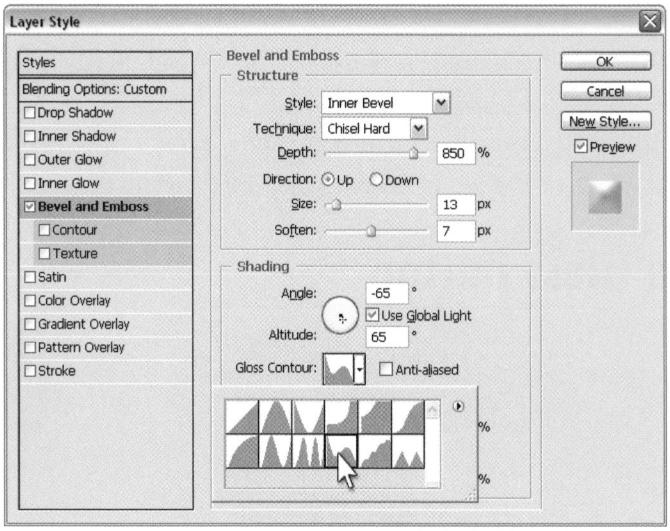

Setting **Gloss Contour**

Your button should be looking like the one shown below.

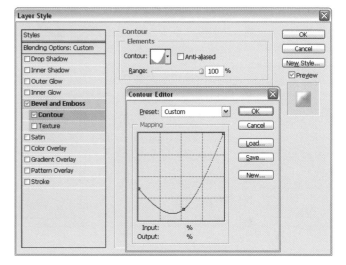

After applying a **Bevel and Emboss** effect

2   In the **Layer Style** dialog box, click
    on the **Contour** style under **Bevel
    and Emboss** to select it. Click on the
    thumbnail image of the contour to
    bring up the **Contour** editor, shown
    at right.

3   Select and move the bottom-left
    point of the contour until it's
    positioned just above the first
    horizontal grid marker. Then, click
    on the contour line to add another
    point and drag it to form a curve.

Changing the contour curve

The image at right shows our button after the contour effect has been applied.

After applying the **Contour** effect

4   Not bad, huh? Now, select the **Satin** layer style and apply the settings shown here:

■   **Blend Mode: Overlay**; black

■   **Opacity:** *30–40%*

■   **Angle:** *126°*

■   **Distance:** *4px* (You may need to adjust this later.)

■   **Size:** *10px* (You may need to adjust this later.)

■   **Contour:** Cone-inverted

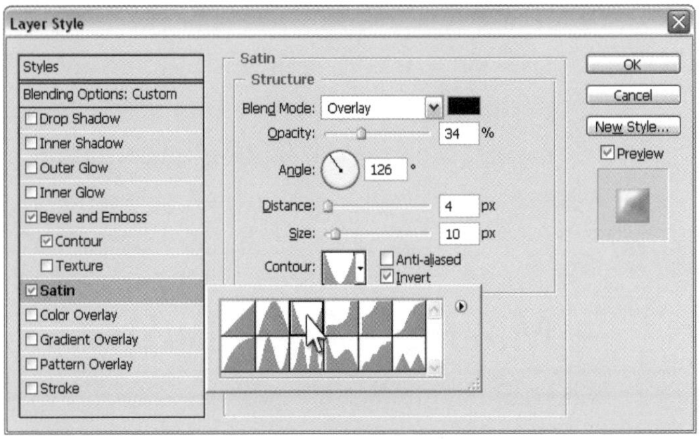

Applying the **Satin** layer style

5   Select the **Drop Shadow** layer style. Change the **Distance** to *4px*, the **Size** to *10px*, and the **Opacity** to *50%*, as shown in the example below.

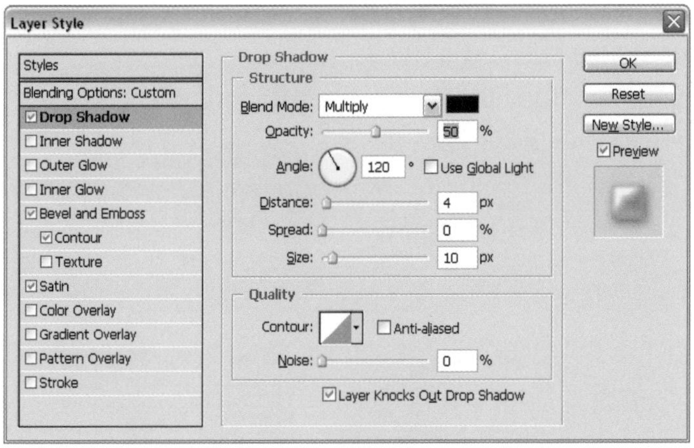

Applying a drop shadow

At this stage, our button's looking quite glassy, as can be seen in the image at right.

Applying a drop shadow

6 All we need to do now is add a simple text layer with a slight drop-shadow! Your completed button should look like the image to the right.

Completed glassy button

You can easily copy this layer style to other shape layers. When you do, remember to set the new layer fill to 0%. Experiment with the layer effects to change the look of your button. The images at right show variations of my glass button.

Glassy button style applied to different shapes

Bevel and emboss shadow set to 20% opacity

Making a Pearl Button

Here's a solution that uses real magic … well, almost! We're going to take the glassy button we created in "Making a Glass Button" and turn it into a pearl button!

Example of a pearl button

Solution

1 Start with the glassy button you created in the solution titled "Making a Glass Button." Change the fill of the button layer to 100%, as shown at right, and use a very light, "pearly" color for the shape. I've used #fae1f9 for my pink, pearly button.

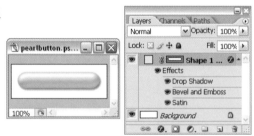

Changing the fill color

2 Enhance the three-dimensional effect of the button by adding a slight inner glow. Double-click on the **f** icon for the layer to bring up the **Layer Style** dialog box, shown at right. Select **Inner Glow** and change the **Blend Mode** to **Normal** and the **Opacity** to *10%*. Increase the **Size** if you need to.

Adding an **Inner Glow** effect

3   We'll also make the drop shadow a bit more subtle. Select **Drop Shadow** and decrease the shadow size to 3px or 4px.

4   Finally, add your text layer. Here we see our final button—all done!

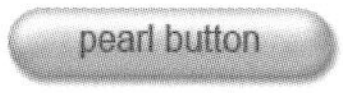

Completed pearl button

Making Angled Tab Buttons

In this solution, I'll show you how to use vector graphic tools to create the angled tab buttons illustrated below.

Examples of angled tab buttons

Solution

Angled Tab

1   Start with a rectangular vector shape in a color of your choice. I've used a light blue in the image below.

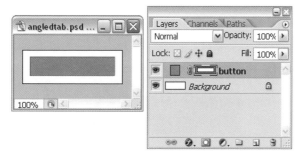

Starting with a rectangular button

2   Using the Direct Selection Tool (**A**), select the top left-hand anchor point of the rectangle. Hold down the **Shift** key and move the point to the right by pressing the right arrow once or twice. Your image should look something like the one at

Moving the anchor point

right. Release the **Shift** key and use the arrow keys to fine-tune the point. We'll go "old school" here and count the number of times we press the arrow key so that we know how far to move the point on the right-hand side when we get to it.

3   Repeat step 2 for the top, right-hand anchor point.

That's it—believe it or not, our angled tab button is complete! If you don't believe me, look at the finished result below.

Completed angle button

Cut-corner Tab

1   This time, we'll make a tab button with a cut corner. Again, start with a rectangular vector shape. Select the Add Anchor Point Tool—you'll find this in the flyout menu of the Pen Tool (**P**), shown at right.

Selecting the Add Anchor Point Tool

2   Add an anchor point to the side of the button as I've done in the example below (you might need to zoom in).

Adding a point to the button

3   Choose the Convert Point Tool, which is also in the flyout menu of the Pen Tool (**P**).

Selecting the Convert Point Tool

4   Click once on the new anchor point to get rid of the direction handlebars, as shown below (left).

Converting the anchor point

5   Using the Direct Selection Tool (**A**), click on the top corner anchor point and use the arrow keys to move the anchor point across to form a "cut corner", as illustrated below.

Moving the anchor point   Completed cut-corner tab

6   If you like, repeat the effect on the other side; otherwise, take a moment to marvel at our cut-corner tab, shown above and to the right.

Making a Rounded Tab Button

The basic rounded rectangle button is very versatile. Here, we're going to convert it into the popular rounded tab button like the one shown at right.

Rounded tab button

Solution

1   Start with a rounded rectangle vector shape, as shown below.

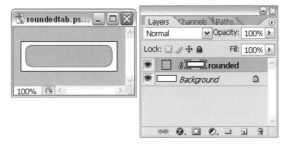

Rounded rectangle shape

2   Select the Convert Point Tool, which is in the flyout menu for the Pen Tool (*P*). Click once on each of the two anchor points, as shown below, to convert them from curve points to angle points.

Converting the anchor points

3   Use the Direct Selection Tool (*A*) to make a selection around the two bottom-most anchor points on the shape. To indicate that they have been selected, the points will turn from white squares to filled squares, as shown at right.

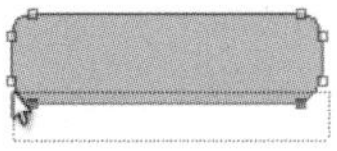

Selecting the bottom two anchor points

4   Delete the anchor points by pressing *Backspace* or *Delete* on the keyboard. Your image should now resemble the one shown at right.

Deleting the two points

5   With the Pen Tool (*P*), click first on the bottom anchor point on the left-hand side, and then on the point on the right-hand side, as shown at right. This will draw a line connecting the two points and complete the shape, which is shown below.

Closing the shape

Completed rounded tab button

Making a File Folder Tab Button

In this solution, you'll learn how to create a nice file folder tab, shaped much like those real folder tabs used in filing cabinets. Remember those old-fashioned things?

Example of a file folder tab button

Solution

1   Using the Pen Tool (*P*), click once to add an anchor point to your Photoshop document (step 1 in the image at right.)

2   Position the cursor over the anchor point. Hold down *Shift* and *Alt* (*Shift* and *Option* on a Mac), click on the point, and drag the mouse towards the right to create a single horizontal handlebar (step 2 at right).

3   Position the cursor as shown in step 3 at right. Click and drag the mouse towards the right to add another anchor point. The line connecting the two points should display a nice curve, thanks to the positions of our control handles.

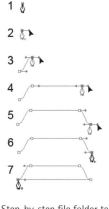

Step-by-step file folder tab

Completed file tab button

4   Holding down *Shift*, click and drag the mouse to the right of the last point we made in order to create another anchor point with horizontal control handles. Press *Shift* to ensure that the two points are aligned horizontally (step 4 at right).

5   Move the cursor a bit lower and to the right so that it's aligned horizontally with our first anchor point (step 5). Click to add another anchor point and drag the handlebars out to the right.

6   Bring the cursor back over the last point we made. Hold down *Alt* (*Option*) and click to remove the right handlebar (step 6).

7   Bring the cursor back to our very first point and click on it to complete the shape (see step 7 at right and the graphic below it).
     Don't worry if your alignment's not perfect—you can use the Direct Selection Tool (*A*) to select individual points, and the arrow keys to fine-tune them.

Summary

In this chapter, I showed you how to make all sorts of buttons! Beyond the obvious navigation buttons, the techniques you've learned here will allow you to make nifty bullet graphics and fancy title bars. For example, you could apply the plastic button effect to a longer rectangle that forms part of your interface, or use it as a bar for text links. You could also use the shiny metal button effect to create shiny metal bullets; you've got a gazillion options!

The experience you've gained with layer styles and vector shapes in this chapter will be invaluable to you later, when you're creating full web site comps. There's a lot more fun to be had in the next chapter—let's bring on those backgrounds!

Creating Backgrounds

If you're looking to create a gradient background, or a realistic texture for use on your web page, you've come to the right place!

In this chapter, I'll show you a stack of different solutions for creating seamlessly repeating backgrounds, realistic textures, and more!

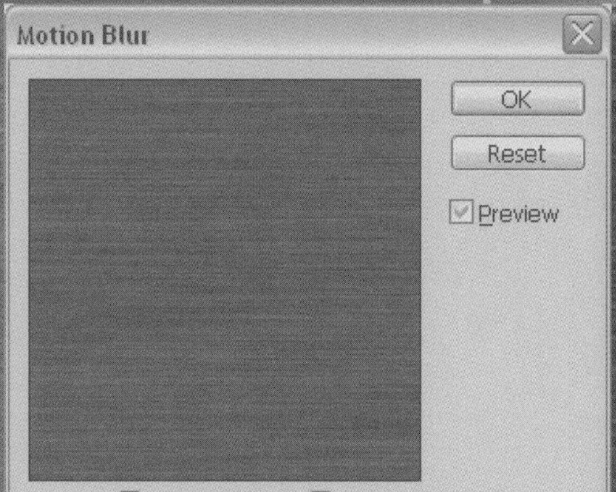

Motion Blur

OK

Reset

☑ Preview

⊟ 100% ⊞

Angle: 0 °

Distance: 80 pixels

Making a Seamless Tiling Background

Tiled backgrounds are a common design element on the Web. In this solution, I'll show you how to create a series of tiling backgrounds that repeat seamlessly, such as the one shown in the image on the right, using any shape or pattern that you like.

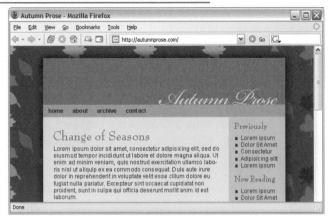

A seamless tiling background in use on a web site

Solution

Custom Shapes

Create a new Photoshop document and draw your shapes. I've used some of the leaf shapes that come with Photoshop's Custom Shape Tool (*U*), and put each shape on its own layer so that I can easily move them around later. While you're creating your shapes, make sure that they're within the boundaries of the document.

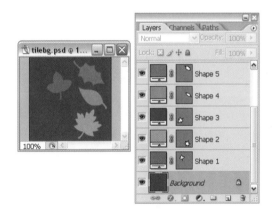

Creating shapes

When you've arranged your shapes as you'd like, hold down *Shift* and click on each shape's layer in the **Layers** palette until you've selected all of them. Right-click (hold *Ctrl* and click on a Mac) on one of the selected layers and choose **Duplicate Layers** from the menu that appears.

Now select **Layer > Merge Layers** or press *Ctrl-E* (*Command-E*). This will merge the duplicated layers onto a single raster layer that contains all the shapes. Hide the original shapes by clicking on their layer eye icons in the **Layers** palette.

You're probably wondering why we went through all the trouble of duplicating and hiding the original

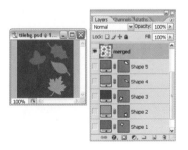

Merging the duplicated layers

layers when we could just have merged them. It's so that we can keep our original layers intact in case we need to revert back to them later.

If we were to use our image as is in a repeating background, we'd get some noticeable "gaps" in the pattern, as shown here.

Background with noticeable gaps

Let's fix this. Select **Filter > Other > Offset**. In the dialog box that appears, set the **Horizontal** field to half your document's width, and the **Vertical** field to half your document's height. Since my document dimensions are 150 pixels by 150 pixels, I've set both the fields to 75 pixels. Select the **Wrap Around** option, and click **OK**. The rasterized shape layer will be moved to the right and shifted down by the number of pixels you've specified, and any leaves extending beyond the document boundary will be "wrapped around," as shown in the example below.

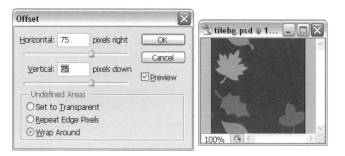

Applying the offset filter

Now you can fill in the empty gap with more shapes, as shown at right. Again, ensure that your shapes stay within the document boundaries.

That's it! Save it for the Web, and your background is ready to be tiled. The example on the next page shows what our final image will look like when it's repeated on a web page (the original tile we created is highlighted with the red square).

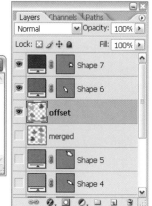

Filling in the gaps

Web page with tiling background

Photographic Backgrounds

We can create tiles for photographic backgrounds in the same way: by applying the Offset filter and filling in the "gap." However, it's a lot trickier to adjust a photographic image in a way that retains its authenticity.

For this solution, I'm using a selection from a photo of coffee beans as my tile. I've used a photo in which the lighting is pretty uniform and there's no perspective to deal with—these are things you should keep in mind when selecting your photo, as you'll be "blending" the edges of the tiles together. I'm using a selection rather than the whole photo to make the blending process a bit easier. For best results, I've chosen an area of the photo in which there's little variation in lighting.

NOTE   To Tile or Not to Tile

The image below shows an example of a photo that I would *not* use as a background tile. The perspective of the photo, which makes the front candies appear larger than the ones at the back, as well as the different colors, would make it almost impossible to "blend" the edges of tiles together.

A selection of good coffee beans

A selection of bad candies

Let's get started! With the original photo open, copy the selection you want to tile and paste it into its own layer in a new document. Select the layer in the **Layers** palette and duplicate it using *Ctrl-J* (*Command-J*). Apply the offset filter to the new layer, as illustrated here.

Applying the **Offset** filter

Position the document windows next to each other so that you can see both the original photo and the tile document. We're going to **clone** areas of the original photo into the new document, then use layer masks to blend the cloned areas.

In the original photo, locate the area from which you made your tile selection. Select the Clone Stamp Tool (*S*), hold down *Alt* (*Option*) and click once within this area. This sets up the "source" for the clone stamp.

Create a new layer in your tile document, and name it *first clone*. Select a medium-sized brush from the options bar and

Setting the source for the Clone Stamp Tool

paint on the new layer. As you paint, you'll see a crosshair cursor moving in the document that contains the original photo, as shown above—this shows you where the information is being cloned from.

In this example, I've dimmed the *offset* layer so that you can see the cloned area more easily. As you can see, I've cloned more than appears in the background picture so that I can hide some of those offset edges.

Cloning an area

After cloning a small patch of the original photo, you may need to switch to the Move Tool (*V*) and carefully line up the cloned patch with the offset layer beneath it.

NOTE   Lining up Layers

When you're lining up the layers, it may help to temporarily lower the opacity of the layer that contains the cloned patch to about 50%, so that you can see the layer underneath. If the two layers are not quite aligned, that particular section of the image will look blurry. You can then adjust the layers until the picture "snaps" into focus, and return the layer's opacity to 100%.

If it's hard for you to tell when the layers are aligned, change the blending mode of the cloned patch to Difference mode using the drop-down menu on the top-left of the **Layers** palette. This compares the clone layer's pixels with the layer below and shows the difference in color between the two. If the layers are aligned, you'll see only black. If this isn't the case, you can use the arrow keys to move the layer until it snaps into place.

Take a look at the example shown here: the top two images are unaligned. The top, right-hand image has lowered opacity and shows a slight blurriness.

The top, left-hand image has the cloned patch set in Difference mode. You can see faint outlines of the shapes, indicating that the layers aren't aligned correctly.

The two images at the bottom of the example show what the layers look like when they are perfectly aligned. The image on the left-hand side shows the black patch that displays in Difference mode.

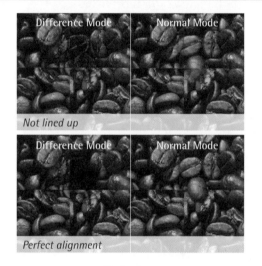

Aligning layers

Add a layer mask to the clone layer by clicking on the **Add layer mask** button at the bottom of the **Layers** palette. Set your foreground color to black and, with a soft-edged brush, paint around the cloned section to blend it into the background, as I've done here.

Adding a layer mask to the clone layer

Create another new layer in your tile document and select the Clone Tool (**S**). Holding down *Alt* (*Option*), click in the original photo document to set up another source point, and clone more areas into the new layer on the tile document as you did earlier. Add a layer mask for this layer as well. The example overleaf shows my *second clone* layer with its layer mask.

The second cloned layer that helps to create a seamless effect

Repeat this process until the image looks suitably blended (you'll probably need to shuffle the layers around a bit and adjust the layer masks to achieve this). As you can see from the example shown at right, I've used five clone layers (I've color-coded these so that you can see which is which).

Final clone layers

The example on the right shows what our final tile looks like, and the example below shows what it looks like when it's repeated on a web page (the original tile is highlighted with a yellow square).

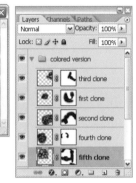

Photographic tiling image

Web page using tiling image

Making a Striped Background

Striped backgrounds are quick and super-easy! In this solution, I'll show you how to create horizontal, vertical, and diagonal striped backgrounds.

Solution

Horizontally-striped Background

Create a new document that's 1 pixel wide and at least 2 pixels high. The height will determine the amount of spacing between the stripes. In this example, my document is 1 pixel wide and 4 pixels high. Then select the Pencil Tool (**B**) and select a foreground color for your stripe. I've used gray. On a new layer, draw a gray dot near the bottom of the canvas, as shown at right (you may need to zoom in to do this).

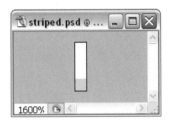

Creating a striped background

Next, hide the background layer by clicking on its eye icon in the **Layers** palette. Select **File > Save for Web...** and save your image as a transparent GIF. You're done!

The image at right shows what this image looks like when it's applied to a web page; the very tiny background tile is highlighted.

Striped background applied to a web page

Vertically-striped Background

This is almost the same as creating a horizontally-striped background. Just make sure that your new document is 1 pixel high and at least 2 pixels wide, and draw your dot on the vertical edge of the canvas.

Diagonally-striped Background

Create a new document with "square" dimensions. I've created a 5 pixel by 5 pixel document to make my diagonal background. Use the Pencil Tool (**B**) to draw a diagonal line from one corner of the document to another. (You'll have to do this pixel-by-pixel, so zoom in for accuracy.)

Hide the background layer by clicking on its eye icon in the **Layers** palette, and save your background using **Save for Web...**. This example shows what our image looks like when it's used on a web page, as well as what the pattern looks like zoomed-in.

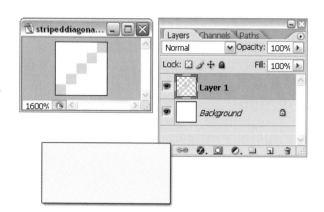

Creating a diagonal pattern

Making a Pixel Background

Earlier, we learned how to use the Pencil Tool to create basic striped backgrounds. Now, I'm going to show you how to use it to create more intricate patterns, like the one shown here.

Pixel pattern

Solution

Create a small document (mine is 25 × 25 pixels) and fill it with a background color. Select the Pencil Tool (**B**) and select a foreground color for your pattern. I'm after a subtle background pattern, so I'm using a lighter shade of my background color.

Creating a design for a pixel background

Zoom in (I went to 500%!) and draw your design on a new layer.

When you're done with your pattern, select its layer in the **Layers** palette and duplicate it using *Ctrl-J* (*Command-J* on a Mac). Hide the original layer and apply the offset filter to the new layer as we did in the solution for "Making a Seamless Tiling Background."

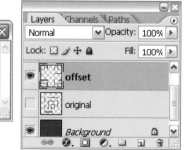

Applying the offset filter

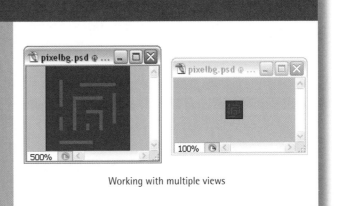

TIP   Two Views at Once

You can open another window to see what your pixel image looks like at its original size (100%) while you're drawing. Select **Window > Arrange > new Window for [your filename]**. This will open a second window for your document (set at 100% zoom). Any changes that you make in one window will be duplicated in the other.

Working with multiple views

If you want, draw more shapes in the center area to fill in the pattern.

Save your completed pixel background using **Save for Web…** .

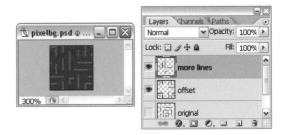

Filling in the center of the background

The examples below show what my completed pixel image looks like, and how it appears when it's repeated on a web page (the original tile image is highlighted with the orange square).

Completed pixel background image

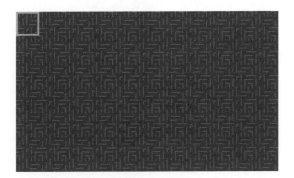

Pixel background on a web page

Making a Gradient Background

Solution

Create a new document in Photoshop. For a horizontal gradient, you'll want your document to have a small width (as small as 1px wide!) and a larger height and, conversely, for a vertical gradient, you'll want a small height and a larger width. You'll repeat this thin image horizontally or vertically on your web page to create a gradient background effect. To get a feel for how your gradient will look, make your image wider than necessary and crop it later.

Once you've got your document set up, set your foreground and background colors to your gradient colors and use the Gradient Tool (**G**) to apply a gradient to your document.

Select **File > Save for Web...** to save your image. The gradient background image is ready to be used on your web page!

In the example shown here, I've created a tall, thin gradient for my background image.

This background image will tile horizontally

Discussion

To use the gradient background image on your web site, you'll need to set up the style sheet with a background color that matches the bottom portion of your gradient graphic. Your style sheet might contain a line that looks something like:

```
body {
    background: #9c9fab url(images/
    gradientbg.gif)
        repeat-x;
}
```

This example shows how the gradient background image integrates with the background color of a web page for a seamless result.

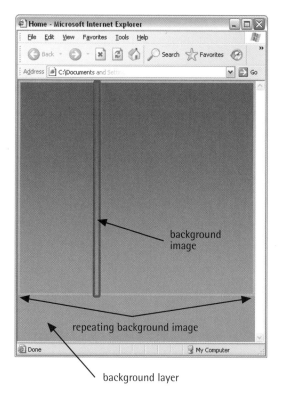

Breakdown of style sheet results

Creating a Brushed Metal Background

Solution

Create a new layer and fill it with a gray color. Select **Filter** > **Noise** > **Add Noise....** In the dialog box that appears, choose **Uniform** distribution with the **Monochromatic** option checked, as shown here. Vary the **Amount** based on how much contrast you want your brushed metal effect to have.

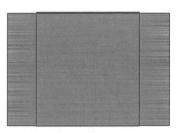

Adding noise

Next, select **Filter** > **Blur** > **Motion Blur....** Set the **Angle** to 0 and adjust the **Distance** until you're happy with the effect. Mine's set to 113 pixels in this example.

Adding the **Motion Blur** filter

You'll notice some discrepancy between the center of your document, which has blurred as you expected it to, and its outer edges, which have not. Crop your document to get rid of the outer edges.

Cropping badly blurred edges

Applying the offset filter

Duplicate the layer in the **Layers** palette using *Ctrl-J* (*Command-J* on a Mac) and apply the **Offset** filter (as described in the solution for "Making a Seamless Tiling Background") to the duplicated layer. Let's call this the *offset* layer.

Click on the **Add layer mask** button at the bottom of the **Layers** palette to add a layer mask to the offset layer. Remove the visible edge by selecting the Brush Tool (*B*), setting the foreground color to black, and painting around the center of the image (make sure that you're painting on the mask and not the image itself). The layer beneath will show through. Continue to blend the offset layer with the original layer by painting on the mask with shades of gray.

The example at right shows the results of my layer mask (shaded in pink so you can see it more easily).

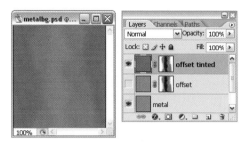

Adding a layer mask

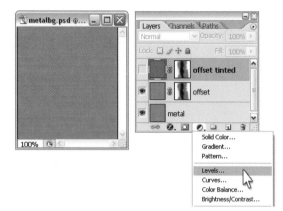

Creating a **Levels** adjustment layer

To adjust the contrast of your background, add an adjustment layer by clicking on the **Create new fill or adjustment layer** button at the bottom of the **Layers** palette and selecting **Levels…** from the menu that appears.

To lighten your background, click on the white slider and drag it to the left in the **Levels** dialog, shown below. Conversely, you can make your background darker by clicking on the black slider and dragging it towards the right.

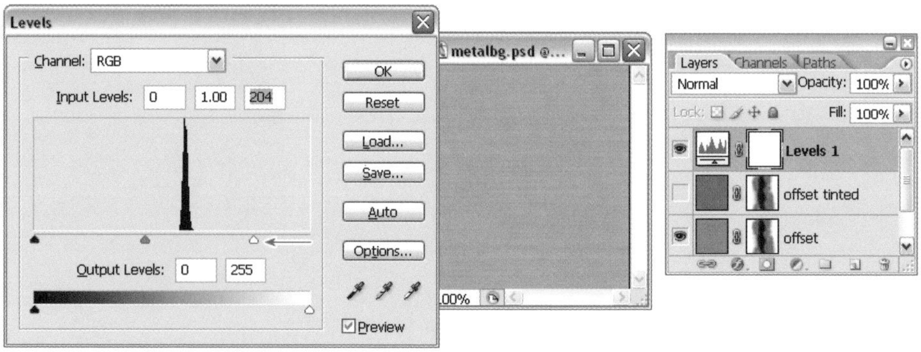

Using the **Levels** adjustment layer to lighten or darken the background

Your brushed metal background is complete! In the example shown here, I've used my background on a button and added some layer styles and other effects.

My metallic button

Creating a Wood-grain Background

Solution

Fill the background layer of your document with a brown color. We're going to add a **Noise** filter as we did when we created a brushed metal background earlier. Select **Filter > Noise > Add Noise**. In the dialog box that appears, set the amount to 65% or thereabouts for a higher contrast, and check the **Monochromatic** option, as shown at right.

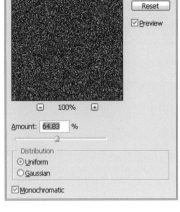

Adding noise

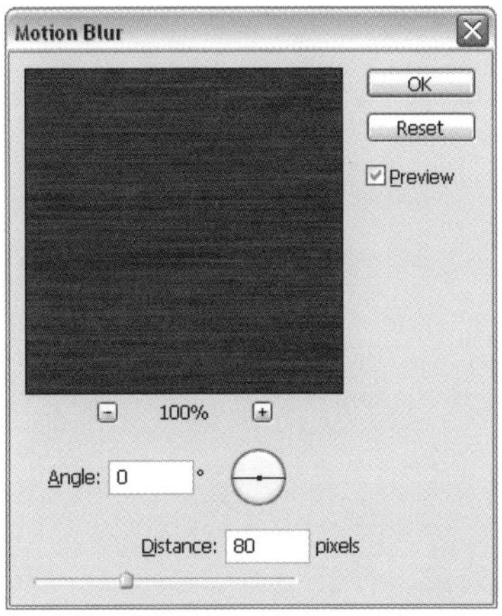

Bring up the **Motion Blur** dialog box by selecting **Filter > Blur > Motion Blur**. Set the **Angle** to *0°* and the **Distance** to about *80 pixels*.

The next few steps can be altered, depending on the type of wood effect that you're looking for. I'm going to use the **Hue/Saturation** and **Levels** commands to brighten the wood and give it a rich hue.

Adding motion blur

Select **Image > Adjustments > Hue/Saturation** or use the shortcut *Ctrl-U* (*Command-U* on a Mac) to bring up the **Hue/Saturation** dialog box. Increase the **Saturation** to an amount that works for you—I used a value of 48.

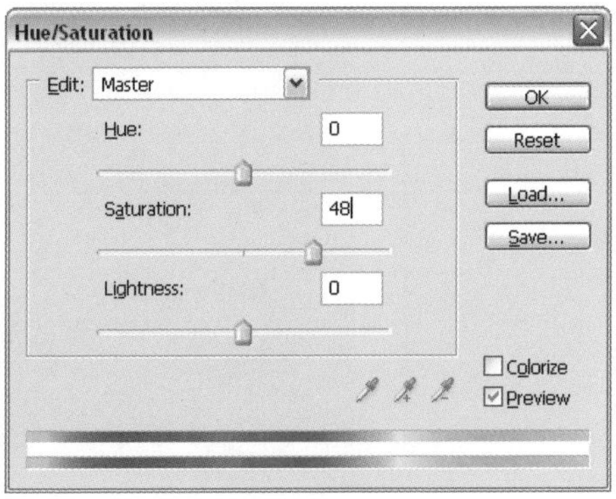

Increasing the saturation

Increased saturation

The colors of my wood-grain now look brighter, as shown here.

TIP   Subtle Beauty

If you're creating an image that you want to tile, you might not want the repeating background to be too obvious. Bear this in mind when you're applying effects. For example, if you use the Bloat Tool to create a "knot" in the wood, the frequency of the repeated knot would hinder the authenticity of your wood-grain background. I'd recommend sticking with more subtle effects.

Next, select **Image > Adjustments > Levels** or press *Ctrl-L* (*Command-L*). Increase the contrast by dragging the black and white sliders towards the center, as shown at right.

Here comes the fun part! Select **Filter > Liquify**. The Liquify filter dialog has several settings that you can use to achieve different effects, as shown below. Select a tool and experiment with it by clicking and dragging, or holding your cursor over the texture.

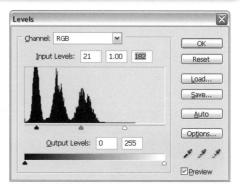

Adjusting the levels

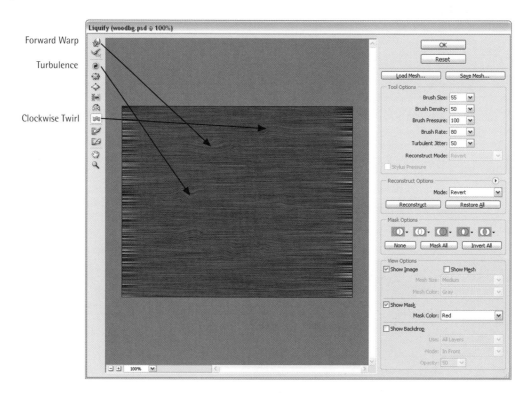

Using the **Liquify** filter

Next, crop the image to remove the edges that were not blurred, as shown below.

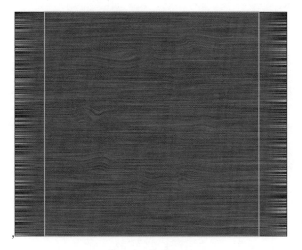

Cropping the image

Duplicate the layer and apply the offset filter, as described in the solution for "Making a Seamless Tiling Background." Then, apply a layer mask to the *offset* layer, as shown at right. Using the Brush Tool (**B**), select a soft-edged brush and paint in black along the middle of the image mask to hide the seam. Blend the *offset* layer

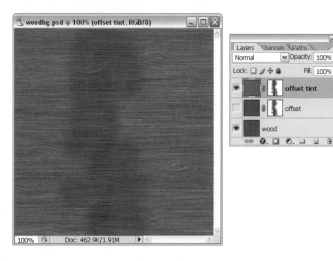

Applying a layer mask

with the background layer by painting in different shades of gray. This example shows my layer mask results (in green).

Export your completed wood-grain texture using **Save For Web...** , and you're done! The example overleaf shows what my image looks like when it's tiled on a web page.

Seamless wood-grain background

Making a Granite Background

Solution

Fill the background layer of your document with a dark gray color. Select **Filter > Noise > Add Noise** to bring up the **Add Noise** dialog box. Set the **Amount** to *50%* and check the **Monochromatic** option, as shown at right.

Adding a **Gaussian Blur** effect

Adding noise

Next, select **Filter > Blur > Gaussian Blur** and set a **Radius** of *.5 pixels* (half a pixel) in the dialog box.

Now select **Edit > Fade Gaussian Blur** or press *Shift-Ctrl-F* (*Shift-Command-F* on a Mac) to bring up the **Fade** dialog box and fade the effect by 90%. Remember, the fade command will be unavailable for the blur effect unless you select it *immediately* after you've added the Gaussian Blur.

Apply the Offset filter (as described in the solution for "Making a Seamless Tiling Background"). You may be able to pick out faint edges. Use the Clone Stamp Tool (*S*) with a hard-edged brush to hide the edges by cloning areas of the existing pattern (for more details on using the clone tool, see the solution using photographs for "Making a Seamless Tiling Background").

Using the clone tool

In the example shown on the right, the blue cross shows the areas I've cloned.

The result is shown below—a seamlessly tiling image that looks like granite stone. If only it were that easy to make granite in real life!

Granite stone background image

Making a Textured Stone Background

Solution

Set your document's foreground color to black and its background color to white. Create a new layer above the background layer and select **Filter > Render > Clouds**. Photoshop will use your foreground and background colors to create a cloud pattern. The filter's random, so you get a different effect each time, but your clouds should look something like the ones shown here.

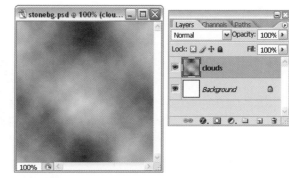

Creating clouds using the clouds filter

Open the **Channels** palette. At the bottom of the palette, click on the **Create new channel** button, as shown below. This will create a new channel called *Alpha 1*.

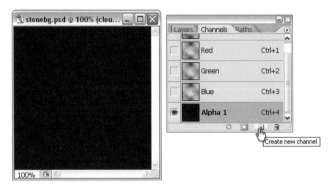

Creating a new channel

Select **Filter** > **Render** > **Difference Clouds**. This will produce an effect similar to the one created using the cloud filter earlier. Now, press *Ctrl-F* (*Command-F*) to repeat the last filter command. Your clouds will intensify. Continue pressing *Ctrl-F* (*Command-F*) until you've got something similar to the example shown here, where the proportions of light and dark tones are almost equal.

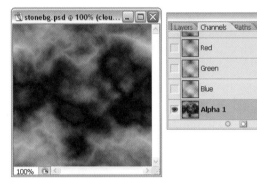

Applying the **Difference Clouds** filter to the alpha channel

Reset your view by selecting the **Layers** palette and clicking on the clouds layer. Select **Filter** > **Render** > **Lighting Effects** and apply the following settings:

- **Light type: Directional**
- **Intensity:** *14*
- **Gloss:** *0*
- **Material:** *0*
- **Exposure:** *5*
- **Ambiance:** *10*
- **Texture Channel: Alpha 1**
- **Height:** *85*

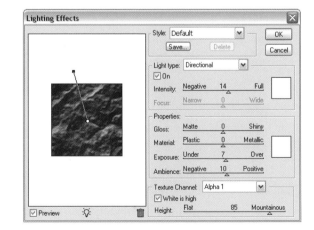

Adding lighting effects

Look at the preview in the dialog box and experiment with some of the settings to see how they affect your image. When you're happy with the way your image looks, click **OK**. Mine now looks like the example shown on the right.

Results of lighting effects

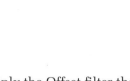

Applying the offset filter

Apply the Offset filter that we used in the solution for "Making a Seamless Tiling Background" at the beginning of the chapter to turn your image into—you guessed it—a seamless tiling background!

I used "special dimensions" (as discussed in the introduction to this chapter) for this document, so the result is practically seamless. My only concern is a very faint line across the center of the image. I'm going to use the Clone Stamp Tool (**S**) with a hard-edged brush to tidy it up.

Using the Clone Stamp Tool

All done! As you can see in the example above, I didn't have to clone too much to hide the seam. The example below shows my final image.

Final rough stone image

NOTE   A Different Look

With this technique, there's a lot of room for variety. Something you might want to try is using the **Noise** filter (**Filter > Noise > Add Noise**) to add noise to the alpha channel before applying the Difference clouds filter. A large amount of noise will give your image a more "pebbly" texture. This example shows an image I created using this technique.

Noisy stones

Here we can see this image used on a web page.

Tiling image used in a web page

Making a Textured Paper Background

Solution

Create a new layer and fill it with an off-white color. I've used beige (#f9f4e2).
Select **Filter > Texture > Texturizer**—this will open the **Filter Gallery** dialog box with the
Texturizer filter selected. Select **Canvas** from the drop-down menu and experiment
with the **Scaling** and **Relief** values until you're happy with the effect (see the example
below). I've used a **Scaling** value of *149%* and set **Relief** to *1*.

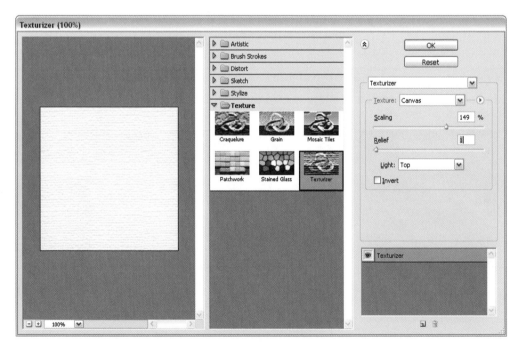

Applying the texturizer filter

You should be quite familiar with this process by now: duplicate the layer, apply the Offset filter (as described in the solution for "Making a Seamless Tiling Background"), and add a layer mask to the duplicated layer. Hide the seam by painting on the duplicated layer mask with gray, as shown in this example.

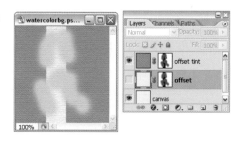

Hiding the seam using a layer mask

Next … there is no next! We've got our textured paper background. Too easy!

Final textured paper background

Making a Rice-paper Background

Yum. Oh, that's right, we're making paper backgrounds, not rice. Let's get to it!

Solution

Create a new layer and fill it with a background color of your choice. In this example I've chosen a dusky rose color (#da9082).

Now create another new document that we can use as a temporary document to create a custom brush. With black as the foreground color, select the Brush Tool (**B**) and use a small, hard-edged brush to paint a few curvy lines (my artistic skills are displayed in this example). This shape will be the base for our custom brush.

Creating a custom brush pattern

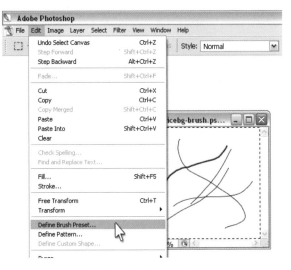

Creating a brush preset

Select your masterpiece using *Ctrl-A* (*Command-A* on a Mac) and create your custom brush by selecting **Edit** > **Define Brush Preset**, as shown in this example. Give it a name in the dialog box that appears, and click **OK**.

Selecting your custom brush

We don't need the temporary document any more, so you can close it (there's no need to save your changes). Back in your original document, select the Brush Tool (*B*) and scroll down the list of brush types in the options bar until you find your brush. Click on it to select it, as shown at right.

Open the **Brushes** palette and select **Shape Dynamics**. Increase the **Size Jitter** and the **Angle Jitter** to *100%*.

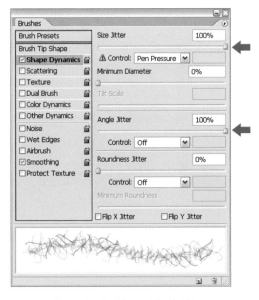

Increasing the **Size** and **Angle Jitter**

Next, click on **Scattering**. Adjust the settings to let your brush run wild. The example at right shows mine doing all sorts of acrobatics!

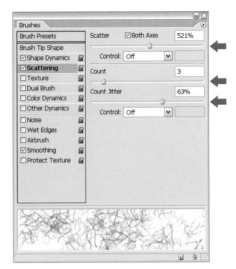

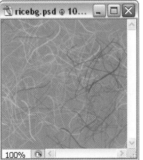

Running wild with the **Scattering** options

Adjusting the **Opacity** and **Flow Jitter**

Finally, select **Other Dynamics** and, as shown on the left, increase the **Opacity Jitter** and **Flow Jitter** until you like what you see.

Right, let's paint! Set the foreground color to white. Create a new layer and paint on it using your custom brush (you'll probably only need to click a couple of times, rather than dragging the mouse around) to add some white lines as I did in the example shown here.

Painting with the custom brush

Happily painting away

If you like, paint on a few more strokes using different colors. I've added some yellow and magenta in the image at left.

Next, choose the Dune Grass brush from the list of brush styles as shown in the example overleaf. Set the diameter of the brush to suit your texture (mine is set at 30px).

TIP   Loading and Saving Brushes

If the Dune Grass brush doesn't appear on the brush list, you can restore the default Photoshop brushes by clicking on the small arrow at the top-right of the brush list and selecting **Reset Brushes.** This action will replace any custom brushes you've created, so before you do this, make sure you've saved your brushes using **Save Brushes** from the same menu.

Set your foreground color to white and create a new layer. Click and drag the mouse back and forth until you've painted over the entire image, as shown below.

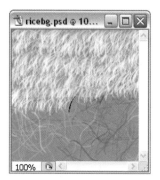

Using the Dune Grass brush

Lower the opacity of the dune grass layer to **20%** or thereabouts, and adjust the opacity on your custom brush layer if you need to. You now have a rice-paper texture!

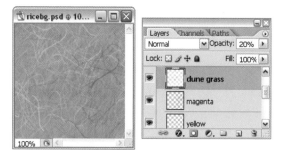

Adjusting the opacity of the layers

To turn it into a seamless tiling background, merge the three layers together, duplicate the merged layer, and apply the Offset filter (we've covered all these procedures in the solution for "Making a Seamless Tiling Background" earlier in the chapter). Hide the seams using the Clone Stamp Tool (**S**). Add a final flourish by using your custom brush to add a few more white or colored lines.

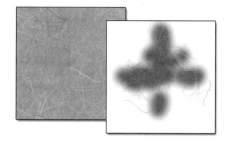

Using the Offset filter and Brush Tool to hide the seams

The example above (right) shows the seams that were created in my image with the Offset filter. The image in the foreground shows the areas I cloned in purple, and my new brush strokes.

And we're done! Our rice-paper background is ready for tiling.

Final rice-paper background image

Summary

In this chapter, we used the Offset filter to create tiling background images, and learned how to use the Clone Stamp Tool in conjunction with layer masks to hide the seams that were created by the Offset filter. I also showed you how to use several other Photoshop filters to create your own textures and backgrounds.

Remember that there aren't any limits to the use of the textures we've created here—you can use them in other design elements as well as in backgrounds!

Photoshop's not just about graphics—you can do a great deal with text, too! In this chapter, I'll start out by showing you how to do simple things, like adjusting the space between lines and letters. Then, we'll move on to working with paths, adding layer effects, and much, much more!

Adding a Single Line of Text

Adding a single line of text to your document is pretty straightforward with Photoshop's Text Tool.

Solution

Select the Text Tool (*T*) from the toolbar, and click once in your document. A flashing text cursor will appear, and a new layer will be created in the **Layers** palette, as shown at right. You can begin typing right away!

Click once to add a single line of text.

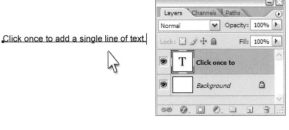

Adding a line of text

When you've finished typing, click on the large tick in the options bar, as shown in the example below, or select a different tool to apply the text. By default, the text layer will be named with the text that you've typed, but you can change this by double-clicking on the layer name.

If you've made a mistake, or decided that you don't need the text after all, you can undo your typing and exit the Text Tool by pressing the *Esc* key.

Applying the text layer

Word-wrapping Text

If you used the Text Tool as I described in the previous solution, you may have noticed that it only creates a single line of text—one that *never* word-wraps! This is bad news for those of us working with multiple lines of text. In this solution, I'll show you how to create text that will word-wrap automatically.

Solution

Select the Text Tool (*T*). In your document, click and hold down the mouse button, and drag the cursor to create a text area. Release the mouse button and type your text— it will automatically word-wrap within the boundaries of the text area that you created.

When you single-click to place text, the text will make one long line of text.

Left-click-drag to create a text area block which will allow your text to word-wrap.

Text word-wrapping within text area boundaries

You can adjust the size and position of the text area by dragging the bounding box handles, as shown in the example below, while the Text Tool (*T*) is selected.

Adjusting the text area

Increasing the Space Between Lines of Text

The term used to describe the spacing between lines of text is **leading** (pronounced "ledding", not "leeding"). In this solution, I'll show you how you can adjust the leading of lines in your text.

Solution

Using the Text Tool (*T*), highlight the text you want to alter. Open the **Character** palette by clicking on the **Toggle Character Palette** button in the options bar, as shown in the example below.

Opening the **Character** palette

In the **Character** palette, adjust the leading amount by selecting one of the existing numbers from the drop-down menu, as shown on the right, or by typing in your own value.

Here, you can see the display that results when two differing leading amounts are applied to the same paragraph.

The spacing between lines of text is called "leading." This block of text has a leading set to 36 pt with 12 pt font.

The spacing between lines of text is called "leading." This block of text has a leading set to 14 pt with 12 pt font.

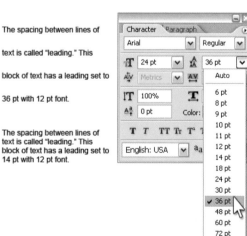

Adjusting the leading

Increasing the Space Between Letters

Tracking is the term used to describe spacing between letters. You can alter the tracking using Photoshop's **Character** palette. The tracking value you choose will apply to all letters in the selected text. You can also adjust the **kerning**, or spacing between two specific letters. In this solution, I'll show you how to do both.

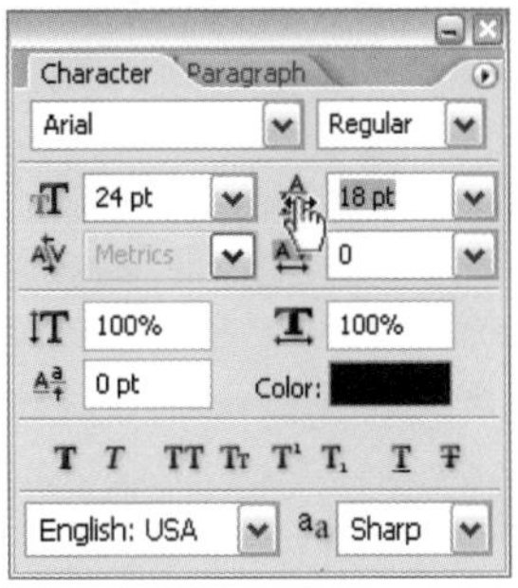

Solution

Adjusting Tracking

Using the Text Tool (*T*), highlight the text you want to alter. Open the **Character** palette by clicking on the **Toggle Character Palette** button in the options bar.

In the **Character** palette, adjust the tracking amount by selecting one of the existing numbers from the drop-down menu, as shown here, or by typing in your own value. This example shows the results when two different tracking values are applied to the same paragraph.

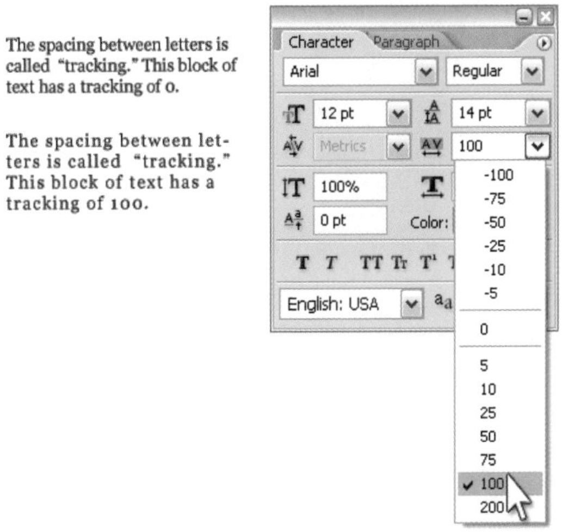

The spacing between letters is called "tracking." This block of text has a tracking of 0.

The spacing between letters is called "tracking." This block of text has a tracking of 100.

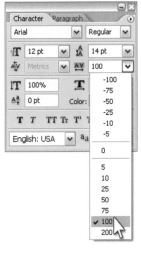

Adjusting the space between letters

Adjusting Kerning

With the Text Tool (*T*) selected, position the cursor between the two letters for which you want to alter the spacing, then modify the kerning value in the **Character** palette. Easy, hey?

This example shows how the spacing between two letters is affected when the kerning value is changed from the Photoshop default to *-170*.

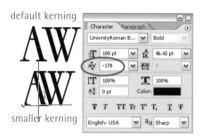

Adjusting the kerning between two letters

Word-wrapping Text Inside a Shape

Solution

To begin with, you'll need a shape. Create a shape of your choice using the Shape Tool (*U*) or the Pen Tool (*U*). If you're using the Shape Tool, make sure that you're *not* using the **Fill pixels** option.

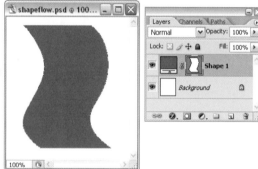

A vector shape created with the pen tool

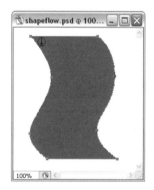

Changed cursor when inside the path

In the **Layers** palette, make sure that the thumbnail for the shape layer's mask is selected, as shown above. Next, select the Text Tool (*T*) and move your cursor inside the shape. The cursor will change to an I-beam with a dotted ellipse around it, as shown in the example on the left.

Click once—a text area will appear. Any text you now type will automatically word-wrap within your shape, as shown in the example on the right.

That's all well and good, but what if you want to alter the shape later? Your first instinct might be to adjust the shape layer, but if you try this you'll soon find

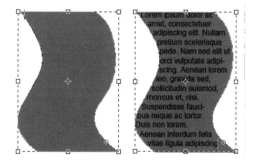

Adding text that flows within the shape

out that the text doesn't adjust to accommodate the new shape. This is because the text and the shape are independent of each other. Look in the **Layers** palette, and you'll see that the text has created its own layer, and the original shape layer remains untouched (see the example below). How do you adjust the shape of your text, then? Let me show you the path!

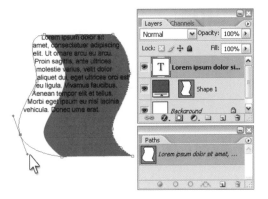

Adjusting the text path

If you select the text layer from the **Layers** palette, then view the **Paths** palette, you'll see your shape there. The path is what's causing your text to word-wrap.

You can adjust the shape of the path using the Direct Selection Tool (**A**). In the example shown here, I've adjusted the path so that the resulting shape is a bit wider than my original vector shape.

Warping Text

Solution

Use the Text Tool (**T**) to type or select the text that you want to wrap, then click the **Create Warped Text** button on the options bar, as shown in this example.

Create warped text

The **Warp Text** dialog box will appear. Create one of the warp options from the **Style** drop-down menu as shown at right.

Selecting a warp style

You can experiment with the values in the **Warp Text** dialog box to fine-tune the effect to your liking.

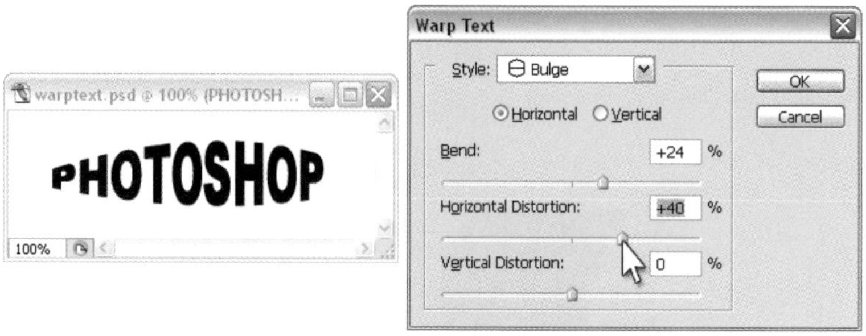

Adjusting the warp effect

Wrapping Text Around a Curved Object

In the previous solution, I showed you how to warp text using Photoshop's built-in text warping options. In this solution, I'll show you how to use the warp options to wrap text around a curved object.

Solution

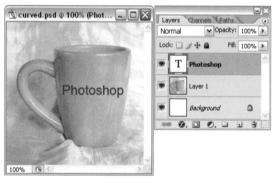

Text layer on top of image layer

I'm using an image of a yellow mug as my curved object, but you might have something else in mind.

Create a new Photoshop document, and place your object on a new layer. Use the Text Tool (*T*) to type some text on your object. This should create a new layer on top of the object layer, as shown at left.

Click on the **Create warped text** button on the options bar to bring up the **Warp Text** dialog box. From the **Style** drop-down menu, select a warp style that works with your object. As you can see from the example shown here, I'm using the **Arch** style with a negative **Bend** amount and a very slight **Vertical Distortion** (to account for the tapering of the mug).

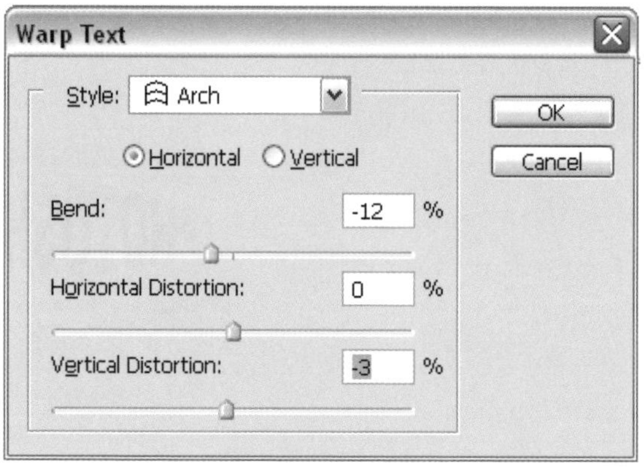

Warp Text settings

You can fine-tune the effect by altering the text color, and by experimenting with the opacity and blend mode settings of the text layer in the **Layers** palette. In the image below, I've set the blend mode for my text to **Multiply**, and lowered the **Opacity** to *65%* to make the text look like it's printed on the mug.

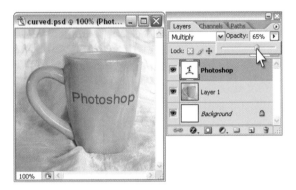

Adjusting **Opacity**

Making Small Text More Readable

If you're working with a "tiny" font, you'll find that the text is much more readable when its edges haven't been smoothed over. Photoshop **anti-aliases**—or smoothes over—text by default, but this is very easily changed.

Solution

From the **Layers** palette, click on the text layer you want to "unsmooth," and select the Text Tool (*T*). In the options bar, you'll see a drop-down menu that allows you to set the anti-aliasing method, as shown in this example. Select **None**.

That's all there is to it!

Creating aliased text

Making Text Follow a Path

The fun with text never ends! In this solution, I'm going to show you how to type text along the edges of a shape or a path you've created.

Solution

Use the Pen Tool (*P*) or the Shape Tool (*U*) to create a path, as shown at right. If you're using the Shape Tool, remember that this won't work if you've got the **Fill pixels** option selected.

Creating a path

Select the Text Tool (*T*) and move the cursor over the path until it changes to an I-beam with a curved baseline, as shown in this example.

The cursor changes when hovering over a path

Click once, and type your text—it will follow your path! In the example shown below, I've typed my text along a curved path.

Text on a curved path

You can change the orientation of your text by clicking on the **Text orientation** button on the top-left of the options bar, as shown below.

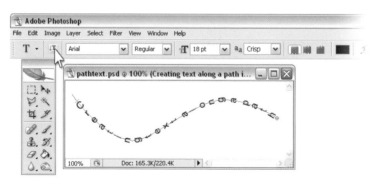

Changing the text orientation

Use the Direct Selection Tool (**A**) to move or flip your text on the path, as shown in this example. Position the cursor near the beginning of the text. When it changes into an I-beam with a small, black arrow, you'll be able to move the text by clicking and dragging the cursor along the curve; flip the text by dragging the cursor downwards.

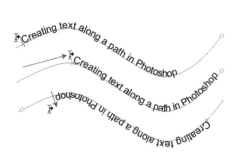

Moving and flipping the text

You can also use the Direct Selection Tool (**A**) to alter the shape of the path, as shown below. Make sure that the text layer is selected in the **Layers** palette when you do this.

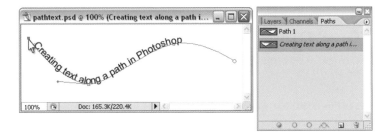

Modifying the path that the text is on

You can enter text along any kind of path, including a vector shape. In the example shown here, I've put two snippets of text along a circular path.

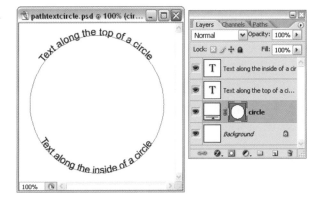

Text on a circular path

Adding an Outline

Adding an outline to a text layer is no different from adding an outline to any other layer. We'll do it using layer styles.

Solution

Select your text layer from the **Layers** palette. Open the **Layer Style** dialog box by clicking on the **Add a Layer style** button at the bottom of the **Layers** palette,

Adding an outline to text

and selecting **Stroke...** from the drop-down menu that appears. Modify the **Stroke** options until you're happy with the effect. In the example shown here, I've given my text a 4-pixel black stroke.

Making Text Glow

Solution

Select your text layer from the **Layers** palette. Open the **Layer Style** dialog box by clicking on the **Add a layer style** button on the bottom-left of the **Layers** palette, and selecting **Outer Glow** from the drop-down menu that appears. Experiment with the settings in the dialog box to create your glow effect. In the example below, I've given my text a blue glow and set the **Blend Mode** to **Normal** so that the effect is more obvious on a white background.

Photoshop

Adding an outer glow

Making Glassy Text

This solution is very similar to the solution for "Creating a Glassy Button" in Chapter 3. We're going to use a combination of layer styles to give our text a glassy effect.

Solution

In the **Layers** palette, select your text layer and set its fill to 0%. First, we're going to add a drop shadow to the text. Open the **Layer Style** dialog box by clicking on the **Add a layer style** button at the bottom-left of the **Layers** palette, and selecting **Drop Shadow** from the menu that appears. Apply the following settings to your drop shadow (you might need to adjust these depending on the size and type of font you use—in this example I've used **Arial Bold** and **Arial Black**, both at *85pt*).

- **Blend Mode: Multiply**; black (by default)
- **Opacity**: *50%*
- **Distance**: *2 pixels*
- **Angle**: *166°*
- **Size**: *4 pixels*

Next, click on **Inner Shadow** in the **Layer Styles** dialog box and adjust the settings for the inner shadow as follows:

- **Blend Mode: Multiply**; black
- **Distance**: *4 pixels*
- **Opacity**: *65%*
- **Size**: *9 pixels*

Almost there! Now click on **Inner Glow**, and use the following settings:

- **Blend Mode: Vivid Light**
- **Color**: white
- **Opacity**: *~38%*
- **Size**: *9 pixels* (increase this for thicker fonts)

Finally, click on **Bevel and Emboss** and adjust the settings as follows:

- **Style: Inner Bevel**
- **Technique: Smooth**
- **Depth**: *90%* (increase this value for thicker fonts)
- **Size**: *9 pixels*
- **Soften**: *2 pixels*
- **Angle** (uncheck **Use Global Light**): *180°*
- **Altitude**: *69°*
- **Highlight Opacity**: *95%* (adjust for different backgrounds—lower values work better with darker backgrounds)
- **Shadow Opacity**: *0%*

Phew! All done. Click **OK** to apply the layer styles. The example to the right shows the final effect.

It's well worth all that effort, in my opinion!

Glassy text

Creating Chiseled or Engraved Text

Solution

Select your text layer from the **Layers** palette, then open the **Layer Style** dialog box by clicking on the **Add a layer style** button at the bottom-left of the palette and selecting **Bevel and Emboss** from the menu that appears. In the dialog box, set the **Technique** to **Chisel Hard**, the **Direction** to **Down**, and experiment with the rest of the settings to fine-tune the effect. The example below shows the settings I used, and the resulting effect.

Applying the **Bevel and Emboss** layer style

If the brushed metal background the text sits on looks familiar, it's because we created it in Chapter 4! (See the solution for "Creating a Brushed Metal Background" within the chapter.)

Giving Text a Stamp Effect

In this solution, I'll show you two techniques that make text look like it was stamped on a surface. In the first method, we'll create a stamp effect for smooth surfaces, and in the second, we'll make one for rough surfaces.

Solution

Smooth Surface Stamp

Select your text layer from the **Layers** palette. Add a layer mask to it by clicking on the **Add layer mask** button at the bottom of the palette, as in the example below.

Adding a layer mask

Select the Brush Tool (**B**), choose one of the spatter brushes from the brush drop-down menu, and lower the opacity of the brush to about **60%** in the options bar, as shown in this example.

Using the Brush Tool

Selecting a spatter brush

Set the foreground color to black. In the **Layers** palette, click on the layer mask thumbnail and paint over the text by clicking on random spots, as shown in the example below. The spatters that you paint on the mask will allow the background to show through, making the text look like it was stamped onto the background.

Using the Brush Tool

In the example at right, I've added a bit more
to my stamp by using a smaller spatter brush
to dab away some of the edges of the text.
I've also created "slice" lines in the text with
a 1px brush, to make it look like a worn-out rubber stamp was used.

Example of worn, stamped text

Rough Surface Stamp

Now we're gong to create text that looks
like it's been stamped onto a rough,
pebbled surface with paint. Arrange
your document so that your text layer
is on top of your background layer.

Text layer over a rough background image

From the **Layers** palette, select the background layer. Use *Ctrl-A* (*Command-A* on a Mac)
to select everything within the layer, then copy it using *Ctrl-C* (*Command-C*). Open
the **Channels** palette by clicking on the **Channels** tab. Click on the **Create new channel**
button at the bottom of the palette.

Still in the **Channels** palette, select the new channel that you just created (it will be
named *Alpha 1*, as shown in the example below), and paste the background layer onto
it using *Ctrl-V* (*Command-V*). Your document will display a grayscale version of the
background.

Creating a new channel

Press *Ctrl-L* (*Command-L*). This will bring up the **Levels** dialog box. Drag the black and
white sliders to increase the contrast of the image. Place them both slightly inside
the main curve of the histogram, as I've done in the example at the top of the next
page.

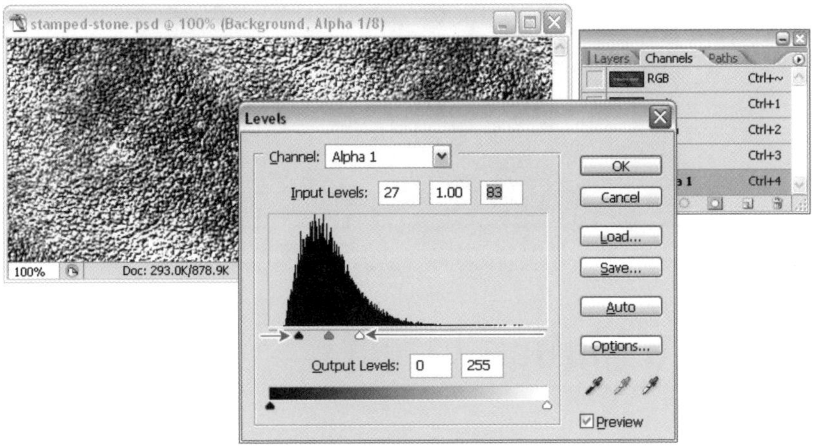

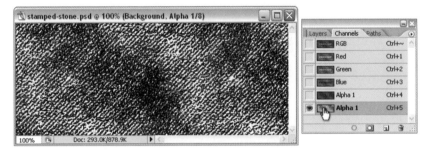

Adjusting the contrast

Hold down the *Ctrl* key (*Command* on a Mac) and click on the **Alpha 1** channel. This will create a selection based on the channel, as shown below.

Creating a selection based on the channel

Click on the **Layers** tab to return to the **Layers** palette, and select the text layer from within it. Add a layer mask to the text layer, as shown below.

Adding a layer mask

Set the document foreground color to black, and paint on the layer mask to fade out areas and add authenticity to the effect. (If you've faded something out by mistake, you can use white to paint it back in.) The final image is shown overleaf.

Final stamped text on rough surface

Giving Text a Motion Effect

Solution

Create your text layer. Use an italic font to enhance the motion effect. Duplicate the text layer using **Ctrl-J** (**Command-J** on a Mac). Right-click (hold **Ctrl** and click on a Mac) on the original layer, and select **Rasterize** from the menu that appears.

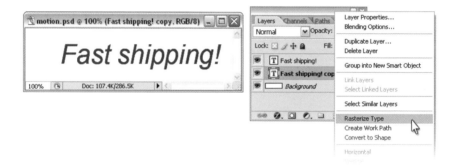

Rasterizing the text layer

Now we're going to apply a filter to make the text look like it's moving. Filters can only be applied to raster layers, which is why we've rasterized our original layer. Select **Filter** > **Blur** > **Motion Blur** to bring up the **Motion Blur** dialog. To make your text look like it's moving horizontally, set the **Angle** to **0°**. Adjust the **Distance** to a value that works with your text.

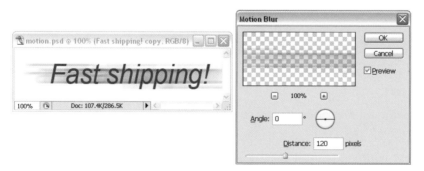

Applying the **Motion Blur** filter

In the finished example below, I've adjusted the **Opacity** of the motion layer in the **Layers** palette to fade it out slightly, and used a layer mask to hide the right-hand side of the blur effect so that the text looks like it's moving towards the right. (If you need a refresher on creating layer masks, see the solutions for "Fading an Image into the Background" in Chapter 2.)

> **WARNING** **Raster Right!**
>
> You can't edit the text that you originally typed once you've rasterized a text layer, so make sure that everything's correct (and spell-checked!) before you go rasterizing your text layers.

Cleaning up the motion effect

Adding a Shadow to Text

Solution

Select the text layer from the **Layers** palette. Open the **Layer Style** dialog box by clicking on the **Add a layer style** button at the bottom-left of the palette and selecting **Drop Shadow** from the menu that appears. That's pretty much all you need to do! If you're not happy with the appearance of the shadow, you can adjust its appearance using the settings in the dialog box, as shown here. Once you're done, click **OK**—and *voila*! Shadow added!

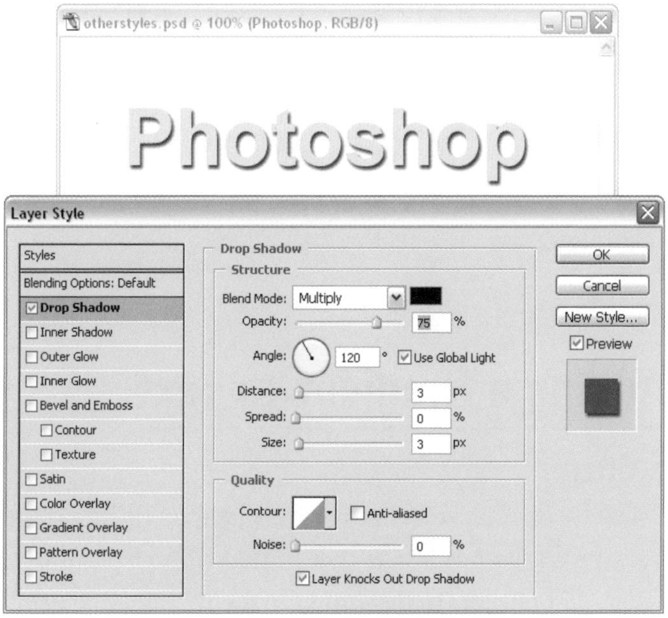

Applying the **Drop Shadow** layer style

Adding a Pattern to Text

If you wanted to go through all the trouble, you could probably add a pattern to your text by rasterizing the text layer, then filling it with the pattern. But why would you bother when you can do it oh-so-simply with a layer style?

Solution

Select your text layer from the **Layers** palette. Open the **Layer Style** dialog box by clicking on the **Add a layer style** button at the bottom-left of the palette and selecting **Pattern Overlay** from the menu that appears. Select the pattern with which you want to fill your text from the **Pattern** drop-down menu in the dialog box—you can choose one of the existing patterns, or use your own image as a pattern. In this example, I've used the coffee bean background tile that I created in the solution for "Creating a Seamless Repeating Background" in Chapter 4. As always, you can experiment with the settings to adjust the effect to your liking. This example shows the effect of the pattern overlay on my text.

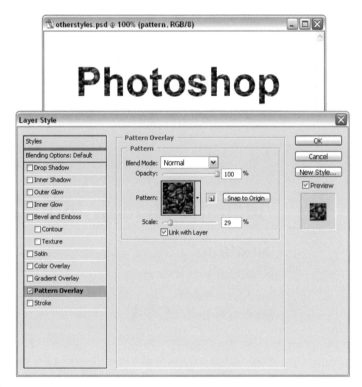

Applying the **Pattern Overlay**

Adding a Gradient to Text

Solution

Select the text layer from the **Layers** palette. Bring up the **Layer Style** dialog box by clicking on the **Add a layer style** button at the bottom-left of the **Layers** palette, and selecting **Gradient Overlay** from the menu that appears. Click on the gradient patch to select a new gradient, or adjust the existing gradient as shown in the example at the top of the next page. You'll find more detailed instructions on how to edit the gradient in the solution for "Making a Gradient Button" in Chapter 3.

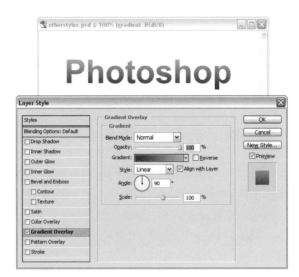

Applying a **Gradient Overlay**

Changing the Shape of Letters

There may be cases in which you need to change the shape of letters—for a stylized logo, for example, or just for fun. You can do so by editing the paths that make up the letters. In this solution, we're going to use the Direct Selection Tool (**A**) and Bezier handlebars to adjust the letter paths.

Solution

In the **Layers** palette, right-click (hold **Ctrl** and click on a Mac) on your text layer and choose **Convert to Shape** from the menu that appears.

Converting text to a vector shape

The text will be converted to a vector shape layer. This will be reflected in the **Layers** palette, as shown in the example on the right.

Converted text layer

Now select the Direct Selection Tool (**A**), and adjust the shape of the text by clicking and dragging the handlebars and anchor points. You may wish to use other tools, such as the Add Anchor Point Tool, Delete Anchor Point Tool, and Convert Point Tool, to adjust the points as necessary.

> **WARNING   Shape Smart!**
>
> As with rasterizing text layers, once you convert a text layer to a shape, you won't be able to edit the text that you originally typed, so make sure that everything's correct and spell-checked before you begin the conversion!

If you can't see the paths and points clearly, double-click on the color patch of the shape layer to bring up the **Color Picker**, and temporarily change the shape color to a lighter shade that's easier to work with.

These examples show how I adjusted the curve of the first "h" to remove the overlap it created. I deleted several of the anchor points, and then adjusted the remaining points to match the curve to the font.

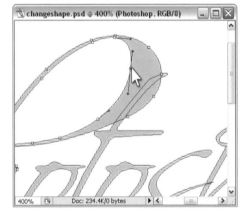

Adjusting the path using the Direct Selection Tool

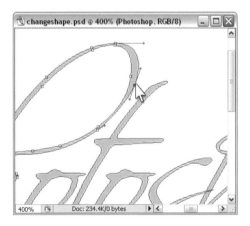

Adjusting the other part of the curve

Here's the final result:

Adjusted text

Summary

In this chapter, we looked at how to use layer styles such as drop shadows, strokes, and overlays to make our text look more interesting. We learned how to use text with paths, and fancy tricks such as writing text along a curvy path, word-wrapping text within a shape, and altering the shapes of letters. The skills you've gained in this fun-filled chapter will help you to create logos, graphic headings, and a lot more.

6 Adjusting Images

Often, you'll find yourself working with photos that just aren't all that great. You know what I'm talking about. We've all seen them (you may even have taken some of them!): the overexposed, the underexposed, the "whoops I forgot to turn on the flash," and the scary red-eye snaps. It's just as well that we've made friends with Photoshop, because it has some handy tools that we can use to salvage *those* photos.

In the following solutions, I'll introduce you to these tools. However, the ways in which you use them will depend on the images you work with. Feel free to make adjustments to make these techniques work for you!

Original photo

Using Overlay blend mode   With Curves

Match Color

Destination Image
Target: matchcolor.psd (mother chil..., RGB/8)
☐ Ignore Selection when Applying Adjustment

Image Options
Luminance   100
Color Intensity   100
Fade   20
☐ Neutral

Image Statistics
☑ Use Selection in Source to Calculate Colors
☑ Use Selection in Target to Calculate Adjustment

Source: motherchild2.psd
Layer: mother child photo 2
Load Statistics...
Save Statistics...

OK
Reset
☑ Preview

Making Whites Whiter

Solution

In this solution, I'm working with a winter photograph that looks like it was taken with a twice-dropped disposable camera.
As you can see, the original photo is very dim, and the snow looks gray and dingy.

Original photograph

Creating a new adjustment layer

Let's fix it. Click on the **Create new fill or adjustment layer** button at the bottom of the **Layers** palette, and choose **Levels...** from the menu that appears, as shown in the image on the left.

The **Levels** dialog box will appear. Make the snow whiter by clicking and dragging the **Input Levels** white slider arrow towards the left, as shown in the example below. I've moved mine so that it's immediately beneath the end of the graph.

Increasing the whiteness

Increase the brightness of the image by dragging the gray slider arrow (the one in the middle) to the left, as shown in the example below.

Increasing the brightness

When you're satisfied, click **OK** to close the **Levels** dialog box. The example below compares the original photograph with my levels-adjusted image.

Original photograph compared with adjusted image

Discussion

Levels Command vs Adjustment Layer

We can achieve exactly the same effect using a **Levels** adjustment (**Image > Adjustments > Levels**). However, using this command applies the adjustment directly onto the image layer, which could cause some problems if you want to alter or remove the adjustment in the future.

In this solution, we used an **adjustment layer** to modify the levels non-destructively.

If you look in the **Layers** palette, you'll notice

Levels adjustment layer in the **Layers** palette

that a special layer has been added. This layer contains the levels adjustment, and affects all the layers beneath it. The original photo layer remains untouched, so if you decide that you don't want the adjustment after all, you can hide the adjustment layer using its eye icon. You can easily alter the adjustment by double-clicking on the adjustment layer's thumbnail (this will bring up the **Levels** dialog box).

While this method is recommended because it keeps the original image intact, as I mentioned earlier, the adjustment layer affects all the layers beneath it. Using an adjustment layer in a document that has multiple image layers can get a bit tricky, particularly if you want the adjustment layer to affect a specific image layer alone. In situations like this, consider adding a layer mask to the adjustment layer (to specify the area of adjustment), or applying the **Levels** adjustment to the image layer itself.

About Using Levels

The **Levels** dialog box displays a **histogram**, which is a graph showing the number of pixels present at each intensity level. The empty space on the right-hand side of the graph for our winter photograph, displayed at right, shows that there are hardly any pixels

Sample histogram

in the higher highlights range. In other words, there are no (or very few) white pixels in the original image.

When you adjust the three sliders underneath the histogram, Photoshop "remaps" the tonal values of the image. In the winter photograph solution, we dragged the white slider to the left and placed it directly beneath the end of the graph. Our image brightened because Photoshop identified the pixels on the graph that were originally gray and remapped them to the whiter end of the spectrum. The rest of the image

was adjusted to accommodate the change. Dragging the gray slider (which represents the "middle" tones) towards the left also increased the brightness of the image, because Photoshop remapped the darker tones to midtones.

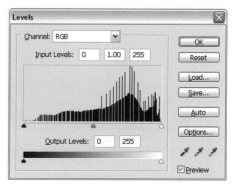

If you're using an adjustment layer, the shape of the histogram itself won't change. However, when you apply the **Levels** command, the histogram is altered to reflect the remapped

Histogram after applying the **Levels** adjustment

tonal values, changing the state of the image permanently (unless you undo the command). As you can see in the example on the previous page, the tonal values now stretch across the entire spectrum (there's no space on the right-hand side of the histogram).

Making Blacks Blacker

Now that you know how the histogram and its sliders work, it should be easy for you to make the blacks in the image blacker. Simply drag the black slider towards the right. This will give your image a little more contrast, making it appear cleaner and less muddy.

Adding Tone Adjustments and Contrast

Using **Levels**, as we did in the solution for "Making Whites Whiter," is a quick and easy way to brighten up dull images. However, it doesn't really allow us to fine-tune the midtones of an image.

Allow me to demonstrate. The example below shows two photographs: on the left is the original image, and on the right is the levels-adjusted image. I've been able to intensify the highlights and the shadows of the image by adjusting the levels. However, when it comes to the midtones, I'm very limited: I can make them all lighter, or all darker. While the darker midtones in this example give the mountains more contrast, they also make the rest of the image appear quite dark. To gain more control over the midtones of the image, we'll need to adjust its curves using either a **Curves** adjustment layer, or the **Curves** command.

Original photo   *With Levels Adjustment Layer*

Levels don't allow fine-tuning of midtones

Solution

Click on the **Create new fill or adjustment layer** button at the bottom of the **Layers** palette, and select **Curves...** from the menu that appears.

Launching the **Curves** dialog

The **Curves** dialog box will be displayed. To start with, you'll see a grid with a diagonal line running from the bottom-left corner to the top-right corner, as shown here. To adjust the contrast, you'll need to alter the shape of the line. Do this by clicking on the line to add points (you can add up to seven points), then dragging the points to change the shape of the line. To increase the contrast, make the line into a roughly S-shaped curve, as shown at right. Remove points by dragging them out of the box. When you're done, click **OK** to close the dialog box and apply the adjustment.

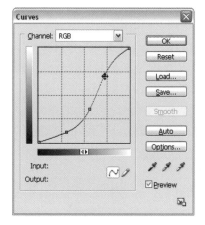

Adjusting the curve

In the example below, the image on the right shows what our image looks like once the Curves adjustment layer has been applied. The mountain still has darker tones, but the sky and clouds look brighter and less washed out.

Levels adjustment　　*Curves adjustment*

Using a **Curves** adjustment to create a lighter image

Discussion

We can achieve exactly the same effect using the **Curves** command (**Image** > **Image Adjustments** > **Curves**). However, using the Curves adjustment layer allows us to modify the image non-destructively by adding a special layer in the **Layers** palette. For details of the differences between adjustment layers and commands, see the discussion for "Making Whites Whiter" earlier in the chapter.

Curves adjustment layer
in the **Layers** palette

Understanding Curves

In the **Curves** dialog box, the horizontal axis represents the input level (or the original color values of the image), while the vertical axis represents the output level (the altered color values). By default, the graph is a straight line because the input and output levels are the same, but these levels change as you alter the shape of the line, as shown in the example below. In this solution, we adjusted the curve to darken the midtones.

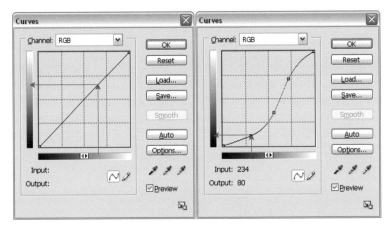

Input and output values affected by curve

Making Colors More Vivid

Solution

Click on the **Create new fill or adjustment layer** button at the bottom of the **Layers** palette. From the menu that appears, select **Hue/ Saturation...** to bring up the **Hue/Saturation** dialog box. To increase the vividness of the colors in your image, increase the **Saturation** value by dragging the **Saturation** slider to the right, as shown in the example at right.

Increasing the saturation

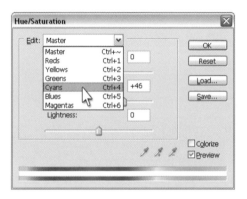

Modifying the saturation of specific colors

If you want, you can modify the saturation value for individual color ranges by selecting a specific range from the **Edit** drop-down menu, as shown in the example on the left. When you're done, click **OK** to apply the effect.

In the examples shown below, I increased the **Saturation** to *46* to turn my overcast ocean photo into a tropical ocean photo. I can now make all my friends "Wish you were here!" postcards using the adjusted photo.

Before and after saturation is increased

Discussion

You can use methods to make colors in a photo more vivid. Let's look at them briefly.

Changing the Blend Mode

In the **Layers** palette, duplicate your image layer using *Ctrl-J* (*Command-J* on a Mac). Change the mode of the duplicated layer to **Overlay** using the drop-down menu at the top of the palette. If you find the effect too striking, try "fading" it by lowering the **Opacity** of the overlay layer.

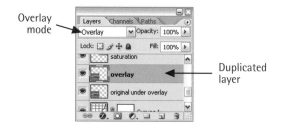

Setting the duplicated layer to **Overlay** mode

Experiment with some of the other blending modes to see the effect that each produces.

Using a Curves Adjustment Layer

Adding a **Curves** adjustment layer, as described in the solution for "Adding Tone Adjustments and Contrast," can also make the colors of an image more vivid. Applying the basic S-curve shown at right to our ocean image produced the result shown at the top of the next page. In this example, the **Curves** adjustment layer and **Overlay** blending mode technique produce very similar results, with the **Curves** adjustment layer providing slightly more contrast.

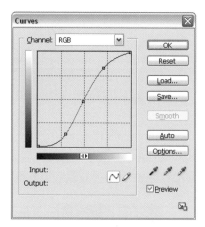

Adjusting the curves

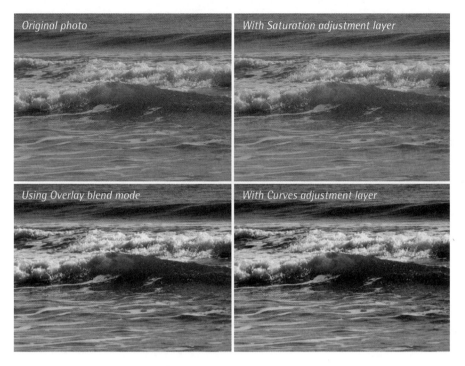

Contrasting different techniques

Removing Color Tints from Photos

Depending on the lighting conditions in which your photos were taken, you may find that your images have a slight color cast. In this solution, I'll be removing the blue tint from a landscape photo of some mountains.

Solution

Click on the **Create new fill or adjustment layer** button at the bottom of the **Layers** palette, and choose **Levels...** from the menu that appears. The **Levels** dialog box will be displayed. Select **Red** from the **Channel** drop-down menu, as shown at right.

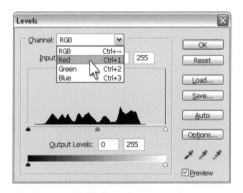

Selecting the **Red** channel

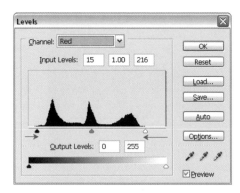

Adjusting levels for the **Red** channel

Adjust the sliders beneath the histogram so that both the white and the black sliders are lined up with the edges of the histogram. (You'll need to drag the white slider to the left, and the black slider to the right, as shown on the left.)

Next, select **Green** from the **Channel** drop-down menu, and repeat the process with the black and white sliders, as illustrated at right.

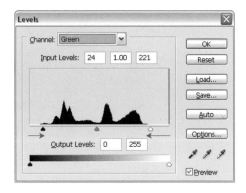

Adjusting levels for the **Green** channel

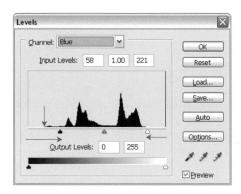

Adjusting levels for the **Blue** channel

Finally, select **Blue** from the **Channel** drop-down menu, as shown at left. Align the white slider with the right-hand edge of the histogram, but drag the black slider *past* the left edge of the graph until the blue color cast clears. The resulting photo is shown below, alongside the original image.

Original photo

With levels adjustment

The final photo at right, with blue tint removed

Discussion

For images in which unnatural coloring is more obvious (such as photos that include people), a levels adjustment layer may not be precise enough to adjust the color tint suitably. In such cases, you'll want to use a Curves adjustment layer instead.

First, open the **Info** palette. Hover the cursor over an area of the image that you know *should* be gray (or close to gray)—in the example on the next page, I chose the wall area in the background. Note down the RGB values of this area, because we'll need them later. My wall has a red value of 128, a green value of 145, and a blue value of 173. Calculate the average of the three values—in this example, it's about 149.

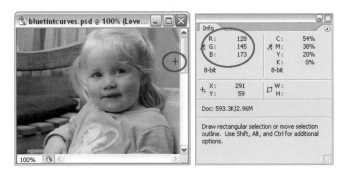

Noting RGB values of the wall

Next, we'll add the curves adjustment layer. Click on the **Create new fill or adjustment layer** button at the bottom of the **Layers** palette, and select **Curves...** from the menu that appears, as shown at right. The **Curves** dialog box will be displayed, as shown below.

Adding a curves adjustment layer

Adding a point to the **Red** channel

In the dialog box, select **Red** from the **Channel** drop-down to display the curve (initially a straight line) for the red channel. You can also jump straight to the red channel using *Ctrl-1* (*Command-1* on a Mac). Click somewhere on the line to add a new point.

In the **Input** field, type in the red value that you noted earlier. In the **Output** field, type in the average of the RGB values. As you can see in the example shown on the right, I've typed in my red value of *128*, and my average of *149*.

Now, repeat the same process for the green and blue channels: click on the line to add a point, enter the original green or blue values in the **Input** field, and enter the average in the **Output** field.

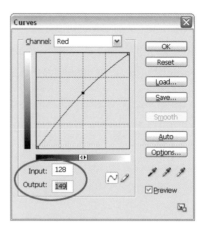

Changing the **Input** and **Output** values

It's unlikely that the gray pixel we initially chose was "pure" gray. If we follow this process, Photoshop will adjust the curves so that the gray pixel *is* really gray (with equal red, green, and blue values). It will then adjust the rest of the image accordingly, so that it looks more natural.

> **TIP   Jumping Around**
>
> Just as you can "jump to" the red channel using **Ctrl-1 (Command-1)**, you can also quickly access the green and blue channels using **Ctrl-2** or **Ctrl-3 (Command-2** or **Command-3)**, respectively.

The examples below show the original photo, plus two adjusted versions of the photo—the first adjusted using levels, the second using curves.

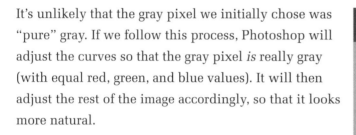

Original   *Levels*   *Curves*

Comparing adjustment techniques

Darkening Areas on an Image

A good way to draw focus to a particular object in an image is to darken the objects or areas around it. In this solution, I'm going to darken the background of the photo shown below, to make the dog stand out.

Solution

Create a new layer on top of your image layer. Fill the new layer by selecting **Edit > Fill**. In the dialog box that appears, select **50% Gray** from the first drop-down menu, and set the **Opacity** to *100%*. Set the blend mode of this layer to **Overlay** by selecting it from the drop-down menu at the top of the **Layers** palette, as shown at right.

Setting the gray layer to **Overlay** mode

Now select the Burn Tool (*O*), as shown at right.

Choose a soft-edged brush from the **Options** palette, and use it to paint over the areas that you want to darken (make sure you're painting on the filled gray layer, not the image layer itself). You may need to adjust the diameter of your brush to suit your requirements. I've set the diameter of my brush to *90px*—this provides me with a stroke that's big enough to cover large areas, but still gives me enough control to avoid painting over Lassie too much. We can see the final result below: a subtle but notable difference.

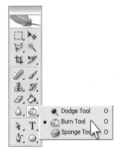

Selecting the Burn Tool

Original photo   *Burn Tool applied*

Burn Tool results

Discussion

Blending Modes

The Burn Tool gradually darkens the areas on which you paint. Let's examine the thumbnail of our gray layer in the **Layers** palette, as shown at right. Since the blend mode of this layer is set to **Overlay**, the 50% gray areas on this layer leave the image underneath unaffected, whereas the "burned" areas (those darker than 50% gray) darken the corresponding areas of the image underneath.

Burn Tool area

You may find that parts of an image that are quite bright are sometimes difficult to darken using this technique. For a stronger effect, try changing the blend mode to **Vivid Light** or **Linear Light**, and using the Burn Tool with more restraint.

Using the Brush Tool

You can achieve the same effect by using the Brush Tool (**B**) to paint on the gray layer with various shades of gray. However, the benefit of using the Burn Tool is that it will darken the image *gradually*, producing a more believable effect.

Using the Burn Tool on the Image Layer

In this solution, we used the Burn Tool with a 50% gray layer and different blending modes to darken areas of our image non-destructively. In fact, there's a lot more that you can do with the Burn Tool. Check out the options bar: you've got a drop-down menu from which you can choose to darken shadows, midtones, or highlights, as well as a field in which to change the **Exposure** level, as shown in the example below.

Changing the burn options

However, to use these options, you'll need to use the Burn Tool directly on the image. As you know, this will alter the image permanently, so you might want to first make a backup of your image by duplicating the original image layer.

Lightening Areas on an Image

In this solution, I'm going to add a ray of light to a photograph of a lighthouse, by lightening certain areas of the image.

Solution

Create a new layer on top of the image layer, and give this new layer a fill by selecting **Edit > Fill**. In the dialog box that appears, choose **50% Gray** from the first drop-down menu, set the **Opacity** to *100%*, and click **OK**. In the **Layers** palette, change the mode of the layer to **Vivid Light** by selecting it from the drop-down menu at the top of the palette, as shown in the image below. Select the Dodge Tool (*O*) from the toolbar.

Selecting the Dodge Tool

With a medium-sized brush (I used one with a diameter of 80 pixels), make a stroke on the gray layer to simulate a ray of light coming down from the sky. This is illustrated below.

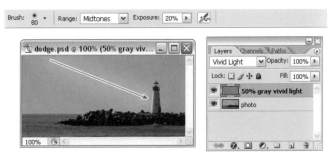

Ray of light

Next, use the Dodge Tool (**O**) along the surface of the object that is being "lit"—in this case, it's the left-hand side of the lighthouse. The image at right illustrates this.

Intensifying the light on the object

Below, we can see the shining lighthouse compared with the original image. The dodge effect is pretty cool, if I do say so myself!

Final results achieved with the Dodge Tool

Discussion

Vivid Light and Linear Light Blending Modes

Using the **Vivid Light** or **Linear Light** blending modes on the gray layer lightens or darkens the image underneath, depending on the layer's gray values. Pixels that are lighter than 50% gray lighten the image underneath, pixels that are darker than 50% gray darken the image, and pixels that remain 50% gray leave the image untouched. The difference between the two blending modes is that **Vivid Light** increases or decreases the *contrast* of the "dodged" area on the image, whereas **Linear Light** increases or decreases the *lightness* of that dodged area.

Experiment with these blending modes to determine which one works best for you. The lighthouses in the images below show the subtle difference between the two blending modes.

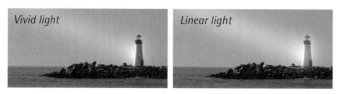

Contrasting the Vivid Light and Linear Light modes

Using the Dodge Tool on the Image Layer

If you look at the options bar for the Dodge Tool, you'll see that additional settings are available. However, to use these settings, you'll need to use the Dodge Tool directly on the image layer. Since this will alter the image permanently, it's a good idea to duplicate the photo first so that you have a backup.

Fixing the Red-eye Effect

With a single click, you can say goodbye to those demonic red-eyes! Let me show you how.

Solution

Select the Red Eye Tool (*J*) from the toolbox, as shown on the left below.

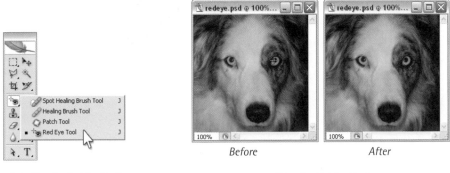

Selecting the Red Eye Tool   Using the Red Eye Tool

The cursor will change into a crosshair. Place the crosshair over one of the red pupils and click for an instant red-eye fix, as shown in the example on the right above.

Repeat the step for the other red eye, and you're done. Below, we can see the final result: she still may not look like the world's friendliest dog, but she definitely seems more approachable!

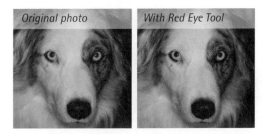

Before and after the Red Eye Tool is applied

As with most of Photoshop's tools, you can fine-tune the Red Eye Tool using the settings that are available for it in the options bar.

Red Eye Tool options

Converting Photographs to Black-and-white Images

Solution

Before you begin, make sure that your image is in RGB mode. Check the title bar of your Photoshop document, as shown at right. If you need to change the image mode, which is circled in the figure at right, select **Image > Mode > RGB Color**. In the dialog box that appears, click the **Don't Flatten** button to preserve any layers that you've created.

Checking the image mode

Open the **Channels** palette. Before you make any modifications, examine your image in different channels to see which ones look better. Click on the **Red** channel to select it. Photoshop will automatically turn off the other channels, and display a grayscale image to represent the red areas of the photo, as shown in the example below. That's right—Photoshop displays a *grayscale* image representing the *red* areas. In this view, white is indicative of "pure" red, and black indicates areas where no red is present.

Examining the red channel

Now compare the **Red** channel with the **Green** and **Blue** channels, as shown in the example at the top of the next page. In my opinion, the **Blue** channel looks the best for this particular example. The **Red** channel is too washed out, and the **Green** channel is too dark (although it does show a bit of detail). I'm going to make a mental note of this, as it will come in handy when I get around to mixing channels later.

When you've made your observations, return to the full-color view of the image by clicking on the RGB channel in the **Channels** palette, or clicking on any layer in the **Layers** palette.

Red   Green   Blue

Comparing the channels

Adding a Channel Mixer adjustment layer

Get your cauldron ready, it's time to mix channels! Click on the Create new fill or adjustment layer button at the bottom of the **Layers** palette, and select **Channel Mixer...** from the menu that appears. The **Channel Mixer** dialog box will be displayed.

Tick the **Monochrome** checkbox in the bottom left of the dialog box. Your image will change to a grayscale image. Since **Red** is set to *100%*, the image will look as it did when we viewed the **Red** channel earlier.

Checking the **Monochrome** option

Remember how we liked the way the **Blue** channel looked? Set the **Red** channel to *0%* and the **Blue** channel to *100%* to view the image as it looked on the **Blue** channel.

Adjusting the **Channel Mixer**

Now you can start mixing the channels until you get an image that you're happy with. In this example, I decreased the **Blue** channel to *82%*, increased the **Red** channel to *18%*, and increased the **Green** channel to *24%* to give my image a bit of detail. When your brew is complete, click **OK** to apply the settings to the image.

Final **Channel Mixer** settings

Discussion

We've just learned one of many techniques that we can use to convert a color image to black-and-white.

Another quick, non-destructive method is to apply a **Hue/Saturation** adjustment layer to the image, and set the **Saturation** level to *-100*, as shown in the example below.

Adding a **Hue/Saturation** adjustment layer

Even simpler still is to select **Image > Mode > Grayscale** to convert your color image into a grayscale image. However, this method does permanently alter your image, so you may want to make a backup first.

The figure below shows three different grayscale versions of the same image. If your aim is to create a sophisticated black-and-white masterpiece, using the Channel Mixer will give you more control over the final image, allow you to preserve detail, and provide you with richer blacks. On the other hand, if all you're after is a simple grayscale image, the other two methods will suffice.

Comparing methods

Making Sepia Images

Solution

Start with a black-and-white image in RGB mode (if you don't have one handy, create one using the solution, "Converting Images to Black-and-white"). The image doesn't need to be flattened; you can keep any adjustment layers you may have used to create your black-and-white image.

Click on the **Create new fill or adjustment layer** button at the bottom of the **Layers** palette, and select **Hue/Saturation...** from the menu that appears.

Adding a Hue/Saturation adjustment layer

In the **Hue/Saturation** dialog box, tick the **Colorize** checkbox, and move the **Hue** slider to your desired color level. Adjust the **Saturation** value to your liking. As you can see in the example shown here, I've set the **Hue** for my image to *38*, and the **Saturation** to *20*. When you're done, click **OK**.

Adjusting the **Hue** and **Saturation** values

The end result is a lovely, sepia-toned image, and since we've produced it using an adjustment layer, our original image remains untouched. Oh, the beauty of it all!

Sepia-toned image

Matching Lighting and Colors between Images

Solution

Open the images you want to match. In this solution I'm using the two photos shown below. While the photo on the left has terrific composition, it's a bit on the dark side. This is the image that I want to modify, so we'll refer to this photo as the "target" image.

The photo on the right has nice, warm colors. This is the photo on which I want to base the lighting and color tones of the target image, so we'll call this photo the "source" image.

Target and source images

Click on the document window of the target image. Select **Image** > **Adjustments** > **Match Color**. In the **Match Color** dialog box that appears, use the **Source** drop-down to select the source image filename, as shown at right.

Move the **Match Color** dialog box so that you can see the photo underneath. The color tones of the target image have been adjusted to match those of the source image. If you're happy with the result, click **OK** and you're done!

Match Color dialog box

Results of Match Color command

I'm having some issues, though. While I like the way the skin tones look after the color match takes place, I'm not happy with the yellow sky in the background. I'm going to click **Cancel** to exit the **Match Color** dialog box *without* applying the change. Instead, I'll adjust only part of the image.

Create a selection in the source image using either the Lasso Tool (**L**), Quick Mask Mode, or any other selection method. Since I want to modify the skintones, I've made a selection that captures the lady and the child, and excludes the background, as shown at right.

Creating a selection

Next, make a corresponding selection in
the target image. Again, I've created a
selection of the lady and child, and
excluded the background.

Creating a second selection

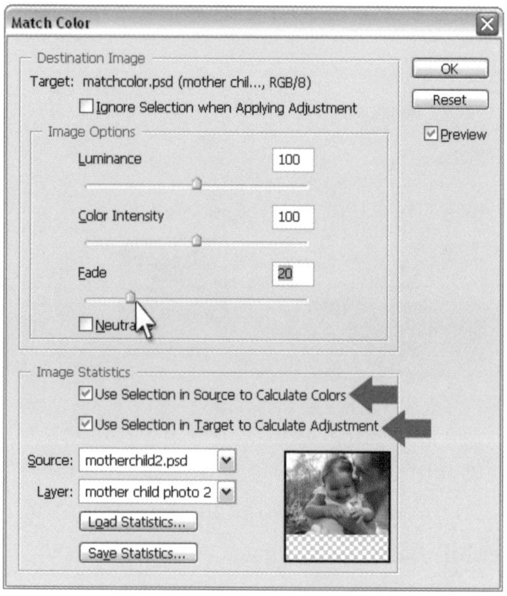

Applying the Match Color command to a selection

Now I'm going to have another go at
matching the colors. In the **Match Color**
dialog box (**Image** > **Adjustments** > **Match
Color**), I'm going to check both the **Use
Selection in Source to Calculate Colors**
checkbox and the **Use Selection in Target
to Calculate Adjustment** checkbox. I've
also adjusted the **Fade** amount to a
value of *20*, as shown at left.

This time, the results look much better. Below, we can see the original photo and the
final, adjusted photo.

Final results using the Match Color adjustment

Combining Two Different Images

A web header graphic or other web graphic that combines two or more images can be enhanced with the use of the **Match Color** command.

Solution

If you're not already familiar with the **Match Color** command, read the solution for "Matching Lighting and Color Between Images."

Arrange your Photoshop document so that the two images that you want to combine are on separate layers, as shown below. In this solution, I'm using the lighthouse photo from an earlier solution, and a photo of some clouds. I want to modify the cloud image so that its colors match those of the lighthouse image.

Photoshop document with images on two layers

First, let's match the colors. Bring up the **Match Color** dialog box by clicking on the cloud layer in the **Layers** palette, and then selecting **Image > Adjustments > Match Color**. In the dialog box that appears, select your currently open document from the source drop-down, and select the source layer (which is the lighthouse layer, in this case) from the **Layer** drop-down, as shown at right.

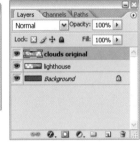

Match Color dialog box

With the **Preview** checkbox ticked, adjust the other settings until the color tones for both images match as closely as possible. Click **OK** to apply the changes.

After applying Match Color adjustment

Because the two images now have similar color tones, it's easy to combine them. In the image below, I've used a layer mask on the cloud layer to create a fade effect. (For more details on how to use layer masks to combine two images, see the solution for "Blending Two Images Together" in Chapter 2.)

Final sample image

Getting Rid of Dust and Scratch Marks

Solution

In this solution, I'm working with a scanned photo that has some obvious dust specks that I'd like to get rid of.

First things first: create a backup of your image layer by duplicating it using *Ctrl-J* (*Command-J* on a Mac). In the **Layers** palette, hide the original image layer by clicking on its eye icon, then select the duplicated layer—this is the one we'll work with.

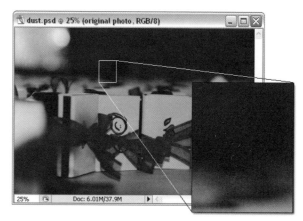

Dust on scanned image

Select the Spot Healing Brush Tool (*J*) from the toolbox.

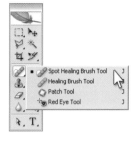

Selecting the Spot Healing Brush Tool

From the options bar, select a brush size that's larger than the specks on the image (I've set my brush to 15px). Click once on a speck—Photoshop will erase it!

Now, if you had the time and patience, you could use the Spot Healing Brush Tool to erase each speck in the photo individually. However, we're going to speed up the process by using the Spot Healing Brush Tool only on areas where the specks are sparse, and applying a filter to the areas in which the specks are more concentrated.

Erase any obvious specks on your image by clicking on them with the Spot Healing Brush Tool (*J*), as we did earlier.

After you've erased all of the noticeable specks, examine your image to determine whether most of the remaining specks lie on the darker or the lighter areas of the image.

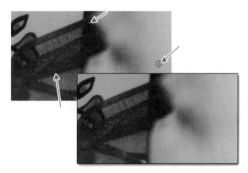

Using the Spot Healing Brush Tool

Applying the Dust & Scratches filter

In the **Layers** palette, duplicate the image layer using *Ctrl-J* (*Command-J* on a Mac). Select **Filter** > **Noise** > **Dust & Scratches** to apply the Dust & Scratches filter to the duplicated layer. The **Dust & Scratches** dialog box will be displayed. To check if the filter has removed all the specks from the entire image, click and drag the mouse around in the preview window of the dialog box to display different areas of the image. If you're not satisfied, adjust the **Radius** and **Threshold** values until all the specks disappear. Click **OK** to apply the filter.

The result is shown below. You may notice that the image is looking a little blurry, but don't worry about that for now. We're not done yet!

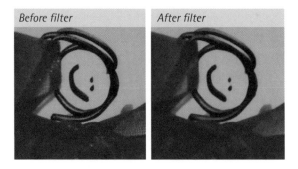

Before and after the filter is applied

Use the drop-down menu at the top of the **Layers** palette to change the blend mode of the filtered layer. Set it to **Darken** if there were more specks in the darker areas of the image, or to **Lighten** if there were more specks in the lighter areas. Most of my specks were in the darker areas, so I've set the blend mode to **Darken**. (If it looks like your specks are evenly distributed over both areas, don't panic! I'll explain how to take care of that in the discussion for this solution.)

Changing the blend mode

This should bring back some of the detail that was lost by the filter earlier. You can use a layer mask for additional detail. Select the filtered layer from the **Layers** palette and click on the **Add layer mask** button at the bottom of the palette to add a layer mask, as shown in the example below. Set the foreground color to black, and use the Brush Tool (*B*) with a soft-edged brush to paint on the layer mask. This will reveal detail from the layer underneath.

Using a layer mask to reveal detail in the layer below

Perform a final cleanup on both layers using the Spot Healing Brush Tool. The example below shows the final result of my image after it's been dusted off. No more specks!

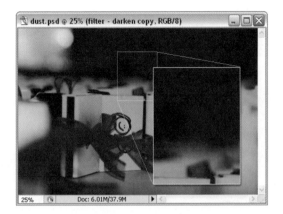

Final image, dusted off

Discussion

About the Darken and Lighten Blending Modes

When you set the blend mode of a layer to **Darken**, Photoshop compares the pixels of that layer (called the **blend layer**) with the pixels of the layer underneath, and displays the darker pixels from these two layers. Can you guess what the **Lighten** blend mode does?

Images with Dust in Both Light and Dark Areas

To fix an image that has dust in both light and dark areas, first duplicate your image layer. Use the Dust & Scratches filter on the duplicated layer, and set the blending mode for the layer to **Darken**. Duplicate the filtered layer (duplicate the duplicate!) and set the blending mode for the new duplicated layer to **Lighten**. You should now have three layers: the original layer, a **Darken** layer, and a **Lighten** layer.

Add layer masks to both the **Darken** and **Lighten** layers as necessary to preserve their detail, and touch up the original layer with the Spot Healing Brush Tool if required.

This method is a lot quicker than clicking on each individual speck with the Spot Healing Brush Tool!

Smoothing Grainy or Noisy Images

High ISO settings on digital cameras and poor quality scanners can sometimes produce grainy or noisy images. With Photoshop's help, you can clean up these images in a few simple steps. In this solution, we'll smooth over a scanned photograph of an orchid, shown below.

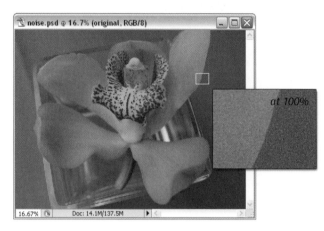

Zooming in on a grainy photo

Solution

For this solution, we'll need to apply a few filters to the image. Before you make any changes, you may want to duplicate the original image layer so that you have a backup.

The first step is to apply a **Despeckle** filter to the image. Select **Filter > Noise > Despeckle**. This will reduce the grain or noise slightly, as shown at right.

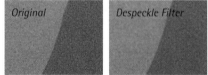

After using the Despeckle filter

Next, we'll apply another filter to reduce the noise further. Select **Filter > Noise > Reduce Noise**. In the **Reduce Noise** dialog box that appears, increase the values for the **Strength** and **Reduce Color Noise** fields, as shown in the example at the top of the next page. If there's a lot of fine detail, try increasing the value of the **Preserve Details** field as well. You can also experiment with the **Sharpen Details** field, although, personally, I prefer to sharpen the image myself as I find that I have more control over it that way. (I'll show you how to sharpen images later in the chapter.)

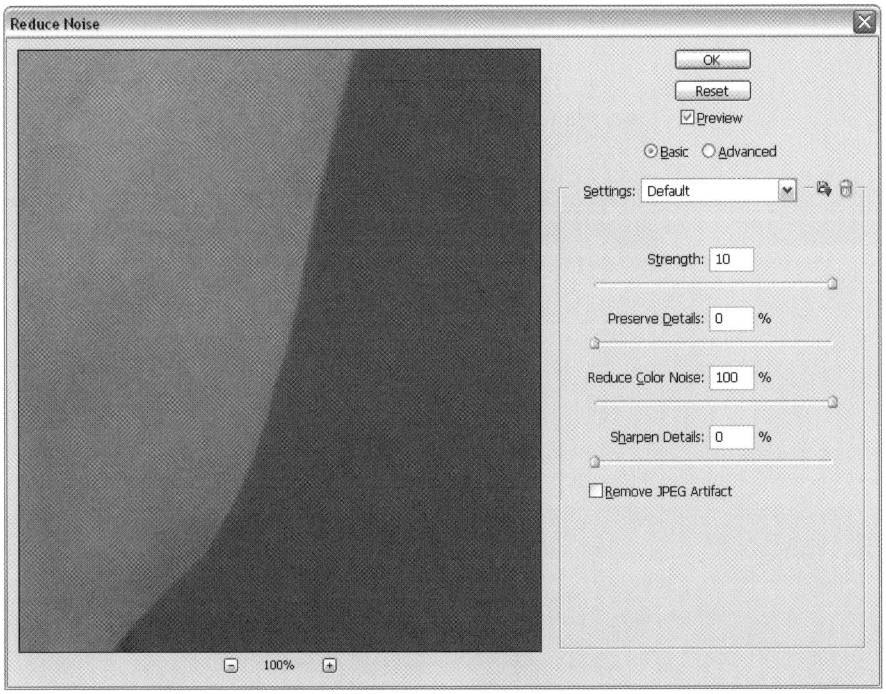

Reduce Noise dialog options

On the far right are the results of the **Reduce Noise** filter, alongside those of the **Despeckle** filter. As you can see, most of the noise has disappeared, and the graininess has been reduced somewhat. Our work is not done yet, though!

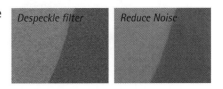

Results of the **Reduce Noise** filter

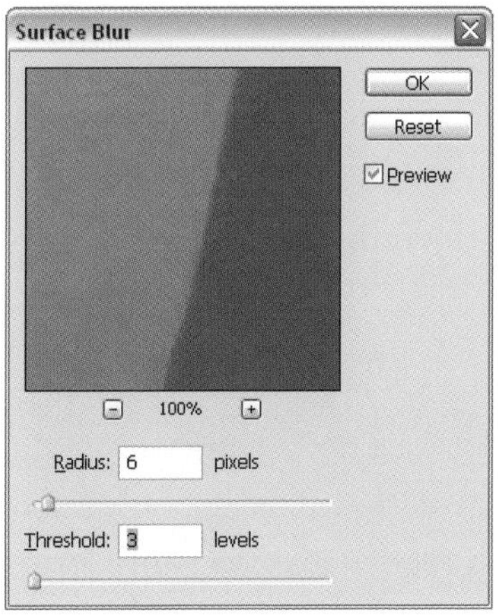

Surface Blur options

The image could still be a bit smoother. Select **Filter > Blur > Surface Blur**. In the dialog box that appears, increase the **Radius** and **Threshold** values by a few pixels, as shown at left. You'll see the effect of this step on the image in the dialog box's preview window. Click and drag the mouse around the window to see how other areas of the image are affected. Once you're happy with the way everything looks, click **OK** to apply the filter.

Here we can see the result of the Surface Blur filter on a zoomed-in portion of the photo.

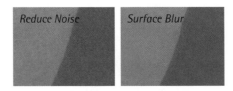

After applying the Surface Blur filter

Take a look at our final image below: a smoother, cleaner photo. If you wanted to, you could take it a step further and sharpen the image as well. I'll show you how to do this in the solution for "Sharpening Images" that follows.

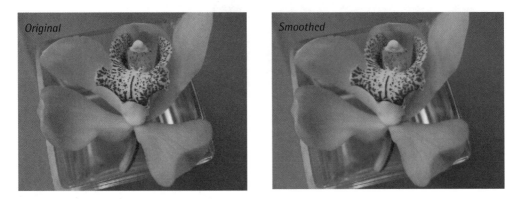

Original photo compared with final photo

Sharpening Images

As you apply filters and make changes to your digital images, you may start noticing that your images begin to lose their sharpness. In this solution, I'll show you how you can sharpen images that have been softened as a result of digital processing.

Solution

Unsharp Mask

Sharpening images is a quick and painless process thanks to the Unsharp Mask filter (there's Photoshop messing with our heads again!). Select **Filter > Sharpen > Unsharp Mask**. In the dialog box that appears, experiment with the settings until you're happy with the result, as shown in the example at the top of the next page. When you're done, click **OK**.

Applying the **Unsharp Mask** filter   Final sharpened image

The example above on the right compares the result of the Unsharp Mask filter with the original photo.

Discussion

The Unsharp Mask finds areas in the image where some contrast exists—usually around the edges of an image—and increases the contrast of the pixels on either side of these areas to create the illusion of a sharper image.

You can adjust the sharpness of the filter by altering the three settings in the **Unsharp Mask** dialog box:

> **NOTE   Just your Average, Everyday Filter**
>
> While the technique I'll show you here is pretty cool, sadly, it's not a miracle worker. If you're trying to sharpen images that were *photographed* blurry or out-of-focus, this technique may not produce dream results. Now if Photoshop could go out and retake the photos for you, it would be another story entirely!

- **Amount:** The amount determines how much contrast is given to the pixels on either side of an edge.
- **Radius:** The radius determines how sharp the edge appears. A smaller radius means that fewer pixels will be affected on either side of the edge, so the sharper the edge will appear.
- **Threshold:** The threshold defines what an "edge" is. A high threshold value requires more contrast in the original image to define the existence of an "edge."

Adjusting Dark Shadows and Bright Highlights

Photoshop has a nifty little feature to help you fix photos with dark shadows and bright highlights.

Solution

The photograph of the quilt below was taken in partial shade. Notice how the quilt appears washed out in areas on which the sunlight fell.

Original photograph

Let's recover some of the detail from those shadowed areas. Select **Image** > **Adjustments** > **Shadow/Highlight**. In the dialog box that appears, check the **Show More Options** checkbox. Adjust the values for **Shadows** and **Highlights**. If the shadowed areas start to look too gray or dull, increase the **Color Correction** amount. Click **OK** once you're happy with the effect.

For additional enhancement, try adding a **Levels** or **Curves** adjustment layer.

The examples at the top of the next page compare my original photo to the adjusted photo. The difference is subtle, but the adjustment allows us to see more of the detail on the quilt, and more of its natural colors.

Shadow/Highlight dialog box

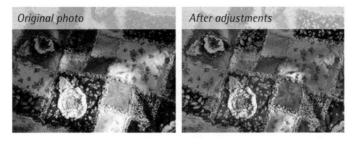

The final, adjusted photo, compared with the original

Summary

In this chapter, we explored the many tools that Photoshop provides for adjusting images. We learned about the powerful Levels and Curves commands, how to add adjustment layers, channel mixing, how to use filters to repair images, and much, much more. With the skills we've learned in this chapter, we can spin the straws of photography into gold, covering the traces of our own embarrassing point-and-shoot blunders, and those of others as well! In the next chapter, we'll explore the tools and effects that can help us to manipulate and use images for web design.

> **NOTE** *Knowing the Limits*
>
> While we've come to expect great things from our good friend Photoshop, it does have its limitations. Unfortunately, even Photoshop won't be able to rescue you from the perils of misguided photography. When using this solution, in particular, bear in mind that Photoshop won't be able to recover detail from images that are too under- or overexposed.

Manipulating Images

In this chapter, I'll show you how you can create your own web graphic effects using existing images, for example, adding scanlines to an image, creating reflections, and "cutting out" objects from a photo. I'll also show you how to remove blemishes from portraits (alas, I have yet to discover how to do this easily in real life!), add color to black-and-white images, and make professional-looking ecommerce graphics. It's a fun-filled chapter! Let's dig in.

Adding Scanlines to an Image

In this solution, I'll show you how to overlay an image with scanlines, as shown below.

Example of a photo overlaid with scanlines

Solution

Start with a one-pixel-wide document that has a white background. Determine how much space you want to appear between your scanlines, then set the height of your document to this value. My starting document is 1px × 1px because I want the spacing between my lines to be 1px.

After you've set up your document, click on the background color swatch at the bottom of the toolbar and set it to a color of your choice (I chose black). Select **Image > Canvas Size** to bring up the **Canvas Size** dialog box shown at right. Add 1px to the **Height**. Your document should now look like the one shown below.

Increasing the canvas height by 1px

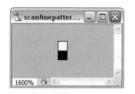

Result of increased canvas height

Click **OK**. The new area will be filled in with your background color.

Make a selection of the entire document using *Ctrl-A* (*Command-A* on a Mac), then select **Edit > Define Pattern**. In the **Define Pattern** dialog box that appears, give your pattern the name scanlines, and click **OK**.

Select the Paint Bucket Tool (**G**) from the toolbox. In the options bar, select **Pattern** from the drop-down menu. Click on the small arrow to the right of the pattern swatch, and choose the pattern you defined earlier, as illustrated below.

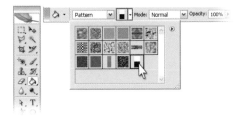

Selecting your striped pattern

Now open the image you want to overlay with scanlines. In the **Layers** palette, add a new layer on top of the image layer. With the Paint Bucket Tool still selected, click once in the document window to fill the new layer with the pattern, as shown here.

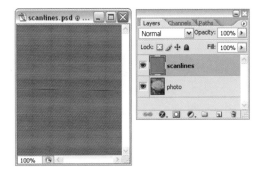

Filling a new layer with the pattern

Back in the **Layers** palette, experiment with the blend mode and **Opacity** value of the scanlines layer until you're happy with the effect. For this solution, the **Multiply**, **Screen**, and **Overlay** blend modes work best. The examples below show how different blend modes and **Opacity** values affect the way my scanlines look on the image.

Changing the blend mode   Comparing blend modes

Discussion

In this solution, we talked about the **Multiply**, **Screen**, and **Overlay** blend modes. They sound great, but what exactly do they do?

The **Multiply** blend mode takes the non-white pixels from a grayscale layer—the layer we set to **Multiply**—and darkens the pixels of the layers underneath. If the blend layer has white pixels, those areas are not affected. So, in this example, setting your scanline layer to **Multiply** allowed the photo underneath to "show through" the white stripes. By lowering the opacity of the scanline layer, we made the darkening effect more subtle. The resulting image with the scanlines is a little bit darker than the original because of the **Multiply** effect.

The **Screen** blend mode could be considered the opposite of the **Multiply** blend mode. In this mode, black areas in the grayscale layer—the scanline layer—allow the layers underneath to show through. Anything lighter than black will lighten the image; white areas will be displayed as white. The opacity of the **Screen** layer in the example at the bottom of the previous page was lowered so that the photo underneath could still show through, and, as a result, the overall image looks lighter than the original.

The **Overlay** blend mode is a combination of the **Multiply** and **Screen** blend modes. Areas that are less than 50% gray will give a screen effect; areas that are greater than 50% gray will give a multiply effect. Images that use the **Overlay** blend mode show greater contrast for this reason.

Creating a Magnifying Glass Effect

In this solution, we'll learn how to use layer styles and filters to produce the cool magnifying glass effect shown in the example below.

Looking for clues

Solution

The first thing to note is that the magnified portion of the image is larger than the rest of the image. It's best to start with a high resolution image, reserve the magnified portion, then resize the rest of the image smaller to create the "background." In this example, I've used a text layer that I could resize easily without losing image quality.

Start with your background image or text on a new layer—I've named mine **text**. We're going to create a magnifying glass object on top of it. (This solution will create a relatively simple magnifying glass, but you can make yours look as realistic as you like.)

First, we'll create the glass. Use the Ellipse Tool (**U**) to create a circle (hold down **Shift** to ensure that the ellipse forms a perfect circle). Next, use the Rounded Rectangle Tool (**U**) to create the handle. The beginnings of my magnifying glass are shown in the example below—you can see that the two new shape layers have been added to the **Layers** palette. We'll call them the **glass** layer and the **circle** layer.

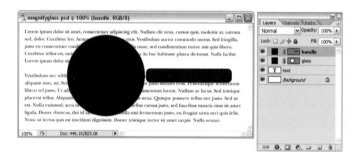

Creating the magnifying glass shapes

Select the **handle** layer from the **Layers** palette and press **Ctrl-T** (**Command-T** on a Mac) to transform the shape. A bounding box will appear around the rectangle. Click and hold down the mouse button outside of the bounding box. Drag the mouse around to rotate the shape. After you've rotated the handle into position, click and hold down the mouse button inside the bounding box. Drag the mouse to move the handle into place. Double-click inside the bounding box, or press the **Enter** key, to complete the transformation.

Your example should look like the image on the right.

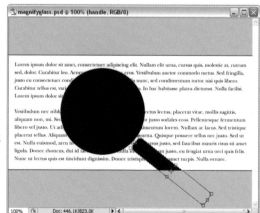

Transforming the handle

In the **Layers** palette, select the *glass* layer and change its **Fill** to *0%*. Bring up the **Layer Style** dialog box by clicking on the **Add a layer style** button at the bottom-left of the **Layers** palette, and selecting **Stroke** from the menu that appears.

Increase the **Size** of the stroke as you see fit, then change the **Fill Type** to **Gradient**, as shown below. Open the **Gradient Editor** dialog box by clicking on the gradient patch. In the **Gradient Editor**, change the white color to a dark gray. Click **OK** to apply the gradient and exit the **Gradient Editor**.

Back in the **Layer Style** dialog box, change the **Angle** to *125°*, so that the gradient starts with a gray on the upper-left and fades to a black on the lower-right. Your image should look something like the one in the example below.

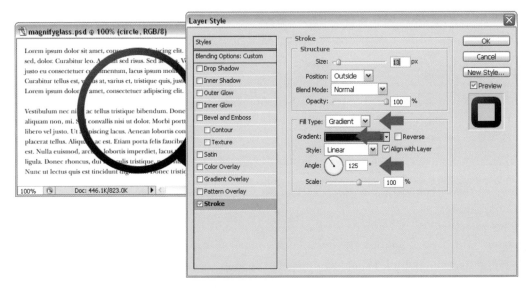

Adding a gradient stroke

Now, select the **Bevel and Emboss** option on the left-hand side of the **Layer Style** dialog box (remember to click on the style name; simply checking the checkbox won't show you the settings you need to change). Make the following changes to the **Bevel and Emboss** settings (these are illustrated overleaf):

- Style: **Inner Bevel**
- Technique: **Smooth**
- Size: *95px* or higher
- Angle: *50°*
- Altitude: *65°*
- Highlight Opacity: *0%*
- Shadow Opacity: *50%* or less

You might need to adjust the **Size**, **Angle**, **Altitude**, and **Shadow Opacity** settings to give the inside of the circle a faint "rounded" shading that makes it appear as though the light is shining on it from the upper-right. When you're done, click **OK**. The example on the right below shows the effect we're aiming for.

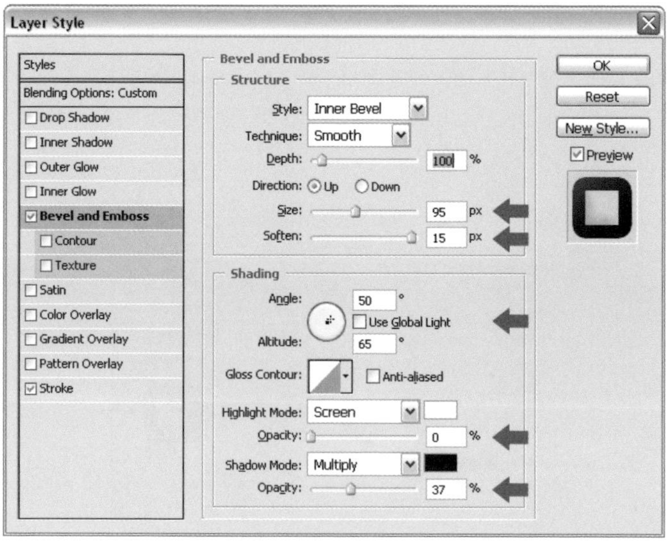

Result of **Bevel and Emboss** style

Applying **Bevel and Emboss** style

Set the foreground color to white, and use the Ellipse Tool (**U**) to draw two highlights on the glass—a larger circle on the upper left, and a small circle on the bottom right. Decrease the **Opacity** of the highlights to **80%** or thereabouts, as shown below.

Let's call on our artistic skills for a second. The highlights are reflections on the magnifying glass, based on the light source that's shining on the object. In this case, our light source, which is behind our point of view, is closer to the upper-left of the magnifying glass and has two reflections. If you're feeling ambitious, find a real magnifying glass and hold it up in different lighting conditions (under light from a window, or from a studio lamp, for example) to see how the reflections look. You can then create your own highlights using Photoshop's drawing tools.

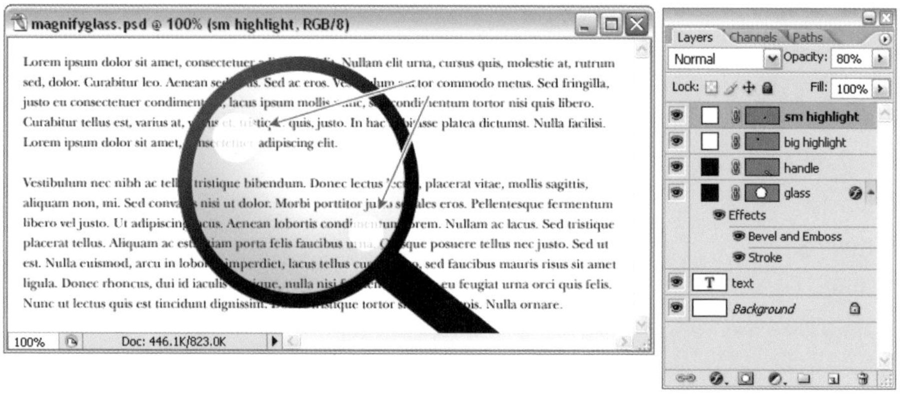

Drawing highlights

Let's add a shadow to the magnifying glass to make our effect look more realistic.

From the **Layers** palette, select the *glass* layer and duplicate it using *Ctrl-J* (*Command-J* on a Mac). Select the duplicated layer and bring up the **Layer Style** dialog box by clicking on the **Add a layer style** button at the bottom-left of the **Layers** palette. Select **Bevel and Emboss** from the menu that appears. In the dialog box, uncheck the **Bevel and Emboss** option, and select **Stroke**. Set the stroke color to black, and change the **Fill Type** to **Color** as shown in the example below. Click **OK**.

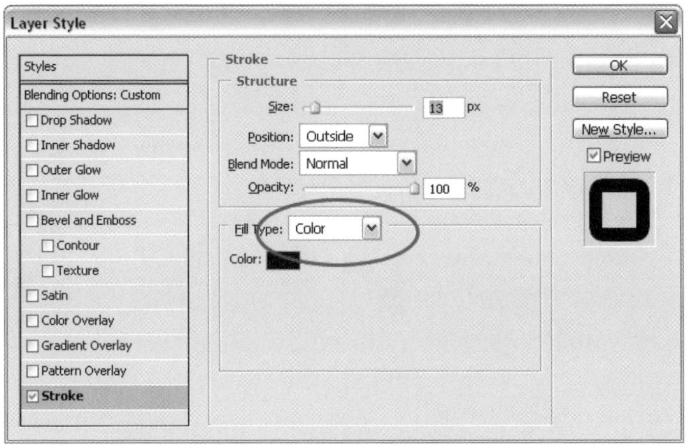

Duplicating the *glass* layer and changing the stroke

Now create a new layer in the **Layers** palette. Hold down *Ctrl* (*Command* on a Mac) and select both the empty new layer and the duplicated *glass* layer. Merge these layers together using *Ctrl-E* (*Command-E*), as shown at right. You should now have a single layer that contains a black circle—we'll call this the *inside shadow*.

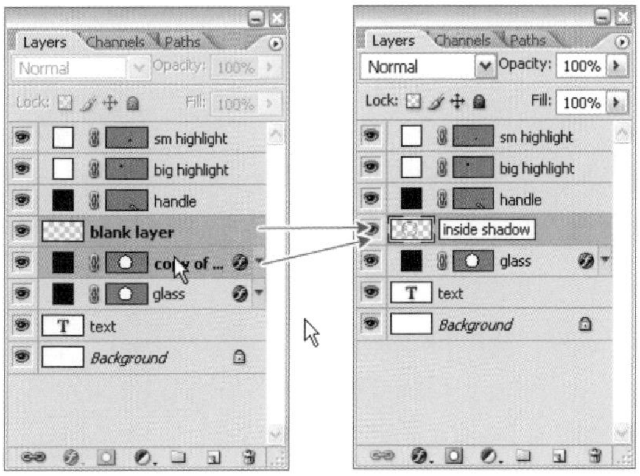

Flattening the ring

Select the *inside shadow* from the **Layers** palette, and transform it using *Ctrl-T* (*Command-T* on a Mac). A bounding box will appear around the circle. Hold down *Shift* and click and drag on one of the corner handles to reduce the size of the ring. Now move the *inside shadow* to place it in a location that's consistent with the light source, as in the example overleaf. When you're done, double-click inside the bounding box to complete the transformation.

Shrinking the ring

Back in the **Layers** palette, hold down the *Alt* key (*Option* on a Mac) and click on the vector mask for the *glass* layer, as shown at right. Drag and drop the vector mask onto the *inside shadow* layer; this will duplicate the vector mask.

Creating the first vector mask

Now duplicate the *inside shadow* layer using *Ctrl-J* (*Command-J*). We'll call this the *outside shadow* layer. We need two shadow layers, since the magnifying glass magnifies the *shadow* that falls behind it, as well as the text. We'll use these two layers to create different drop shadow effects for the inside and outside of the glass.

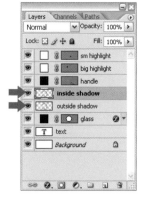

Duplicating the ring

Now we're going to invert the vector mask for the *outside shadow*. To do this, first extend the size of your document's window so that the gray areas beyond the canvas area are visible. Select the Rectangle Tool (*U*), and choose the **Paths** icon in the options bar, as shown in the example below.

Setting the Rectangle Tool with the **Paths** option

Select the *outer shadow* layer's mask by clicking on its thumbnail in the **Layers** palette. Click and hold down the mouse button, and drag the mouse to draw a rectangle that's bigger than the canvas, as shown below.

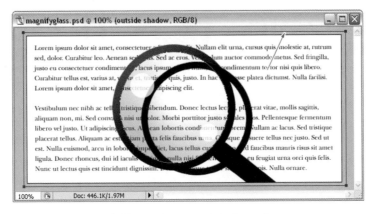

Adding a vector rectangle to the mask

A large rectangle will be added to the existing circle on the vector mask. When two paths intersect, Photoshop inverts the area of intersection. In this case, our *outer shadow* circle is intersecting with the rectangle we just drew, so Photoshop will invert the vector mask for the *outer shadow*. This means that the area *inside* the circle will be hidden, and the area *outside* the circle (but within the rectangle) will be visible. That's why our rectangle needed to be larger than the document canvas—so that everything in our document that's around the *outer shadow* circle would be visible.

Let's look at the result in the **Layers** palette, shown at right. The vector masks for both the *glass* layer and the *inside shadow* layer have white circles against gray backgrounds. The vector mask of the *outer shadow* layer, on the other hand, is a gray circle against a white background. (Remember: gray signifies areas that are hidden by the mask, while white signifies visible areas.)

Inverting the vector mask for the *outside shadow* layer

Now let's make our shadows look more realistic. Select the mask for the *inside shadow* layer by clicking on its thumbnail in the **Layers** palette. Select **Filter > Blur > Gaussian Blur**. In the dialog box that appears, increase the **Radius** to a value that gives your shadow a soft blur while retaining its shape. As you can see in the example overleaf, I've blurred mine by 15 pixels. Click **OK** to apply the blur.

Blurring the inside shadow

Do the same for the mask of the *outside shadow* layer, but this time use a lower value for the **Gaussian Blur**. I've set it at nine pixels, as you can see below.

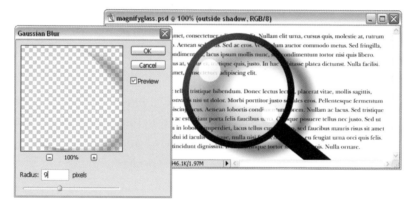

Blurring the outside shadow

Let's work on the handle now. Select the *handle* layer from the **Layers** palette. Bring up the **Layer Style** dialog box by clicking on the **Add a layer style** button at the bottom-left of the **Layers** palette, and selecting **Drop Shadow** from the menu that appears. In the dialog box, decrease the **Opacity** of the shadow, and adjust its **Angle**, **Distance**, **Speed**, and **Size** settings until it lines up with the *outside shadow*, as shown in the example at the top of the next page. (You'll just have to rely on your artistic skills for this!)

You may want to decrease the opacity for both the *inner shadow* and *outer shadow* layers, as shown in the second example on the next page, so that the shadows are subtle and believable.

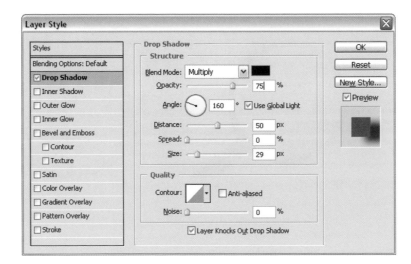

Adding a shadow for the handle

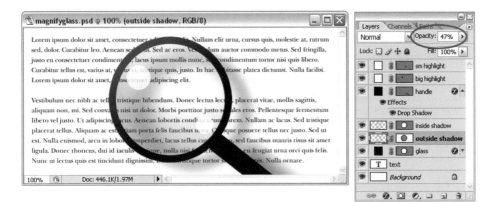

Decreasing the opacity for the shadows

The magnifying glass is done! Now let's make it magnify the text.

At the beginning of this solution, I asked you to reserve a large version of the image that you wanted to magnify. Place this version of the image onto its own layer. We'll call this layer *magnified*. Line up the layer so that you have the part of your image that you want to "magnify" correctly positioned underneath the magnifying glass, as shown in the example at the top of the following page. Your background text (or image) should be on another layer.

Now, create a layer mask so that the circular section of the *text* layer that's underneath the magnifying glass is invisible. An easy way to do this is to drag and drop the vector mask of the *outside shadow* layer onto the *text* layer in the **Layers** palette, as illustrated in the second image overleaf.

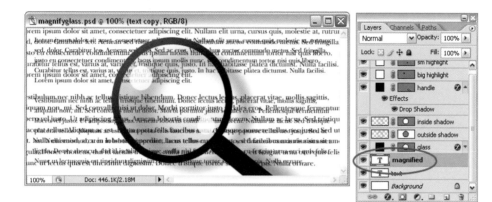

Two layers of text: normal-sized and magnified

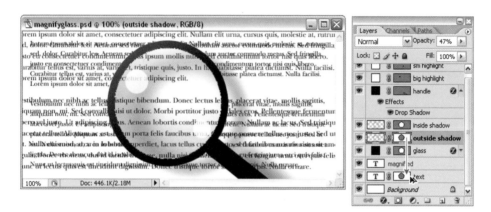

Hiding the normal-sized text inside the glass area by copying a layer mask

We'll get rid of the magnified text outside of the lens in the same way. Drag and drop the layer mask from the *inside shadow* layer onto the *magnified* layer, as shown below.

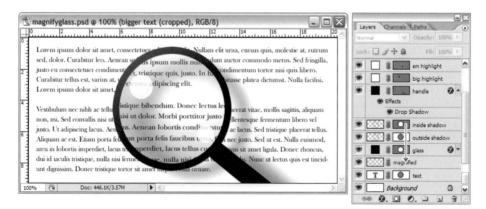

Hiding the magnified text outside the glass area by copying a layer mask

It's looking pretty good, but we're not quite there yet! Let's add a touch of realism to the magnified text. If you're using a text layer, as I am, right-click on the *magnified* layer in the **Layers** palette, and select **Rasterize Type** from the menu that appears, as shown at right. This will convert the text layer to a raster layer. (If you're using a layer other than text—such as a photo—your layer will already be a raster layer.)

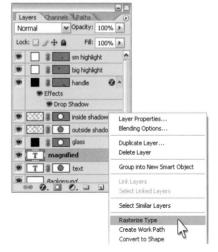

Rasterizing the text layer

Make a circular selection by holding down *Ctrl* (*Command*), and clicking on the vector mask thumbnail for the *glass* layer in the **Layers** palette. Select the *magnified* layer and, with the circular selection still active, use *Ctrl-J* (*Command-J*) to duplicate the selected portion of the *magnified* layer onto a new layer. Hide the original *magnified* layer by clicking on its eye icon, as shown below.

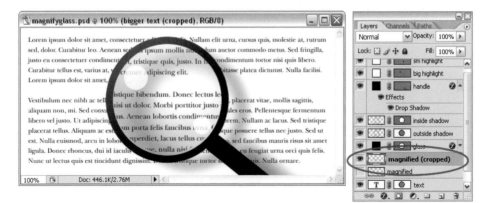

Copying to a new layer

Next, we're going to create a **displacement map**, which is a filter that will distort the words around the edges of the magnifying glass.

Create a new layer and select **Edit > Fill** to bring up the **Fill** dialog box. From the first drop-down menu, select **50% Gray**. Set the **Opacity** to *100%*, and click **OK**.

Filling a new layer with 50% gray

Create another new layer. Make a circular selection by holding down *Ctrl* (*Command*), and clicking on the vector mask thumbnail for the *circle* layer in the **Layers** palette. Select **Edit** > **Fill**, and select **50% Gray** from the first drop-down menu.

Let's recap: we've just created two new layers. The first one is a 50% gray layer, and the second one contains a 50% gray circle, since we made a circular selection before we filled it.

Select the gray circle layer. Bring up the **Layer** style dialog box by clicking on the Add a layer style button at the bottom-left of the **Layers** palette, and selecting **Inner Glow** from the menu that appears. Set the **Blend Mode** to **Normal**, the color to black, and increase the **Size** until a fuzzy, black edge appears around the circle. The examples below show the settings I've used, and their results.

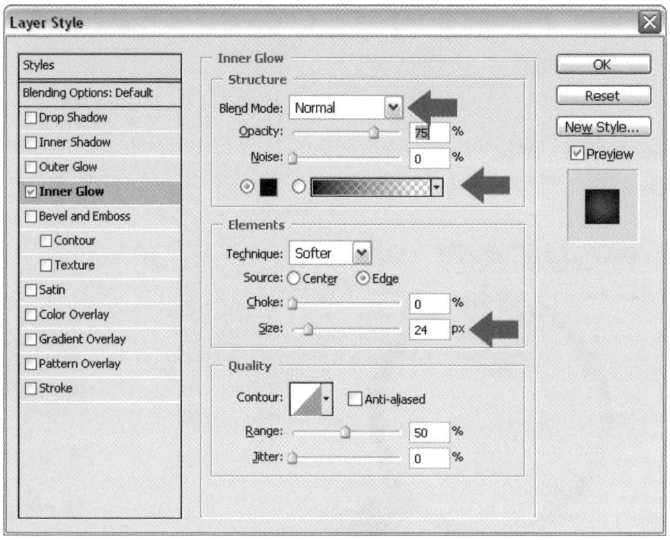

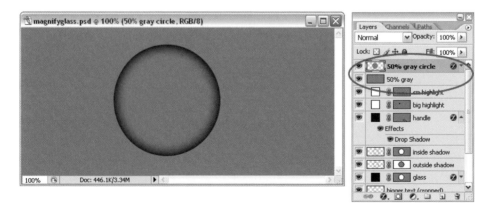

Inner Glow settings

Inner Glow results

Let's create our displacement map.

1   Select both of the gray layers from the **Layers** palette, and merge them together using *Ctrl-E* (*Command-E*).

2   Now make a complete selection of the merged layer using *Ctrl-A* (*Command-A*).

3   Copy the selection using *Ctrl-C* (*Command-C*).

4   Create a new document using *Ctrl-N* (*Command-N*).

5   Use *Ctrl-V* (*Command-V*) to paste the selection into the new document.

This is our displacement map. Save the document (I've called mine *magnifyglass-map.psd*), and remember where you put it!

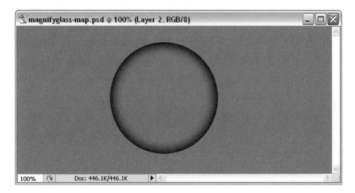

Creating a map file

Close the displacement map, and return to your magnifying glass document. Hide the layer that we used to create the map by clicking on its eye icon in the **Layers** palette.

Select the *magnified* layer, and select **Filter** > **Distort** > **Displace**. In the dialog box that appears, enter a small value for the **Horizontal Scale** (I entered *2*) and click **OK**. Another dialog box will appear, asking you to choose a displacement map. Select the map file you saved earlier, and click **OK** to apply the displacement map. This will make the outer edges of the text appear as though they are bending, just as they would if you were using a real magnifying glass!

Applying the Displace filter

The result? Below we can see the final image, a true masterpiece.

The completed magnifying glass effect

Discussion

Understanding the Displace filter

The Displace filter distorts a layer in your Photoshop document based on the grayscale values from a map file (another Photoshop document). Photoshop uses the displacement map as a stencil to distort the layer to which the filter has been applied. Pixels that are lighter than 50% gray get pushed in one direction, pixels that are darker than 50% gray get pushed in another, and the remaining pixels (which are 50% gray) remain untouched.

In this solution, we created a 50% gray layer. If we'd turned this layer into a map file, applying the Displace filter would have done nothing! However, creating the second layer gave our displacement map a dark outer ring. Those darker areas were used by the Displace filter to distort the text around the edges of the glass.

Thinking Outside the Box

In this solution, we used a combination of Photoshop's filters, layer styles, and other tools in non-conventional and creative ways to achieve our final effect.

For example, while we used the **Drop Shadow** layer style to create a drop shadow for the handle, we couldn't use this effect to provide us with the varying levels of "fuzziness' that we needed for the rest of the magnifying glass. Instead, we created that effect by duplicating and masking a ring layer, and applying to it different levels of the Gaussian Blur filter.

Let's also revisit also how we used the Bevel and Emboss effect in this solution. While the name Bevel and Emboss may lead you to think that you can only use this filter to make solid objects look three-dimensional, we were also able to use it to shade the bottom-left portion of the magnifying glass to a pale shade of gray, while leaving a rounded, clear area on the right-hand side, creating the effect of focused light.

By thinking outside the box (or at least, beyond the name of a tool), you'll find that you can achieve countless cool effects using Photoshop's tools.

Making the Foreground of a Photo Stand Out

Solution

Creating a selection

Using your preferred selection tool or method, create a selection of the object to which you'd like to draw attention, as with my image of a duck on the left.

Saving the selection as an alpha channel

Save your selection using **Select > Save Selection**. In the dialog box that appears, enter a name for your selection and click **OK**. Photoshop will create a new alpha channel for your selection. As you can see in the example on the right above, I've called my selection *lens blur*.

Open the **Channels** palette, and select your new alpha channel. Invert the channel using *Ctrl-I* (*Command-I* on a Mac). This will create a black silhouette of the selected object against a white background, as shown at right.

Inverting the channel

Adding a gradient to the alpha channel

In the toolbox, set your foreground color to black and select the Gradient Tool (**G**). Using the **Foreground to transparent** gradient option, click and hold the mouse button down near the bottom of the foreground object, then drag the mouse upwards while pressing **Shift**. Release the mouse button at a suitable position to create the gradient.

Select the photo from the layers palette. Select **Filter > Blur > Lens Blur**. In the dialog box that appears, which is shown below, select the alpha channel that you created from the **Source** drop-down.

Applying the Lens Blur filter

Change the **Blur Focal Distance** to *0*, and increase the **Radius** until you're happy with the effect (I set mine to *11*). If you're feeling a bit adventurous, you might also want to experiment with the other settings to see how they affect the image. When you're done, click **OK** to apply the filter.

The result is shown below.

Original photo

Lens Blur effect

Effects of using the Lens Blur filter

Creating a Polaroid Photo Effect

Solution

Select the layer that contains your photo. Bring up the **Layer Style** dialog box by clicking on the **Add a layer style** button at the bottom-left of the **Layers** palette, and selecting **Stroke** from the menu that appears. Increase the **Size** of the stroke to *10px* or thereabouts, depending on how thick you want your border to be. Select **Inside** from the **Position** drop-down menu, and set the stroke **Color** to white, as shown in the example overleaf.

The original photo

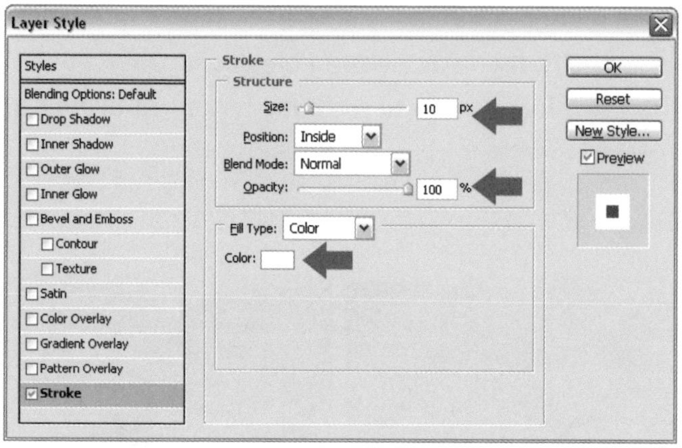

Applying a stroke

Next, select the **Drop Shadow** layer style from the right-hand side of the **Layer Style** dialog box. Keep the default settings of the shadow for now. Click **OK** to apply the layer styles, as shown below, and close the dialog box.

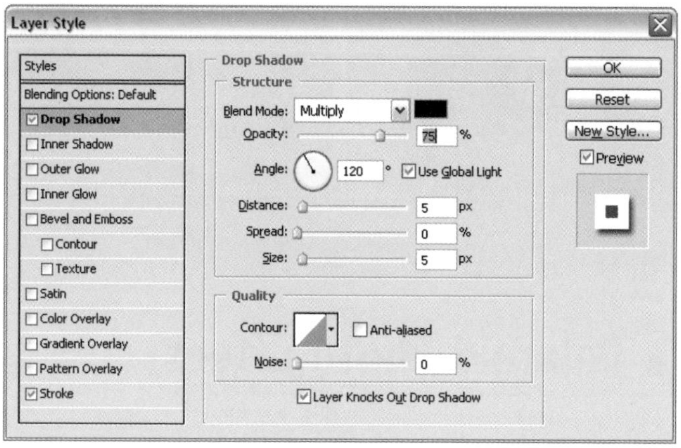

Applying the Drop Shadow style

Free-transform the photo layer using *Ctrl-T* (*Command-T* on a Mac). A bounding box will appear around the image, as shown at right. Use the bounding box to rotate, resize, and move the photo so that neither the edges of the image, nor the drop shadow, extend beyond the canvas area. Resize the image by clicking and dragging on the handles of the bounding box; rotate the image by clicking and dragging outside of the

Shrinking and rotating the image

bounding box; and move the image by clicking and dragging inside the bounding box. Double-click inside the bounding box to apply the transformation.

Right, all we need to do now is adjust the drop shadow. Select the photo layer from the **Layers** palette. Bring up the **Layer Style** dialog box by clicking on the **Add a layer style** button at the bottom of the palette, and selecting **Drop Shadow** from the menu that appears. Alter the values to your liking. The most important thing to remember is that the value for **Size** should be several pixels greater than the value for **Distance**, otherwise the upper edges of the photo won't be visible against a white background. I used the following settings, as shown below:

- Angle: *120˚*
- Spread: *0%*
- Distance: *2px*
- Size: *5px*

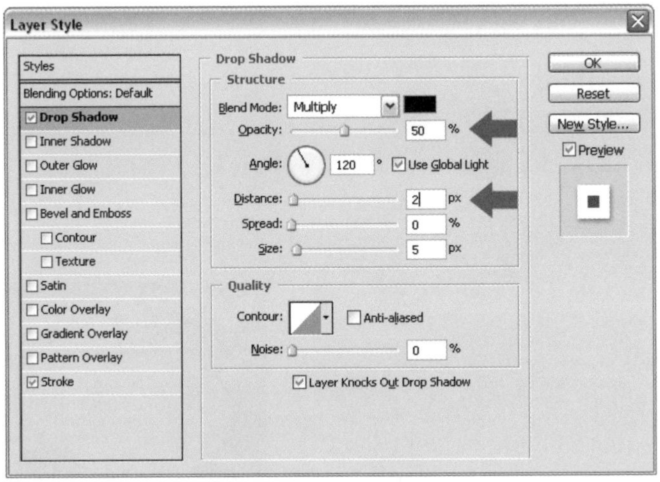

Adjusting the drop shadow

The figure below shows the final result.

The completed Polaroid effect

Isolating an Object from an Image

When you're isolating or cutting out objects from an image, the method of extraction you should use will depend on the image with which you're working. Clipping Paths work best for objects with hard edges, an Extract filter works best with objects on detailed backgrounds (such as hair or branches), and a layer mask will help with those photos in which there is little contrast between the object and its background.

"Can't I just make a simple selection?" you might wonder. Of course you can! However, if the original image is modified later, selections won't always allow for the changes you want to make. The approaches I'll show you here will provide you with greater flexibility.

Solution

Clipping Path Method

As I mentioned earlier, this method is effective for hard-edged objects. Select the Pen Tool (**P**), and choose the **Paths** button in the options bar.

Selecting the **Paths** option for the Pen Tool

Create a path that tightly follows the outline of your object as shown at right. If you need to, zoom in and use the Direct Selection Tool (**A**) to adjust the handlebars for the path.

Creating an outline using the Pen Tool

Select your image layer from the **Layers** palette and select **Layer > Vector Mask > Current Path**. A vector mask, based on the path we just drew, will be created for the layer, as shown in the example at the top of the next page. Notice that my image has a slight color halo.

Creating a vector mask

With the Direct Selection Tool (**A**) I'm going to adjust the path of the vector mask to get rid of the halo. As you can see in the example shown at right, I've moved some of the anchor points inside the edges of the image. We can see what my final extraction looks like here—a nice, clean cut with no halo.

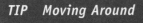

Adjusting the vector mask

The final extracted image

> ### TIP Moving Around
>
> If you've zoomed in and need to move around to view different portions of the image, hold down the spacebar. The cursor will temporarily change to the hand tool, and you can then click on the document window and drag the image around. Release the spacebar when you're done.
>
> You can use this handy shortcut with almost any of Photoshop's filters or tools, unless, of course, you're in the middle of using the Text Tool—then, you'll need the spacebar for spaces!

Extract Filter Method

This method works best for finely detailed objects, such as hair or branches, and images in which there's plenty of contrast between the background and the object that you're extracting.

Before we begin, select your photo layer from the **Layers** palette and duplicate it using *Ctrl-J* (*Command-J* on a Mac) for backup purposes.

Select the duplicated layer from the **Layers** palette, and select **Filter > Extract**. The **Extract** dialog box will appear. Select the Edge Highlighter Tool (*B*) from the left-hand side of the dialog box as shown below, and draw an outline around the edges of the object you're cutting out. Your outline should be thick enough to overlap some of the background as well as the edges of the object, because the Extract filter will be looking inside it for contrast between the object and the background. Use a larger brush to catch finer details, as I've done with the fuzzy stem.

Outlining the object

When you've made your outline, select the Fill Tool (*G*) from the dialog box, as shown in the figure at the top of the next page, and click inside your outline to fill the area you want to cut out.

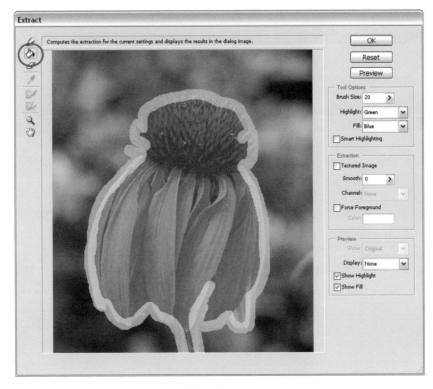

Filling the object

Click **OK** to apply the filter and close the dialog box.

Next, open the **History** palette (**Window > History**). You'll see a list of the last 20 actions that you performed on your image. Click on the column on the left-hand side of the **Duplicate Layer** action, as shown at right.

Setting a state for the History Brush Tool

Now we're going to paint with the History Brush Tool (*Y*). By toggling the column on the left-hand side of the **Duplicate Layer** action, we've set up a "state" for the History Brush Tool—it's going to use that version of the image to paint.

There'll probably be some areas where the Extract filter has erased too much. You can use the history brush to paint these areas *back into* the image. I'd recommend using a smaller brush size to paint back finer details, such as the fuzziness on the stalk. Don't worry if you paint some of the background back in as well—we'll fix that later.

Using the History Brush Tool

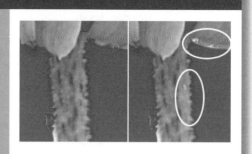

Painting with the History Brush Tool

Finally, we'll use the Eraser Tool (**E**) to clean up any stray pixels around the edges, and to remove any of the original background that we brought back when we were painting with the History Brush Tool. A comparison that shows the result of work with the Eraser Tool (**E**) is shown at right.

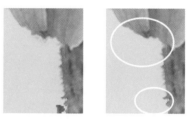

Using the Eraser Tool

Below, we can see the final result.

The image isolated using the Extract filter method

Layer Mask Method

The layer mask method is a bit more time-consuming than the solution we worked through above, but works well with most images—particularly those in which there is little contrast between the object and its background. Take a look at the example at right. I tried to extract the owl using the Extract filter, and found that most of the selection's edges were erased by the filter.

Extract filter results not satisfactory

Adding a layer mask

I'm going to use a layer mask instead. Select the image layer from the **Layers** palette and click on the **Add layer mask** button at the bottom of the palette. Set the foreground color to black, and use a large brush to hide most of the background by painting on the layer mask, as shown at left.

Use a smaller brush to fill in the edges around the object: you'll need to zoom in to get a clean result, as the image at rights shows. Instead of zooming in all the way and using the Pencil Tool to modify one pixel at a time, I've chosen to zoom in partially and use the Brush Tool (B) with a small brush, to keep the edges of the object slightly transparent so that the masking effect doesn't look too stark.

Zooming in for precise brushwork

Clean up the image by using white to paint back the areas you deleted accidentally, and using different shades of gray to get rid of color halos.

Here we can see the final extracted image.

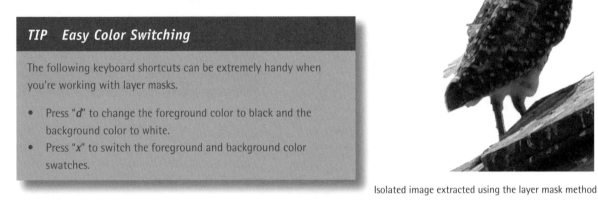

> **TIP** *Easy Color Switching*
>
> The following keyboard shortcuts can be extremely handy when you're working with layer masks.
>
> - Press "*d*" to change the foreground color to black and the background color to white.
> - Press "*x*" to switch the foreground and background color swatches.

Isolated image extracted using the layer mask method

Saving an Object on a Transparent Background for a Flash Movie

Solution

Extract your object using one of the methods described in the solution for "Isolating an Object from an Image." Hide any background layers so that your object layer is the only layer visible. Select **File > Save For Web…**, and save your image as a transparent PNG-24 image. Images saved in the PNG-24 format retain their transparency when imported into Flash movies.

Creating a Reflection for an Image

Solution

To start with, make sure that the object for which you want to create a reflection is on its own layer. Duplicate the layer using *Ctrl-J* (*Command-J* on a Mac). If you're using a text layer, as I am, you'll need to turn it into a vector shape layer by right-clicking on the layer in the **Layers** palette, and selecting **Convert to Shape** from the menu that appears.

Transform the duplicated object using *Ctrl-T* (*Command-T*)—a bounding box will appear around it. Click and hold the mouse button down on the middle control point at the top of the bounding box. Hold down *Shift* and drag the mouse downwards

Transforming the object

until you've flipped the object upside-down, as shown in the example above. Double-click inside the bounding box, or press *Enter* (*Return*) to apply the transformation.

In the **Layers** palette, lower the **Opacity** of the flipped layer to *75%,* as shown at right.

Now click on the **Add layer mask** button at the bottom of the **Layers** palette to add a layer mask to the flipped layer. Add a white-to-black gradient to the layer mask to fade out the bottom part of the layer, as shown below.

Lowering the opacity

Adding a layer mask

In the case of text shapes, you may notice that when the straight edges of the bottom of the object and the top of the reflection line up, the curved letters overlap each other slightly. In many fonts, the curved letters (such as the O in the example shown below) are slightly taller than the rest of the characters. To line them up, you'll need to edit the paths for the reflections of these letters manually.

Using the Direct Selection Tool (*A*), draw a box around the letter to select all the points in its path, as shown at right. Then, press *Ctrl-T* (*Command-T* on a Mac) to transform those points. Drag the top-center control handle down slightly to compress the shape until the top of the shape no longer overlaps the object.

Adjusting the paths of the curved letters

Double-click inside the bounding box to apply the transformation. Repeat this process for the other curved letters.

And *voila*! Our reflection is complete. Below, we can see the final result.

Reflected object

Discussion

If you wanted to, you could add a ripple effect to your reflection. Duplicate the background layer using *Ctrl-J* (*Command-J* on a Mac), then select both the duplicated background layer and the reflection layer from the **Layers** palette. Right-click on one of the selected layers, and choose **Merge Layers** from the menu that appears.

Merging an object into a background.

Now select the merged layer and open **Filter > Brush Strokes > Sprayed Strokes**. Use the following settings in the dialog box that appears (and is illustrated below):

- **Stroke Direction**: **Horizontal**
- **Spray Radius**: *8*
- **Stroke Length**: *11*

Click **OK** to apply the filter and close the dialog box.

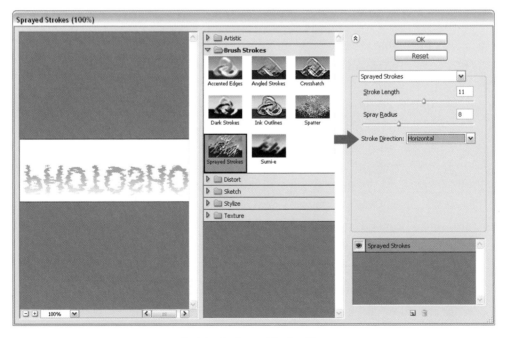

Applying the Sprayed Strokes filter

Your image will now look like it's reflected in rippling water, as shown below.

Rippling reflection

Creating an Image Thumbnail

Solution

A quick and simple way to create an image thumbnail is to select **Image > Image Size**. In the dialog box that appears, check the **Constrain Proportions** checkbox, as shown at right, and enter a **Width** or **Height** value for your thumbnail (Photoshop will automatically calculate the other value).

Click **OK** to create the thumbnail. Mine's shown below.

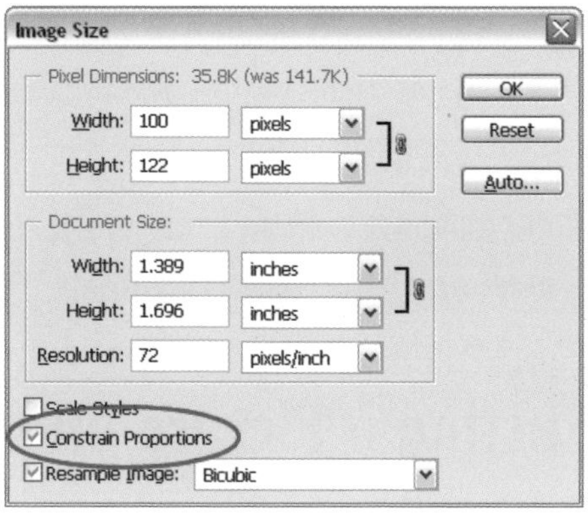

Creating a thumbnail using the **Image Size** command

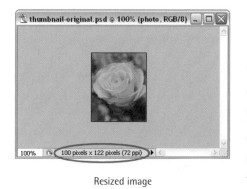

Resized image

You can also create an image thumbnail using the Crop Tool (**C**). Select the Crop Tool (**C**) from the toolbox, and enter the width and height values of your thumbnail in the options bar, as shown below. Make sure that the **Resolution** is set to *72 pixels/inch*.

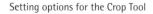

Setting options for the Crop Tool

Now, when you use the Crop Tool, Photoshop will ensure that the dimensions of your final image are the values that you specified, regardless of the size of the rectangle you create with the Crop Tool. This is illustrated overleaf.

Using the Crop Tool to create a crop
that is larger than 100×100 pixels

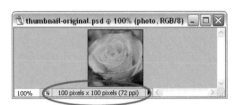

The dimensions are adjusted automatically

Save an optimized version of your image thumbnail using **File** > **Save For Web**....
When you're done, close your original image without saving the changes (unless you
want to overwrite it).

If you need to create lots of thumbnails, you can streamline the process using
Photoshop's batch processing tools. We'll learn more about these in Chapter 9.

Putting a Picture onto a Product Box

Solution

What could be more innovative than a lighthouse-in-a-box? In this solution, I'm
going to place a picture of a lighthouse onto the side of a box to simulate the
packaging of my fantastic new product.

As you can
see from the
example at left,
I've got two
documents
open: one is
my box, and
the other is
the lighthouse
(the image I'm
going to place
onto my box).

The box and the lighthouse

Select the box document. The first step is to measure the size of the box's surface. We'll do this using the Measure Tool (*I*), which can be found in the flyout menu of the Eyedropper Tool. With the Measure Tool selected, click and hold the mouse down on one corner of the box, then drag the cursor along the edge to measure it, as shown at right. The measurement will be displayed in the options bar.

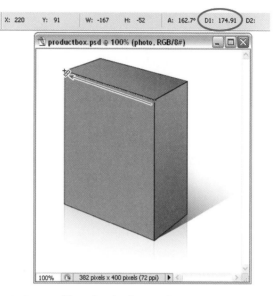

Measuring the distance of an edge

My box measured as follows:

- top edge: *175px*
- right edge: *250px*
- bottom edge: *180px*
- left edge: *240px*

I'm going to use 250×180pixels as the base dimensions for my lighthouse image. However, instead of cropping to these values, I'm going to crop to an area that's 1.5 times larger (270×375 pixels). This will give me the ability to preserve image quality if my image stretches when I'm distorting it later.

Select the Crop Tool (*C*), and enter the dimensions of the cropping area into the options bar, as shown below.

Setting dimensions for the Crop Tool

Select the lighthouse document, and click and drag within the document window to define the crop area of the image, as shown at right. Double-click in the bounding box when you're ready to crop the image.

Make a selection of the newly-cropped document using *Ctrl-A* (*Command-A* on a Mac), and copy it using *Ctrl-C* (*Command-C*).

Cropping the image

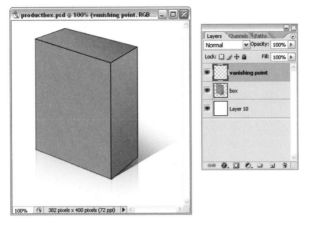

Creating the *vanishing point* layer

In the **Layers** palette of the product box document, create a new layer and give it a relevant name. I've called mine *vanishing point*.

Select **Filter > Vanishing Point**. In the dialog box that appears, make sure that the Create Plane Tool (**C**) is selected, as shown below.

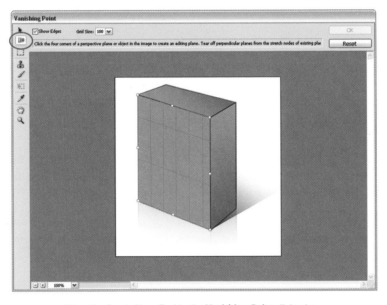

Using the Create Plane Tool in the **Vanishing Point** dialog box

Click on the four corners at the front of the box to define the perspective plane, as illustrated at right. Zoom in and adjust the corners if you need to.

Creating a perspective plane

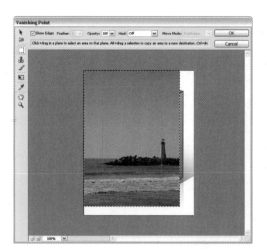

While still in the **Vanishing Point** dialog box, paste the copy of your cropped image using *Ctrl-V* (*Command-V*).

Pasting the cropped image in the **Vanishing Point** dialog box

Drag the picture onto the perspective plane, as shown below. It will snap into place.

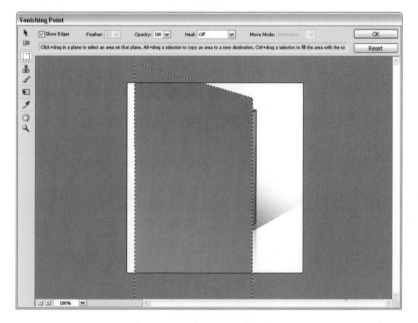

Image snapped to perspective plane

Press *T* to transform the shape. Drag the edge and corner control handles inwards until they are aligned with the edges of the box, as shown overleaf.

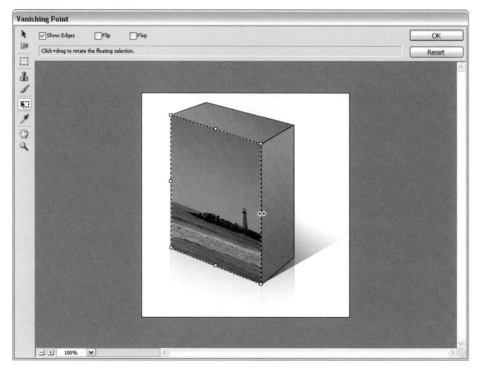

Transforming the shape

Click **OK** to commit the transformation and exit the **Vanishing Point** dialog box.

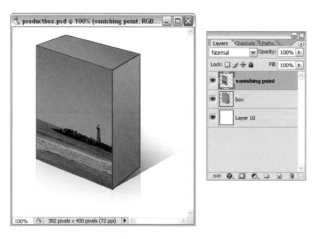

Applying the transformation

In the example above, the product box has a slight reflection. We'll create a reflection of the photo to match. In the **Layers** palette, create another new layer and name it *reflection*.

Bring up the **Vanishing Point** dialog box by selecting **Filter > Vanishing Point**. You should see the grid you created earlier. Press *Ctrl-V* (*Command-V*) to paste another copy of the cropped image into the document. Repeat the transformation, but this time, check the **Flop** checkbox to turn the image upside-down, as shown below.

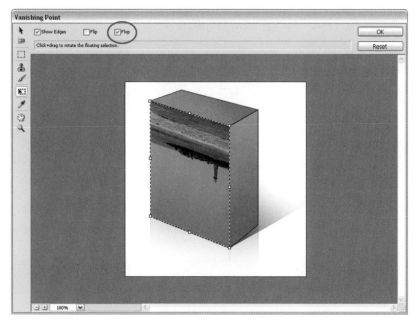

Transforming the reflection layer

Click and drag the image to move it down so that the top edge of the flipped image meets the bottom edge of the box, as shown below. Click **OK** to apply the transformation.

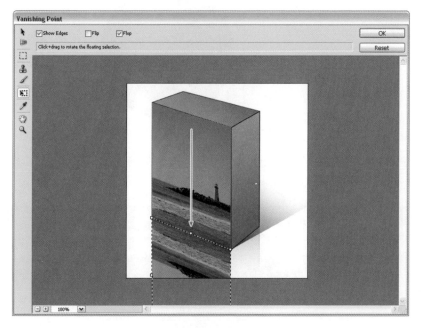

Creating the reflection

Add a layer mask to the reflection layer by clicking on the **Add layer mask** button at the bottom of the **Layers** palette. Select the layer mask and use the Gradient Tool (**G**) to add an angled black-to-white gradient to fade out the reflection from the bottom-left. The results are shown at right.

The completed product box

With this solution, you're not confined to adding images to the surfaces of boxes. You could also put images onto an image of a computer screen, add posters and paintings to images of walls, place your own photos on the covers of books, and even replace someone's picture in a magazine—the possibilities are endless!

Placing a Picture onto a Curved Surface

Solution

In this solution, I've put a logo on a vector shape layer, and an image of a Christmas ornament on the layer below it. I'm going to combine them using a bit of Photoshop magic. As you can see from this example, I've also created a *guides* layer. I've drawn some guides on this layer with the pen tool, to help me align the logo to the ornament. I'm going to hide this layer when the effect is complete.

Text layer, guides, and the ornament

NOTE   Convert your Text to a Shape

If you're using a text layer in this or other similar solutions, you'll first need to turn the text into a vector shape by right-clicking on the text layer in the **Layers** palette, and selecting **Convert to Shape** from the menu that appears. Make sure the text is as you want it, though, because once you do this, you won't be able to edit the text that you originally typed.

Select **Edit** > **Transform** > **Warp**. Your image will be overlaid with a three-column, three-row grid, as shown in the example at right. You can adjust the grid by clicking and dragging on its points. First, pull the corners of the grid in, then adjust the handlebars for each point along the edge of the grid so that the logo curves to match the curve of the ornament, as shown at right.

Warping the right side of the logo

Dragging the center of the logo

Once you've got the corners sorted, adjust the inner parts of the grid. As you can see in the figure at left, I've moved the center of the image down to bend and warp the text to "fit" the curvature of the ornament. Press **Enter** (**Return**) to commit the transformation when you're ready.

There are a few additional steps that we can take to further blend the text into the ornament. In the final image overleaf, I've added some lightening and darkening effects to the logo. We covered most of the techniques I used here in Chapter 6 (have a look at the solutions for "Darkening Part of an Image" and "Lightening Part of an Image" in that chapter).

1   Add a new layer, and fill it with **50% Gray** using **Edit** > **Fill**.

2   Hold down the *Alt* key (*Option* on a Mac) and click and drag the vector mask from the shape layer to the gray layer. (If you aren't using a vector shape, create a selection that's the same size as the warped object, and use that to create a layer mask for the gray layer.)

3   Set the blend mode of the gray layer to **Hard Light**, as illustrated at right.

4   Use the Burn and Dodge tools (**O**) with a soft-edged brush to paint shadows and highlights on the gray layer.

5   Finally, lower the **Opacity** of the gray layer to *50%*, and the **Opacity** of the logo layer to *85%*, for a more natural effect. The results of our efforts are shown below

Setting the blend mode to **Hard Light**

After warp transform   After burn and dodge

The logo successfully placed on the ornament

Making Product Photos for an Ecommerce Site

To create product photos for an ecommerce site, you'll need good quality images to start with. In this solution, I'll give you some ideas for creating eye-catching product images.

Solution

Enhancing Detail in Product Photos

This technique will allow you to enhance the detail in different areas of your product shot. As I mentioned, use a high-resolution image of your product.

Create a new document, and set the dimensions of this document to the dimensions that you'll want your final image to have. Open your product image and make a selection of the entire image using *Ctrl-A* (*Command-A* on a Mac). Copy the selection using *Ctrl-C* (*Command-C*) and paste it onto the new document using *Ctrl-V* (*Command-V*).

Use **Ctrl-T** to transform the selection. A bounding box will appear around the image. Hold down **Shift** and drag the corners of the bounding box inwards until the image is approximately half the size of the document. Leave plenty of room to the right of the image, as I've done in the example at right. Commit the transformation by double-clicking inside the bounding box.

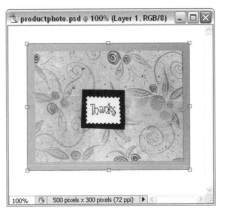

Transforming the image

Back in the document window of your high-resolution image, create a selection of an area that you'd like to use for the product detail, and copy it using **Ctrl-C** (**Command-C**). As you can see below, I've made a circular selection on the top right-hand side of the card.

Copying a selection

Return to the new document and paste in the selection using **Ctrl-V** (**Command-V**). Use the Move Tool to position the selection to the right, so that it overlaps the product image slightly, as shown at right.

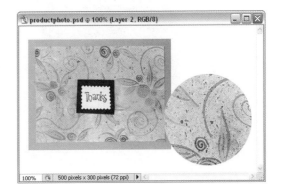

Pasting the selection over the image

In the **Layers** palette, select the product image layer and click on the **Add a layer style** button at the bottom of the palette. Select **Drop Shadow** from the menu that appears to add a drop shadow to the layer. Repeat the process with the detail layer, but instead of applying the style when you're done, click on **Stroke** in the **Layer Style** dialog box to give it a stroke as well.

The resulting image is a neatly shadowed image of your product, with a "magnification" of its detail, as shown below.

A magnification of the product

Labeling Product Images

This technique provides a simple but professional method to assign labels to different features of a product.

Make sure that your product photo document allows enough room for you to add labels to it, as shown below. Resize the document's canvas if you need to. Use the Text Tool (*T*) to add labels that identify the product features that you want to highlight, as I've done below.

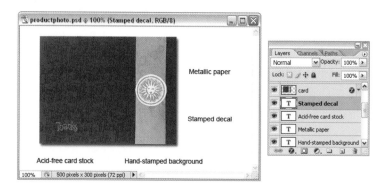

Text labels applied to the product image

Select the Line Tool (*U*). Click on the small triangle to the right-hand side of the Custom Shape Tool button in the options bar. This will display the **Arrowheads** dialog box. Check the **End** checkbox, and enter the following values:

- **Width:** *750%*
- **Length:** *1000%*
- **Concavity:** *33%*
- **Weight:** *1 px*

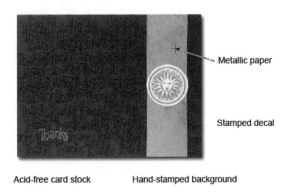

Modifying the Line Tool options

Draw lines from the labels to the corresponding areas on the product image.

Creating an arrow

The end result will be a neatly labeled product image, with arrows that tell you what's what, as shown below.

The labeled product image

Removing Distracting Elements from an Image

Solution

In the example below, we have a nice photo of a flower, but the surrounding leaves and plants draw focus away from it. I'm going to use the Clone Stamp Tool (**S**) to remove these other foreground elements, so that the focus is mainly on the flower.

Original photo

Create a new layer on top of the photo layer. We'll use this layer to hold all our cloned information.

Select the Clone Stamp Tool (**S**) from the toolbox. In the options bar, check the **Use All Layers** checkbox. Hold down the *Alt* key (*Option* on a Mac), and click once on the background area of the image to set up the tool's source, as shown in the example at the top of the next page. As a general rule, set the source using a sample area that's close to the area that you're painting over, as the lighting and color tones around this area will be similar to those of the object to which you're trying to draw focus.

With the new layer selected in the **Layers** palette, click and drag the cursor over the stem to paint over it. Use a soft-edged brush with a diameter of 25–50px (depending on the size of your image) for a subtle, realistic effect. Reset the source after every few brush strokes, sampling from different areas of the background. Preserve finer details by zooming in on, and cloning them, using a smaller brush.

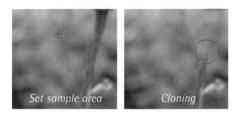

Using the Clone Stamp Tool

The image below shows the results of using the Clone Stamp Tool. I've lowered the opacity of the original image so that you can see clearly which areas were cloned.

Highlighting the cloned areas of the image

The final result is shown below.

Comparing the original and cloned images

Removing Blemishes from a Portrait

Solution

In this solution, we'll first remove blemishes from the portrait in the example below using the Spot Healing Brush Tool. Then we'll use the Healing Brush Tool to get rid of the wrinkles underneath the person's eyes.

Select the Spot Healing Brush Tool (J) from the toolbox. In the options bar, select a brush size that's slightly larger than the blemish you want to remove. Center the cursor on the blemish and click once. Photoshop will magically remove the blemish, as the image at right shows.

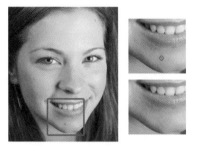

Using the Spot Healing Brush Tool

For large blemishes, wrinkles, or smudges, we'll use the Healing Brush Tool (J). You can find this in the flyout menu for the Spot Healing Brush Tool (J).

Hold down the **Alt** key (**Option** on a Mac), and click in an area that's similar to the area that you're fixing, but has no blemishes or wrinkles. As you can see in the example below, I've sampled the area just below the wrinkles.

Click and drag the mouse to paint over the wrinkles. This process is pretty similar to using the Clone Stamp Tool, but with the Healing Brush Tool, Photoshop takes into account the difference in lighting and color to create a smooth surface. The final result can be seen below.

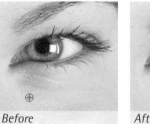 

Before *After*

Using the Healing Brush Tool

Original photo   *After healing brush*

Before and afer the Healing Brush Tool is applied

Merging Partial Scans into a Single Image

If you have a document that is too big for your scanner bed, you can scan it in pieces and use Photoshop to merge the scanned pieces together.

Solution

As you prepare to scan your image, be sure to arrange the different areas of the image on the scanner so that they scan with significant areas of overlap. The example below shows the two scans that I'm going to merge.

Two different scans with significant overlap

Create a new document that's big enough to hold the final merged image. Use *Ctrl-A* (*Command-A*) to make a selection of one of your scanned images, and paste this into the new document using *Ctrl-V* (*Command-V*). Repeat the process with the other image.

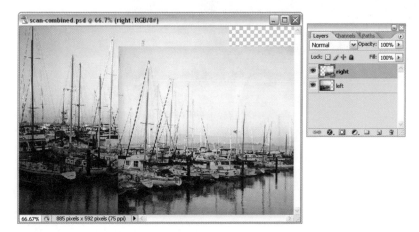

Putting the two scans into one document

To line the images up correctly, lower the **Opacity** of the top layer, as shown below, so that you can see the layer beneath, and move the top layer into its correct position. Don't worry if the alignment isn't exact. Increase the **Opacity** of the layer back to *100%* when you're finished.

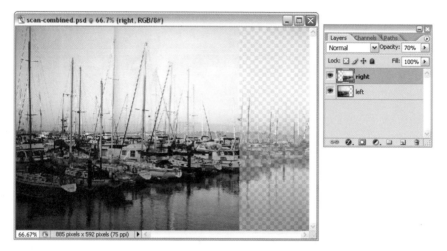

Roughly aligning the images

Use the drop-down menu at the top of the **Layers** palette to set the blend mode of the top layer to **Difference**. This will darken part of the image, as shown below.

Setting the layer to Difference mode

Black areas indicate that the pixels on the top and bottom layers are perfectly aligned. Fine-tune the positioning of the top layer using the arrow keys so that most of the overlapping section is black. It's unlikely that scanned images will give you a perfect overlap, but focus on the edge where the two images are combined. As shown at the top of the next page, the edge of the top layer corresponds to the left of the black area, so I need to align the image so that the region near this edge is as black as possible.

Lining up the images

Set the **Blending Mode** of the top layer back to **Normal**, and see how it looks. As you can see below, my layers do match up, but a faint edge is visible along the top layer. This is because the edge of the photo was raised slightly when I scanned it, so a shadow has been cast by the scanner.

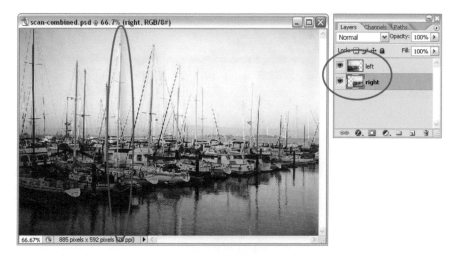

Checking the image

To fix this, I'll just reorder the layers to bring the bottom layer to the top.

Voila! Problem fixed! The figure below shows the final result.

Before and after: merging two images into one

Coloring a Grayscale Image

Solution

In this solution, I'm going to color in a grayscale illustration, but you can also use this technique for grayscale photos. The example here shows my image. As you can see in the **Layers** palette, the image has been flattened onto a single layer.

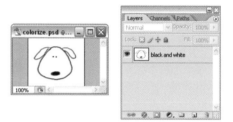

Flattened grayscale image

Create a new document. Make a selection of the illustration using *Ctrl-A* (*Command-A*). Copy the selection using *Ctrl-C* (*Command-C*), then paste it onto its own layer in the new document using *Ctrl-V* (*Command-V*). Set the **Blending Mode** of this layer to **Multiply**, as shown in the example below.

Setting the blending mode to **Multiply**

In the new document, create a new layer underneath the grayscale image layer. Now if you paint on this layer using the Brush Tool (*B*), the color will "show through" the white areas of the grayscale image. Add as many layers, and paint with as many colors, as you like.

My final image is shown below. I've used a blue background, and painted the dog's face and ears using two different layers.

Colored layers add life to a grayscale image

Summary

In this chapter, we really unleashed our creativity! We created a magnifying glass, a rippled reflection, a lighthouse-in-a-box, and added a logo to a Christmas ornament, among other things. We looked at how to use a few more filters and blending modes, and learned to appreciate Photoshop's tools beyond their conventional applications. In the next chapter, we'll look at how we can use Photoshop to create layout comps for web site design—there's a lot more fun to be had!

8 Designing a Web Site

Up to this point, we've covered solutions for creating different graphical and type elements. You've probably amassed quite a collection of techniques by now, and you may be wondering what you're going to do with them all!

This chapter covers techniques on creating web site "comps"—mockup layouts—in Photoshop. I'll show you how to evaluate your layout to determine which parts can be styled using CSS, and I'll also show you how to optimize and save the necessary images from your layout for use on the Web.

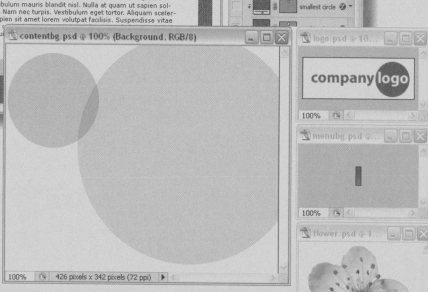

Designing a Web Site Using Photoshop

Let's start by learning how to create a comp. First, I'll go over the concept, then I'll give you a practical example to illustrate the steps involved.

Solution

The Concept

We'll begin by creating a new, web-page-sized document. A common starting size is 750×550 pixels—this will allow you to create a layout for a minimum screen resolution of 800×600 pixels. Create your layout design on this document. The techniques to create navigation buttons, backgrounds, and other design elements that you learned in the earlier chapters will come in handy here!

Once you've completed your design, determine which parts of it will be implemented using web-optimized images, and which parts will use CSS. Consider these questions:

- Will you be able to use one button image for all your navigation buttons? Forget about the button text for a minute. Do all your buttons look the same? If so, you'll be able to use the same background image for all of them, and overlay the text using HTML and CSS.
- Which background images can be tiled or repeated?
- Have you used layer styles or special effects on text? If you can't replicate these effects using CSS, you'll need to create graphics for the text in question.
- What other images will you need to create?

Next, you'll slice, dice, optimize, and save your layout's images. You can do this using Photoshop's Slice Tool (*K*), or by cropping and saving (I'll talk about both these methods later in the chapter).

Once you've saved all your images, you'll be able to use your HTML editor to piece the jigsaw of saved images together. Leave your Photoshop document open so you can quickly access any hexadecimal color codes that you may need for your style sheet.

An Example

To demonstrate this process, I'm going to create a mockup. As I mentioned earlier, my document is 750×550 pixels, and I've set its color mode to RGB by selecting **Image > Mode > RGB Color**.

I've placed each design element on a separate layer so that it's easier for me to extract them later. In the design shown overleaf, I've used many of the techniques we covered in previous chapters. For example:

- I've created a repeating pixel background image.
- I've added an outline (stroke) to the white content area.
- I've created a gradient background for the horizontal navigation menu.
- I've made the circles partially transparent.
- I've created a wrapped text area to hold dummy text.
- I've set the text within this area to be aliased.
- I've cut the flower out from a photo.

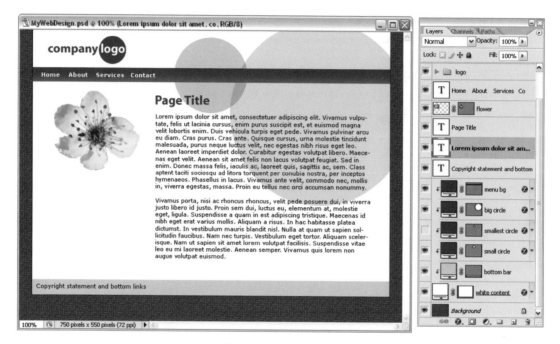

The web site design comp

Now, I've got to decide which parts of my layout will require graphics, and which aspects I'll be able to format using CSS. I've determined the background images I'll need, and the other images I'll want to use—they're shown in the examples on the next page.

I've also made the following mental notes:

- This design doesn't need individual navigation button images. I can design the navigation bar by selecting a background image and setting it to tile in my style sheet, and use simple HTML text links for the navigation buttons.
- I'll need a small image that I can tile to create the repeating pixel pattern on my page background. Fortunately, this won't be a problem—I created this image in Chapter 4!

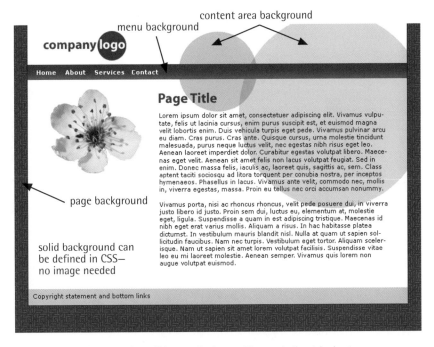

Elements that will become background images in the style sheet

- I'll be able to create the main, white content area, and its small border, using CSS. However, I will need to save the colored circles as a single image, and use this image as the background for our web page's content area.
- I'll need to save the logo as a separate image.
- I'll need to save the flower as a single image.

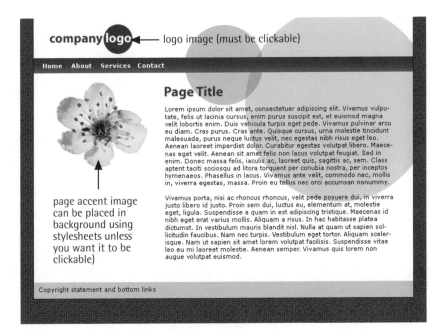

Other images to be used in the web page

- I'll be able to define solid colors, such as the background behind the copyright statement at the bottom of the page, using CSS.

The example below shows all the images that I've saved for my layout.

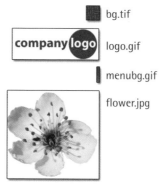

bg.tif

logo.gif

menubg.gif

flower.jpg

contentbg.gif

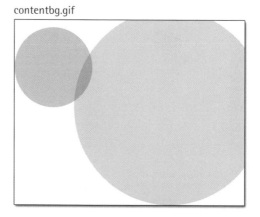

The saved, web-optimized images

> ### TIP   Best Practices
>
> Here are a few tips, or best practices, to keep in mind when you're designing a web site layout in Photoshop.
> - Group related layers together using the **Group** button at the bottom of the **Layers** palette. For example, if you have several layers that comprise your navigation menu (such as the background, the buttons, and the text) then it makes sense to put them all in a group called *Navigation*.
> - Give your layers and layer groups intuitive names. This will make it easier if you need to change an element later, or if you pass on the file to another designer.
> - Use vector shapes instead of raster shapes when possible, so that you can tweak the design more easily.
> - When possible, edit your image using non-destructive tools, such as layer styles and adjustment layers—they'll make your life easier if you need to make changes later on.
> - Allow site properties and considerations to affect your design. For example, if you think your web site will have a long list of menu links, you may want a vertical menu area instead of a horizontal menu area. If you need a super-fast-loading site, stick to solid blocks of color that can be defined in the style sheet, rather than backgrounds that require the use of multiple images.

Right! I'm ready to lay out my web page. I'm going to do this using HTML and CSS, but I won't discuss the details here, as the topic's well beyond the scope of this book. You can see on the next page that I've left my Photoshop layout open while I work on my CSS file—this way, I can quickly grab the hexadecimal color values as I need them.

Finding hexadecimal color values for the design

Discussion

Cascading Style Sheets (CSS) is a language that lets you capture the size, color, font, and other presentational aspects of your web site in a single file (called a **style sheet**). In fact, CSS can also be used to control the position of every element on a page, including the background images for the web page body (or individual parts of the web page).

Using CSS to design your web site gives you the following benefits:

1   HTML files become easier to maintain, because the site's content and structure are separated from presentation.

2   Site-wide changes to the presentation of the site become easier (and quicker), since all of the presentational information is located in one place.

3   Pages load faster, because the style sheet is cached on the visitor's computer and therefore loads more quickly on subsequent visits.

4   The site is more easily indexable by search engines, so it may enjoy a better position in the search results.

5   The accessibility of the site is automatically improved, because an HTML page that is properly structured is more easily navigated by visually-impaired users who may be using screenreaders (software that reads the site aloud to them).

If you're interested in learning more, a great place to start is Ian Lloyd's *Build Your Own Web Site The Right Way Using HTML & CSS* [http://sitepoint.com/books/html1/].

There are many other beginners' books that teach out-dated methods of web design (such as letting a tool generate a table-based layout for you), but this book will teach you to build your site *the right way*, as the title suggests!

Or, if you already have a handle on the basics, but need a CSS refresher, *HTML Utopia: Designing Without Tables Using CSS, Second Edition* [http://sitepoint.com/books/css2/] is a very thorough and up-to-date reference.

Experimenting with Different Layouts

It would be no fun if, once you'd completed your layout, you couldn't do anything else to it! There'll be times when you want to experiment with your mockup layout—for example, moving design elements around or trying different adjustment layers—without losing your original ideas. The Photoshop **layer comps** feature allows you to save the different states of the layers in a document.

Solution

Open the **Layer Comps** palette (**Window > Layer Comps**) and click on the **Create New Layer Comp** button at the bottom of the palette, as shown at right.

Creating a new layer comp

The **New Layer Comp** dialog box will appear. Give your comp a name, and add comments about it if you like. Use the checkboxes to select the information you'd like to save for each layer in the comp (you can choose to save the layer's visibility, its X- and Y-positions, and the styles applied to it). For now, we'll check all three checkboxes. When you're more comfortable with this feature, you may find that you need only to store one or two layer aspects for each comp.

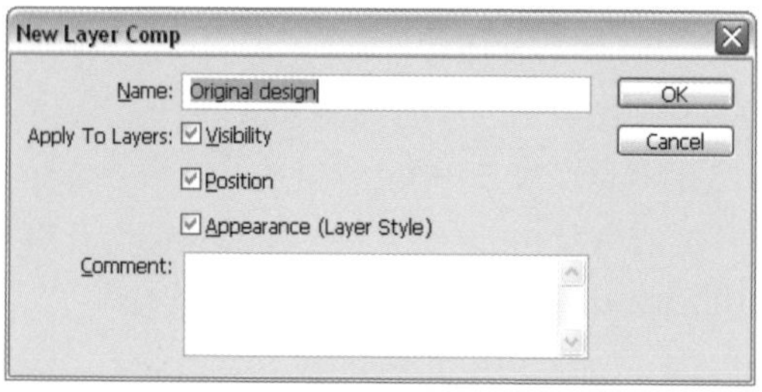

Naming the layer comp

Now create a new version of your layout by reshuffling the document. In the example at the top of the next page, I've moved the background circles, and added a third circle. I've created a new layer comp for this version, called *Three circles*.

Creating another layer comp

You can switch back and forth between your layer comps by clicking in the column next to the layer comp name in the **Layer Comps** palette. For example, clicking to restore the *Original design* layer comp, as shown below, hides the third circle layer, and moves the other two circles back to their original positions.

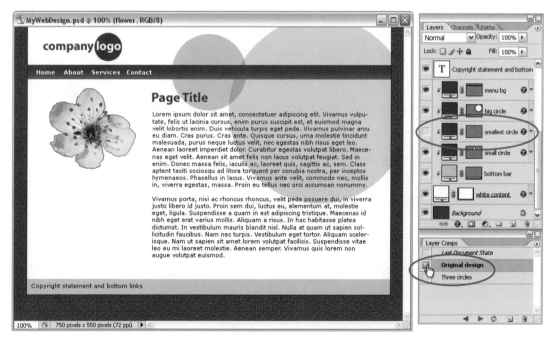

Restoring the first layer comp

Discussion

Layer comps remember a layer's visibility, its position, and the styles associated with it. The key to using layer comps well is to duplicate the layers that you'll be changing, and to create your new layer comp using the duplicated layers. For example, if I wanted to make one of my circles green, I would duplicate the circle, hide the original circle layer, change the circle's color to green on the duplicated layer, and create my new layer comp using the green circle layer.

You can update or resave a layer comp if you've made a few changes to it since you first created it. To select it, simply click on the *name* of the layer comp in the **Layer Comps** palette. Then click the **Update Layer Comp** icon (found at the bottom of the **Layer Comps** palette). Don't click in the left-hand column, as that will restore the layer comp and remove the changes you just made!

Creating Web-optimized Images from a Photoshop Site Mockup

In this solution, I'll talk about two methods that you can use to generate web-optimized images from a site mockup you've created in Photoshop: the slice, and crop-and-save methods.

Solution

The Slice Method

To use the slice method in all its glory, switch to ImageReady. While Photoshop does have its own slice tools, the palettes in ImageReady give you additional options that can make the process a whole lot quicker.

The ImageReady icon

If your site mockup's already open in Photoshop, you can "jump to" ImageReady by clicking on the **Edit in ImageReady button** at the bottom of the toolbar.

Select the Slice Tool (*O*) in ImageReady (the keyboard shortcut in Photoshop is *K*). We're going to create slices that contain the elements that we need, then save them as web-optimized images to use with our web pages.

Create a slice simply by drawing a rectangular area in your layout document using the Slice Tool (*O*). ImageReady will help you create a clean slice by snapping the slice boundaries to the edges of pixels. If you don't want its help, you can turn off ImageReady's snap feature by toggling **View** > **Snapping** or pressing *Ctrl-Shift-;* (*Command-Shift-;* on a Mac).

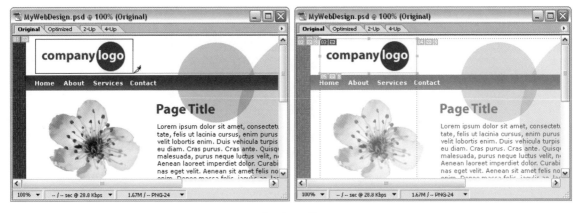

Creating a slice

Move your mouse over the slice after you've drawn it. The Slice Tool will temporarily turn into the Slice Select Tool. Double-click inside the slice to bring up the **Slice** palette, shown in the example below. Give your slice a name in the palette—this will become the filename of your final, optimized image. In the example below, I've called my slice *logo*.

Naming the slice

Create slices for the other elements that you need, and save them. The example overleaf shows the different slices I created, and the names I gave them. I haven't created a slice for the repeating pattern in the background because chances are that the slice I create won't repeat seamlessly. Instead, I've used the techniques covered in "Making a Pixel Background" in Chapter 4 to create a tile image for the background.

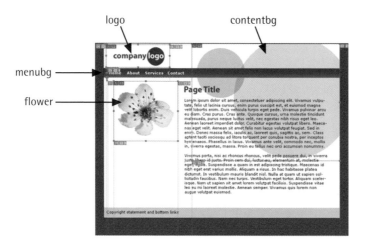

Slices and slice names

Next, open the **Optimize** palette (**Window > Optimize**) and select one of the slices. Adjust the settings in this palette to optimize your slice for the Web. The palette contains options similar to the ones in Photoshop's **Save For Web** dialog box (we covered these in the solutions for "Saving Images for the Web" in Chapter 2). The image at right shows the settings I used to save the logo slice as a 16-color optimized GIF.

Setting optimization options

Creating a new layer comp

When you're optimizing a slice that has objects on top of it, like the *contentbg* slice, you'll need to hide the obstructing layers. This is where layer comps come in handy. Open the **Layer Comps** palette (**Window > Layer Comps**) and click on the **Create New Layer Comp** icon at the bottom of the palette.

In the dialog box, check the **Visibility** checkbox and name the layer comp. I've called mine *Normal*.

Now I need to hide the menu background and text layers. Create another layer comp, check the **Visibility** checkbox, and give the layer a name. I've called mine *Background*, as you can see in the image at the top of the next page.

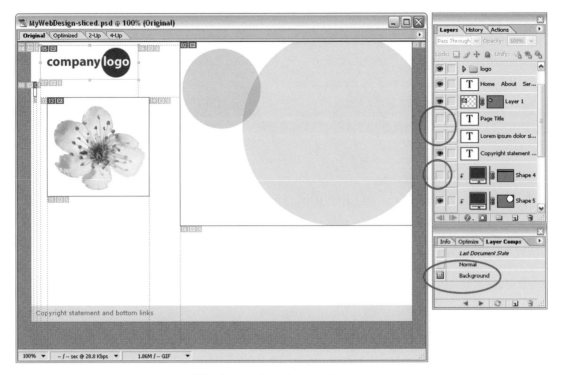

Hiding layers and creating a new layer comp

Now, you can switch between the *Normal* and *Background* versions easily without having to show or hide layers each time.

Another useful feature ImageReady provides is the ability to place slices into sets. This may be useful if you want to group existing slices that are related—for example, you might want to group all the background images, or all the branding-related images.

Creating a slice set

ImageReady makes this easy. To place multiple slices in a set, as illustrated at the top of the following page:

1   Hold down *Ctrl* and select all the slices from the **Web Content** palette.
2   Click on the **New Slice Set** button at the bottom of the palette. The selected slices will be grouped into their own slice set.
3   Rename the set to something more intuitive by double-clicking on its name.

To move slices between slice sets, drag them from one set to another.

You're ready to optimize! We'll save each slice set separately. I'm going to save my content background first. Select **File > Save Optimized As...** and select the folder in which you'd like to save your files. In the dialog box that appears, choose the following options from the drop-down menus:

- **Save as type: Images only**
- **Slices**: Choose the slice set to save. In the example on the previous page, I selected *Slice Set 1*.
- **Settings**: if this is set to **Default**, ImageReady will place all of your optimized images into a subfolder called *images*. If you don't want that to happen, select **Other**, and choose your own location.

Creating a second slice set

Click **Save** to save your slices as web-optimized files. The saved file from my first slice set is shown at right.

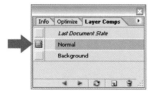

Showing the *Normal* layer comp

Let's save another set. Select the *Normal* comp we saved earlier from the **Layer Comps** palette, as shown above.

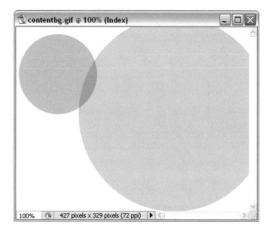

A web-optimized file from a slice set

Again, select **File > Save Optimized As...**. Choose your slice set from the drop-down menu, and click **Save** to save your second set of slices for the Web. This set is shown below.

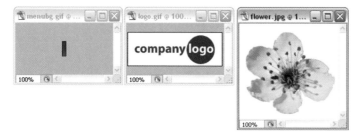

More web-optimized files

The Crop-and-save Method

The concept of the crop-and-save method is simple:

1   Duplicate your web design mockup image.
2   Use the Crop Tool (**C**) to chop out a slice for the image you need to optimize.
3   Delete the layers that you don't want.
4   Export the optimized file.

You can use this technique in both Photoshop and ImageReady. First, duplicate your image by selecting **Image > Duplicate**. In the **Duplicate Image** dialog box that appears, type in a name for the image that you're creating, and click **OK**. As you can see below, I'm saving the *logo* image.

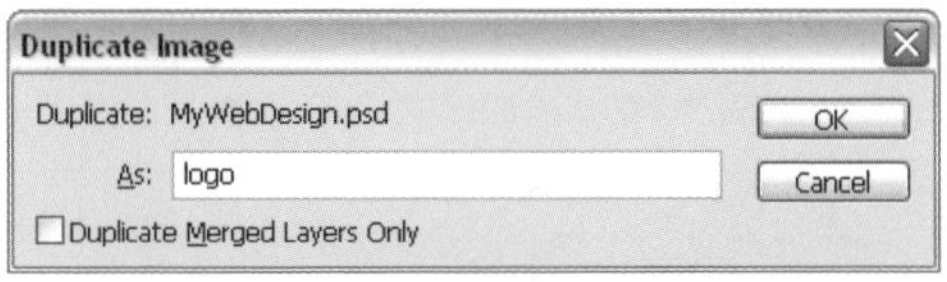

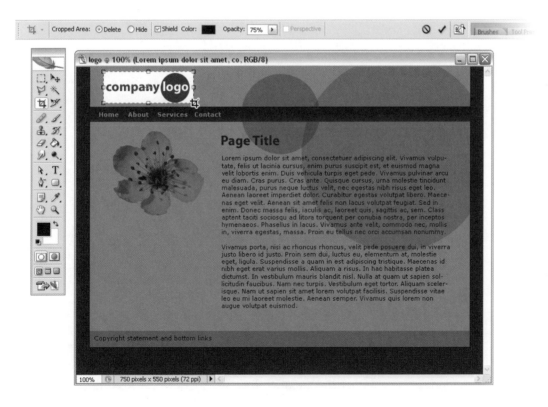

Naming the duplicate image

Now I'm going to use the Crop Tool (**C**) to draw a rectangle around the logo, as shown below.

Cropping the logo

Apply the crop command by double-clicking within the boundaries of the crop area. Then, in the **Layers** palette, select all the layers that aren't needed and click the **Delete Layer** icon at the bottom of the palette. In the example at right, I'm keeping the layers that make up the logo, and deleting everything else.

Keep this

Delete these

Deleting unnecessary layers

Save the file. We're ready to optimize the file for the Web. Select **File > Save For Web…**. Optimize your image using the settings in the **Save For Web…** dialog box, and save your image. The example below shows the Photoshop files that I created for the example site—I optimized and saved each of these for the web individually using **File > Save For Web…** .

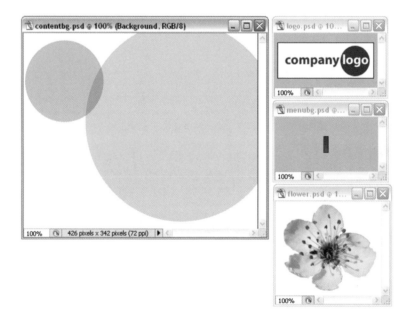

Photoshop files created: *contentbg.psd*, *logo.psd*, *menubg.psd*, and *flower.psd*

Discussion

The slice method works nicely with web design mockups that involve lots of layers, layer styles, and integrated design elements. For example, imagine you've got a box with rounded corners and a drop shadow that you'd like to cut up into a top, a bottom, and a middle image. If you did this using the crop-and-save method, any changes that you made to the box in the future would involve modifying each individual piece of the box, or going through the crop-and-save process again. By using the slice method, you can keep your box intact in one document, and define slices to cut it into the necessary pieces. This way, you'll just need to resave the slices if you modify the box.

The crop-and-save method works well with independent graphic elements. For example, if you had a graphic for a banner ad that you needed to change regularly, it wouldn't make sense for you to open your entire design comp each time you needed to do so. Instead, you could crop-and-save the banner image, then open that file whenever you needed to change it.

However, there are no set rules as to which method you should use—at the end of the day, it all comes down to your personal preference.

Filling an Area with a Pattern

In Chapter 4, we learned how to make a variety of tiling backgrounds. This solution helps you to apply those backgrounds to an area when creating site mockups in Photoshop.

Solution

Open one of the tiling background images you created in Chapter 4. Press *Ctrl-A* (*Command-A* on a Mac) to make a selection of the entire document, then select **Edit > Define Pattern**. In the **Pattern Name** dialog box, type a name for the background, and click **OK**.

Defining a pattern

You can use this pattern with the Paint Bucket Tool, or in Layer Style Pattern Overlays, which we'll look at in a moment.

Select the Paint Bucket Tool (**G**). In the
options bar, select **Pattern** from the **Fill** drop-
down menu. Then, click on the arrow to
the right of the pattern swatch to display
the available patterns, and choose the
pattern you created earlier.

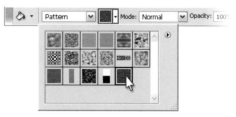

Setting the Paint Bucket Tool to a custom pattern

To use this pattern as the repeating background on a particular layer comp, open the
comp and, with the Paint Bucket Tool still selected, click once on the background
layer to fill it with the pattern.

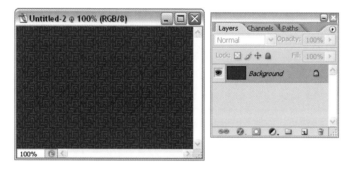

Filling a background with a custom pattern

You can also fill a shape layer with your pattern by creating a pattern overlay for the
layer. Click on the **Add a layer style** icon at the bottom-left of the **Layers** palette. Select
Pattern Overlay from the menu that appears—this will bring up the **Layer Style** dialog
box. In the dialog box, click on the arrow to the right of the pattern swatch and
choose your pattern, as shown below.

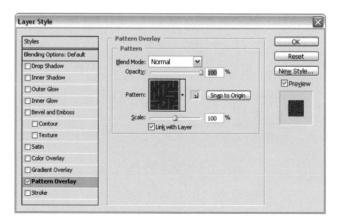

Adding a pattern overlay

Click **OK** to apply the pattern overlay to the layer, as shown below.

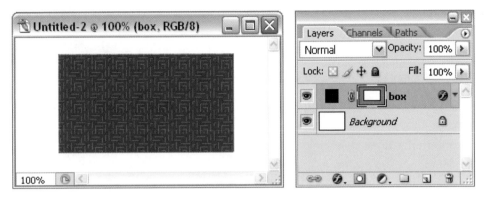

Results of the pattern overlay style

Adding a Shadow Effect to the Content Area

You can make your content area stand out by adding a shadow effect to it, as I've done below.

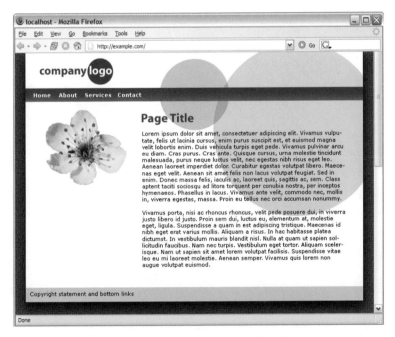

The site's content area, accented with a drop shadow

Solution

Shadow on a Solid-colored Background

Create a rectangular shape layer to represent your site's content area, as shown at right.

Creating the content area shape

Click on the **Add a layer style** icon at the bottom of the **Layers** palette, and select **Drop Shadow** from the menu that appears. This will bring up the **Layer Style** dialog box. Set the shadow's **Distance** to *0px*, and increase the **Size** and **Spread** values until you're happy with the effect. As you can see, I've set my shadow to have a **Size** of *22px*, and a **Spread** of *18px*. The result is shown below.

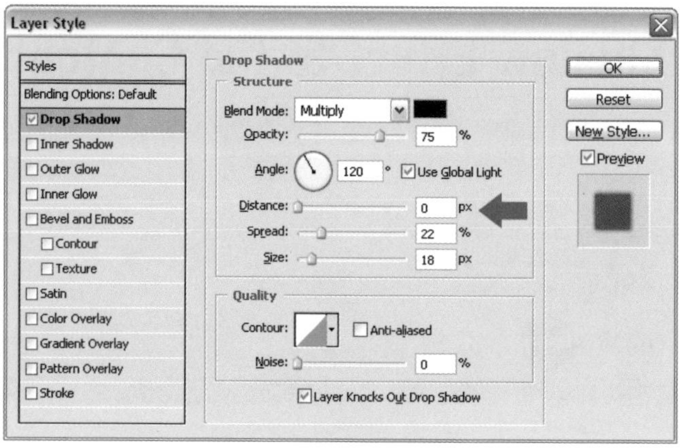

Adding a drop shadow layer style

Content box with drop shadow

Now, create two optimized images using either the slice method or the crop-and-save method (both were discussed earlier in this chapter). One image will become your vertically repeating background image; we'll place the other at the bottom of the content area to complete the rectangle, as shown in the example below.

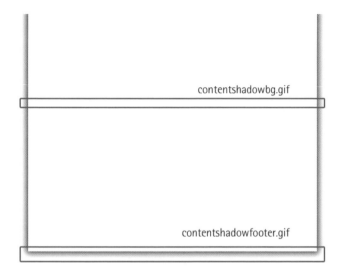

Web-optimized images

To create a shadowed content area on your web page, you'll need to reference these two images in your stylesheet.

Shadow on a Patterned Background

Unfortunately, the solution I've described for solid-colored backgrounds won't work as reliably on patterned backgrounds. Because your web site's visitors will have different screen sizes and browser resolutions, the part of the pattern that falls outside of the content area (and, therefore, outside of *contentshadowbg.gif*) in the saved tiling image won't necessarily line up with the background pattern on the page. In these situations, you'll need to create a fixed background without a footer shadow area.

First, resize your canvas so that it's extra-wide using **Image** > **Canvas Size**. I resized my canvas to 2000 pixels. Fill in the background layer with your pattern, as shown at right (see the solution for "Filling an Area with a Pattern" earlier

Creating the extra-wide background image

in the chapter if you're not sure how to do this), and create your shadowed content area. Create a slice across the width of the entire document; we'll tile this vertically with CSS to create the background image of the web page.

Use CSS to center your background image, tile it vertically, and adjust it so that it does not scroll with the page content. Here's the CSS you might use:

```
html { margin: 0px; padding: 0px; }
body {
  background: url('images/contentsshadowpatternbg.gif') 50% 0%;
  background-attachment: fixed;
  margin: 0px;
  padding: 0px;
  text-align: center;
}
```

Placing a Person or an Object onto a Background

Solution

We'll start with a basic web page header that has been mocked up in Photoshop, such as the one shown below.

Web page header mockup

Take an extracted image (see the solution for "Cutting out Part of an Image" in Chapter 7) and paste it into its own layer in the document. The examples here and at the top of the next page show the two extracted images that I've pasted into my Photoshop mockup.

Adding an extracted image

Overlaying a second extracted image

Creating the mockup in Photoshop is easy enough, but it gets a little trickier when you're overlaying the images across a web page layout.

First, I'm going to create a background image that contains both the top gradient area and the menu bar. Then, I'm going to create a new image that includes my extracted image (as well as portions of the background), and overlay this new image on top of the background image.

The image below compares the slices I would have needed for my original layout with the slices I need for the layout with the extracted image. Once I've optimized and saved these images for the Web, I can reference them in my stylesheet.

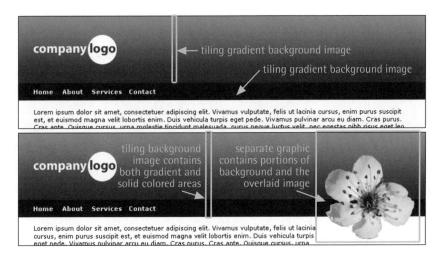

Images needed for the original layout and the extracted image layout

Making Graphics for CSS Rollover Buttons

Solution

Create a new document that's wide enough to hold your button, and about 200 pixels tall. Place your button at the top of the document, and a rollover version of the button towards the bottom of the document, as shown at right.

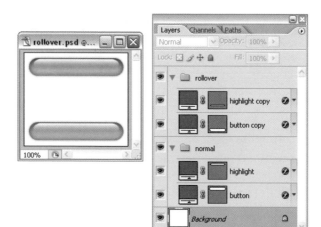

Creating the button file

Save a web-optimized version of your file, then reference the graphic in your stylesheet. You'll need to use CSS to change the background position of the image so that the rollover portion of the button graphic shows.[2]

Discussion

One of ImageReady's primary features is the ability to create different states for rollover buttons. ImageReady will even create the JavaScript functions, HTML, and CSS code for you! It sounds great, right? So, why don't we just use this feature?

Unfortunately, as of this writing, ImageReady's code generators are notorious for creating some pretty ugly code, which simply won't cut it if you're aiming for clean, semantic markup, and a CSS-based layout. While generators may be improved in the future, currently, most web developers find it easier to write their own code, and use Photoshop and ImageReady purely for graphical purposes.

In examples such as this, it's better to create one optimized image graphic that contains both button states than it is to create two separate images, because, if you use the former approach, you won't have to worry about preloading your button images.

---

[2] Be sure to check out Simon Collison's excellent tutorial and script for generating the CSS to create rollovers like this [http://www.collylogic.com/scripts/rollover.html].

Summary

In this chapter, we learned how to tie graphical elements into a cohesive web site mockup. I showed you how to slice and dice your layout comps using the Slice Tool and the crop-and-save method, and how to optimize and save elements to use on your web pages. I also explained a few other tips and tricks along the way to help you convert your Photoshop mockups into fully-fledged web sites.

Advanced Photoshop Techniques

In this final chapter, we'll be covering some more advanced topics, such as task automation, batch processing, and animation. I'll show you tools that will help save both your time and sanity when you're working on tedious, repetitive tasks. We'll do some fun things, too, like creating GIF and Flash animations with Photoshop and ImageReady. Let's get on with it!

Creating Thumbnails for Multiple Images

Back in Chapter 7, we used the **Image Size** dialog window to create thumbnails for images. Here, we'll use the same window, in conjunction with actions and batch processing, to create thumbnails for multiple images automatically.

Solution

I've started with 12 photos of the same size (2560×1920 pixels), oriented as shown at right. I want to create a 150 pixel-wide web-optimized thumbnail for each photo, while keeping the original images intact.

The first step is to create a Photoshop **action**—a saved set of commands for the process. Open one of the images in Photoshop, then display the **Actions** palette by selecting **Window > Actions**. Click on the **Create New Action** icon at the bottom of the palette, as shown on the left below.

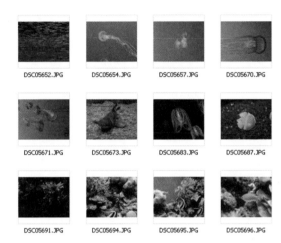

Original photos

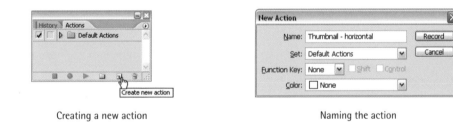

Creating a new action   Naming the action

The **New Action** dialog box will appear as in the example above, on the right. After you've given your action a descriptive name (I've called mine *Thumbnail – horizontal*), click **Record**.

Back in the **Actions** palette, shown at right, you'll see that the name of your new action (*Thumbnail – horizontal*) has been highlighted, and the **Record** button (which was gray earlier) has turned red. Photoshop is now recording your commands!

Record button activated

Select **Image** > **Image Size**. In the dialog box that appears, enter the size details of your thumbnail. As you can see in the example shown at right, the dimensions of mine will be 150×113 pixels. Click **OK** to apply the new size.

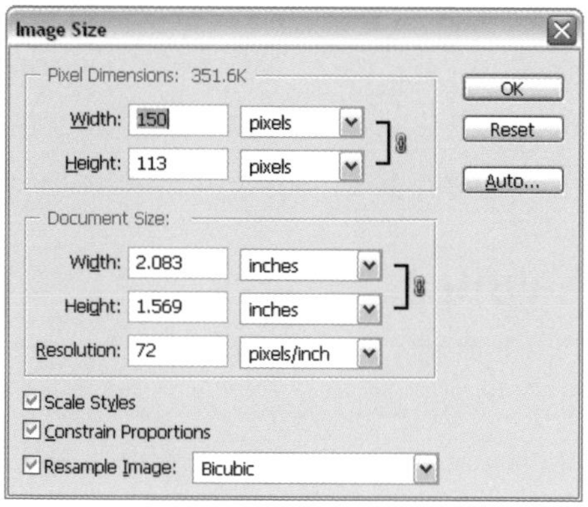

Adding the Image Size
command to the action

Resizing the image

Let's revisit the **Actions** palette. As you can see at left, a new line has appeared under *Thumbnail – horizontal*. This is the **Image Size** command we've just performed.

Now, let's add a command to save our thumbnail for the Web.

Select **File** > **Save For Web...** and choose your web optimization settings. (If you need a refresher on saving images for the Web, see "Saving Files for the Web" in Chapter 1.) Use settings that will work reasonably well with all of your images. I'm saving my thumbnail as a JPEG with a **Quality** value of *60*. When you've finalized your settings, click **Save**.

To prevent your original file from being overwritten, create a new folder called *Thumbnails* to store your thumbnail images in.

After saving the thumbnail, close the original image *without* saving any changes. The process is complete—click the **Stop** button at the bottom of the **Actions** palette, as shown at right, to stop recording the action.

To see your action in progress, open another photo, select the *Thumbnail – horizontal* action from the **Actions** palette, and click on the **Play** button, as shown in the example at the top of the next page.

Stopping the recording

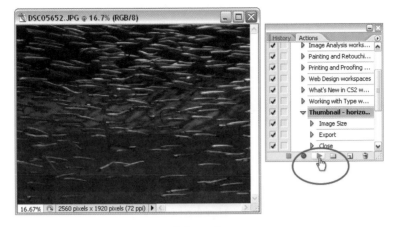

Action replay

Photoshop will quickly run through the steps you recorded earlier. Check your *Thumbnails* folder to make sure everything's in order.

That's your action completed. Now, let's run a *batch command*, which will let us use the action to process multiple images at once. First, make sure that all the photos you want to work with are in the same folder. Select **File > Automate > Batch**. The **Batch** dialog box will appear.

Select your action from the **Action** drop-down menu in the dialog box. As you can see from the example above, I've selected **Thumbnail – horizontal**.

From the **Source** drop-down, select **Folder**. Click the **Choose** button and select the folder that contains your photos.

You'll notice that, by default, the **Destination** drop-down is set to **None**. If you keep this setting, the thumbnails that are created will be saved into the folder that you specified in your action. If you want to save your thumbnails to a different folder, select **Folder** from the **Destination** drop-down and click on the **Choose** button to pick a folder. Photoshop will provide additional options for naming your files.

Setting the destination folder

Click **OK** to run the **Batch** command. Photoshop will apply the *Thumbnail – horizontal* action to each file in the source folder. When it's done, you'll find a collection of shiny new thumbnails in the destination folder!

> **TIP   *Saving Time with Custom Actions***
>
> I've found it useful to create custom actions for tasks that I perform frequently, such as rotating images clockwise or counter-clockwise, then saving to overwrite the original image; or creating thumbnails for portrait- and landscape-orientated images using the method that we used for the action in this solution. It's a great time-saver!

Saving Settings for a Batch Command

Batch settings in Photoshop need to be reconfigured with each new action or process that you run. **Droplets** are mini-applications that can save you time, as they allow you to run batch processes without needing to reconfigure them each time. To use this solution, you'll need to be familiar with creating an action and using the batch command, both of which were covered in the solution to "Creating Thumbnails for Multiple Images."

Solution

First, set up a droplet by selecting **File** > **Automate** > **Create Droplet**.

In the dialog box that appears, click on the first **Choose** button to specify a location to which you want to store the droplet—this could be your desktop, or a special folder. Update the rest of the settings in the dialog box as you would for a **Batch** command, then click **OK** (there's no source folder, because your droplet can be placed anywhere).

Now look in your droplets folder. You'll see a new file that's represented by the Photoshop droplet icon shown here. On PCs, droplets have an *.exe* extension.

Photoshop droplet

Simply drag-and-drop your folder of photos onto the icon to run the droplet. Photoshop will process the photos using the action and batch settings you specified earlier. You don't even have to start Photoshop beforehand: the droplet will open it for you! This provides you with the perfect opportunity for a cup of coffee, and perhaps that nice lunch you keep thinking about. When you return, there'll be a folder of thumbnails ready for you!

TIP Log Errors for Uninterrupted Batching

When you're creating your droplet, change the **Errors** dropdown menu to **Log Errors To File**, and click on the **Save As...** button to specify a location for your error log. This will ensure that Photoshop doesn't stop if it encounters a problem during batch processing.

Instead, it will note the error in a text file and move on to the next photo, allowing you to review and fix the problem later.

Errors: Log Errors To File
Save As... C:\...\My Photoshop Projects\errors.txt

Changing the Errors setting

Pausing an Action to make Customizations

In this solution, I'm going to create a series of thumbnails using the Crop Tool (**C**). I want to be able to define the crop area for each image individually *and* enjoy the ease of batch processing. Will Photoshop allow me do this? You betcha!

Solution

Open one of the photo files for which you'd like to create a thumbnail. Let's record a new action like we did in the solution for "Creating Thumbnails for Multiple Images." Click on the **Create New Action** button at the bottom of the **Actions** palette, and give your action a name (I've named mine *Thumbnail – square*).

Select the Crop Tool (**C**), and change the settings in the options bar to suit your thumbnail. I used the following:

- Width: *100px*
- Height: *100px*
- Resolution: *72px/inch*

Now use the Crop Tool (**C**) to draw a square that defines the crop area, and double-click inside it to apply the crop command.

Select **File > Save For Web...** and save the file. You might want to create a new folder for your saved thumbnails, so that your original images remain unaltered.

Close the file without saving changes, and click the **Stop** icon at the bottom of the **Actions** palette to stop recording the action.

Click in the empty column to the left of the **Crop** action label in the **Actions** palette. A small square icon will appear, as in the example shown at right.

Now, when you run the action, it will pause at the crop step and allow you to customize the crop area, as shown below. After you've applied the crop command, the rest of the action will play on as usual.

Pausing an action to crop

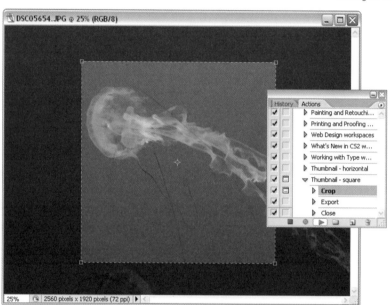

Customizing the crop area

Watermarking Multiple Photos

In this solution, we're going to create an action that will help us to watermark multiple photos. You'll need a separate file that contains your watermark image. The image should have its own layer, and it shouldn't be on the background layer. The example below shows one I prepared earlier.

Solution

Open the photo that you want to watermark. Record a new action by clicking on the **Create New Action** icon at the bottom of the **Actions** palette. Name your new action *Watermark*.

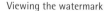

Viewing the watermark

If you're not sure about creating actions, see the solution for "Creating Thumbnails for Multiple Images" earlier in the chapter.

If the photo you're watermarking is a high-resolution file, resize your image to optimize it for the Web. I've adjusted mine to a width of 400px.

Now open the file containing your watermark and create a selection of the entire document using *Ctrl-A* (*Command-A* on a Mac). Select the watermark layer and copy it using *Ctrl-C* (*Command-C*).

Return to the photo document and paste your watermark onto it using *Ctrl-V* (*Command-V*). Lower the opacity of the pasted watermark layer to make it transparent. I've used an **Opacity** value of *50%* for mine, as you can see below.

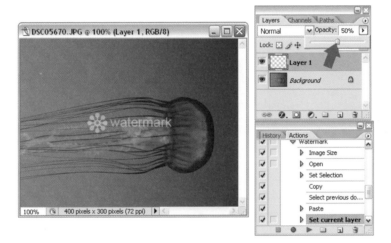

The transparent watermark

Select **File > Save For Web...** and optimize your image for the Web. You may want to save your watermarked images into a new folder, so as not to overwrite the original files. When you're done, close both files, and stop recording the action by clicking on the **Stop** icon at the bottom of the **Actions** palette.

You can now use this action on individual images of your choice, or as part of a batch process. (For a refresher on batch processes, see the solution for "Creating Thumbnails for Multiple Images" at the beginning of the chapter.)

Saving Photoshop Actions

There may be moments during your action-packed Photoshop adventures when you feel a bit generous, and decide to share your clever actions so that your friends can use them, too. Or maybe you just want to show them off! Whatever the reason, if you want to save and share your Photoshop actions with other Photoshop users, you can!

Solution

Create a new set of actions by clicking on the **Create New Set** button at the bottom of the **Actions** palette, as shown in the example on the left below. A **New Set** dialog box will appear, requesting a name for your set. Enter a name, as shown in the middle image below, and click **OK**.

In the **Action**s palette, drag and drop the actions that you want to share into this new set, as shown in the image on the right below. With your action set selected, open the **Actions** palette menu by clicking on the small triangle on the top right-hand side of the palette, as illustrated in the image at the bottom of the page.

Creating a new set	My Cool Actions	Adding actions to the set

Select **Save Actions...**, as shown at right, and specify a location for your actions file. You can save your actions anywhere you like, but if you save them in the default Photoshop *Actions* folder, Photoshop will automatically load them for you when it starts up. (If you've saved your actions elsewhere, you can load them by selecting **Load Actions...** from the **Actions** palette menu.)

The actions file will have an *.atn* extension. You can now send it to your friends, or share it on the Web. Be sure to specify the version of Photoshop you were using when you created your actions, and check with your friends to see that they have the same version as you—your actions may not work for them otherwise!

Saving your actions for future use

Saving Layer Style Sets

In the previous solution, we talked about saving and sharing action sets. You can also save and share layer styles, which can come in handy when, for example, you're trying to explain how you achieved a particular effect to a co-worker who's had very, *very* limited experience with Photoshop.

Solution

From the **Styles** palette, delete any styles that you don't want to save by dragging them onto the trash bin icon at the bottom-right of the palette.

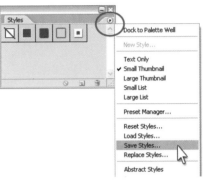

Open the **Styles** palette menu by clicking on the small triangle on the top-right of the palette, and select **Save Styles...** to save the remaining styles, as shown in this example.

Saving styles

Name your customized style set and click **Save**. The file that stores your styles will have an *.asl* extension. If you want Photoshop to load your styles whenever it starts up, save the style set in the Photoshop *Styles* folder; otherwise, save it in a destination of your choice. The next time your co-worker asks you for instructions, all you'll need to do is send through the files!

Discussion

You can save custom-created shapes, brushes, patterns, gradients, and more, using this approach. As well as sharing your files, you enjoy added bonus of having backups of your customizations. However, do remember that some of your shared files may not work with different versions of Photoshop.

Creating a Web Photo Gallery

You may or may not be aware that Photoshop provides automated routines that allow you to create web-based photo galleries, complete with thumbnails, from folders that contain photos. Since Photoshop's automatically-generated HTML contains non-semantic markup, this method is not recommended, but I'll show you how it works anyway. You can always correct the HTML later!

Solution

Put all the photos that you want to include in your gallery into one folder, then select **File > Automate > Web Photo Gallery**. The **Web Photo Gallery** dialog box will appear. Photoshop provides several gallery styles, which you'll see in the **Styles** drop-down menu. Select a style —a small preview will appear in the right column, as you can see in the image at right. I'm going to choose the **Flash – Gallery 1** option. This particular style creates Flash content rather than HTML content.

Setting the banner options

Now, click on the **Browse** button and select the folder in which you keep your photos. Then, click the **Destination** button and select the folder in which you want to save your gallery files.

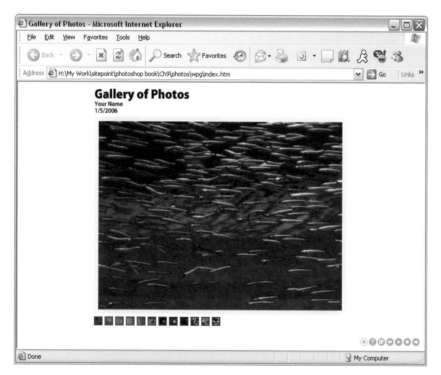

Completed web photo gallery

As you can see in this example at the top of the previous page, I've set the **Options** drop-down menu to **Banner**. The settings that you enter for the banner, including the **Site Name**, **Photographer** and so forth, will appear in the gallery banner area that's been circled.

When you're ready, click **OK** and sit back. Photoshop will open and close several windows as it creates the files for the photo gallery. When it's done, it will launch a browser window that displays your completed gallery.

Discussion

The Photoshop web gallery page templates are stored in *Presets/Web Photo Gallery*, which is in the Adobe Photoshop CS2 program folder.

- On a PC, this is usually *C:\Program Files\Adobe\Adobe Photoshop CS2\Presets\Web Photo Gallery*.
- On Mac OS X, this is usually */Applications/Adobe Photoshop CS2/Presets/Web Photo Gallery*.

If you're proficient with HTML, you can modify the code in the page template files to customize the layouts, but be sure to keep the file and variable names the same. (This only works for the HTML web page templates, not the Flash page templates.)

Saving Multiple Comps for Presentation

In Chapter 8, I showed you how you could use layer comps to save different design mockups (if you don't remember this, see the solution for "Experimenting with Different Layouts on one File" in Chapter 8). In this solution, I'll show you how to save each comp as its own flat image file, so that you can easily present each version of the layout to your client.

Solution

I'm starting with three layer comps—all are variations of the site mockup that we created in Chapter 8. The example below should look familiar!

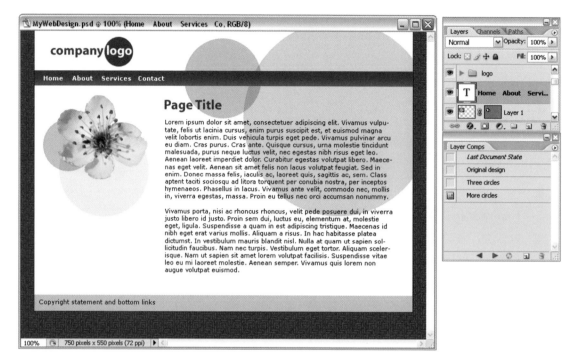

Mockup with three layer comps

Select **File > Scripts > Layer Comps to Files**. In the dialog box that appears, specify your destination folder, and change the **File Name Prefix** to something suitable (the project or client name perhaps). Select the format of your file from the **File Type** drop-down menu, and click on the **Run** button. The image at right shows the settings I used.

You'll see Photoshop open and close windows as it runs through the process of saving your comps. When it's done, it will display a dialog box to inform you that the process was successful. Close the dialog box and use

Layer Comps To Files settings

Windows Explorer (or Finder on a Mac) to open the folder in which your files were saved. You'll see the flat image files of your comps, as shown at the top of the next page.

MyWebDesign_0000_Ori   MyWebDesign_0001_...   MyWebDesign_0002_...
   ginal design.jpg   circles.jpg   circles.jpg

Layer comp files created

You can now email these files to your client, post them on a web site for viewing, or use them in a PowerPoint presentation!

Discussion

You may have noticed that the **File** menu contains two other options related to layer comps:

- **Layer Comps to PDF:** Photoshop will create a PDF slide show of your layer comps. The options for this process are fairly straightforward.
- **Layer Comps to WPG:** Photoshop will create a Web Photo Gallery of your comps. To set this up, you'll need to have a little more understanding of how Photoshop's Web Photo Galleries work. We covered this in the previous solution, "Creating a Web Photo Gallery". Let's look at this now.

As usual, you'll first specify the destination folder in the **Layer Comps to WPG** dialog box, as shown below. The tricky bit is to specify the gallery style in the **Style** field—there's no drop-down menu, so you'll need to type the name of the gallery layout you want to use! (Don't ask me why—perhaps, since it's made everything so easy for us thus far, Photoshop's decided to challenge us!) You'll probably need to launch the **Web Page Gallery** window and make note of the style that you want to use beforehand. In this example, I've used **Flash – Gallery 1** again.

When you're done, click on the **Run** button and Photoshop will create the files your gallery will need.)

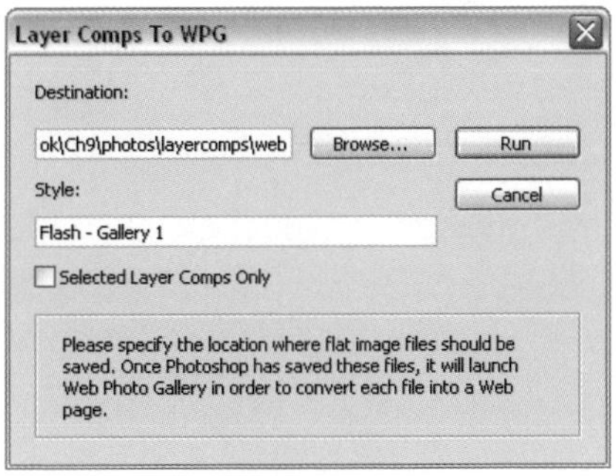

Layer Comps to WPG options

Here's the completed gallery page.

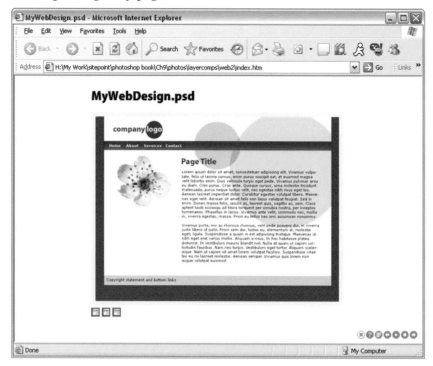

Web photo gallery page created with layer comps

Creating an Animated GIF

You can create animations with both Photoshop and ImageReady. In this example, I'm going to use Photoshop to animate some snowflakes.

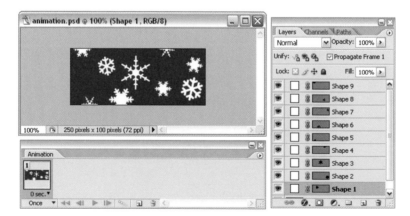

Layered Photoshop document

Solution

Arrange your document so that each component that makes up the animation is on its own layer, and open the Animation palette by selecting **Window > Animation**. If you're unsure of how your document should look, take a look at mine, which is displayed in the example on the previous page.

In the **Animation** palette, you'll see the starting frame of your animation—this is what the animation will look like when it first loads. If it's making you unhappy, reorder, modify, and adjust the layers until you've got something you like. In the example below, I've moved all the snowflake shapes off the canvas so that they're hidden initially.

Photoshop can easily animate layer positions, opacity changes, and layer style effect changes. However, it can't animate changes in shape (known as "shape tweens" in Macromedia Flash). If you've transformed a shape in one frame, the transformation will affect all the other frames.

> **WARNING** *Off Canvas, Still Selectable*
>
> If you're using ImageReady, you'll find that when you move an object outside the canvas's boundaries, you can no longer see or click on that object to select it! This can confuse you into thinking that the object has disappeared, but it's still there. You can select it using the **Layers** palette, and move it using the arrow keys on your keyboard. Once it's back on the canvas, you can select and move it using the mouse as usual.

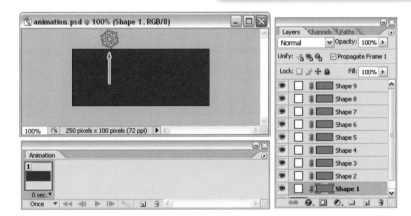

Moving the shapes into the starting lineup

In the **Animation** palette, click the **Duplicates selected frames** icon at the bottom of the palette to make a copy of the first frame, as shown below.

Adding a new frame

Animations proceed frame by frame, so you'll want your objects to move (or transition) slightly with each new frame that you add, until they reach their final positions (or states). Photoshop quickens this process for you with **tweening**: the process by which Photoshop fills in the movement between two frames. In this example, Photoshop will use your initial frame as a beginning point, and your new frame as an end point (or keyframe); it will create the movement between these two frames using the information they provide.

The frame you duplicated earlier is your first keyframe. Move the elements in the layers on this frame to a transition point in your animation. For example, in the image below, I've moved a couple of snowflakes down. I've done this because at this stage, I'd like some, but not all, of my snowflakes to float across the screen.

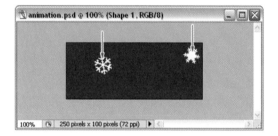

Moving layers in the keyframe

Now we're ready to tween the two frames. In the **Animations** palette, hold down *Shift* and click on the frames to select them both. Then, click on the **Tweens animation frames** icon at the bottom of the palette, as shown at right.

Tweening frames

In the **Tween** dialog box, specify how many frames you want to add—I've added five to mine, as you can see at left. Leave the other settings at their default values for now. Click **OK**.

Look in the **Animation** palette. Photoshop's created the additional frames that were required for the animation to progress between the two frames.

Specifying the number of frames

Photoshop tweens the animation

Continue adding frames and tweening as you need to. As you can see from the example below, my completed animation has 30 frames all up, including several keyframes. If I'd wanted to, I could have produced this animation using only one keyframe, but I've used a few to give myself more control over the animation's timing.

Now, let's imagine that I want to add some text that fades at the end of the animation. When you add a text layer (or any new layer), it shows up on every single frame in the **Animation** palette, as shown in the example below.

Added text shows on every frame

That's not what I want! To get the text to fade in on just the last few frames, I'm going to have to hide it during the rest of the animation. The best way to do this is first to hide the text for all of the frames. Select all the frames in the **Animation** palette by clicking on the first frame, holding down *Shift*, and clicking on the last frame (you'll probably need to scroll to get there). Now, in the **Layers** palette, hide the text layer by clicking on its eye icon—the text layer will no longer be visible on the selected frames, as you can see in the image at the top of the next page.

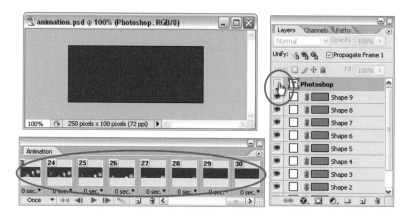

Selecting all the frames and hiding the text

Now we need to delete some of the frames towards the end of our animation—not the very last one, though! Don't worry: we'll restore the animation in these frames later. In the image at right,

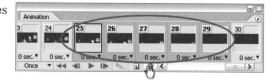

Deleting frames

I deleted frames 25–29 by pressing **Shift** and selecting them, then clicking on the **Delete** icon at the bottom of the **Actions** palette.

Let's make the text layer visible for the last frame. First, select the frame; then, in the **Layers** palette, click on the text layer's eye icon to make it visible within the frame, as shown below.

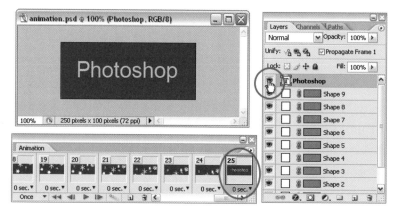

Showing the text layer in the last keyframe

We'll replace the tween that we deleted earlier by adding a tween of five frames between the last two frames—24 and 25, in my case.

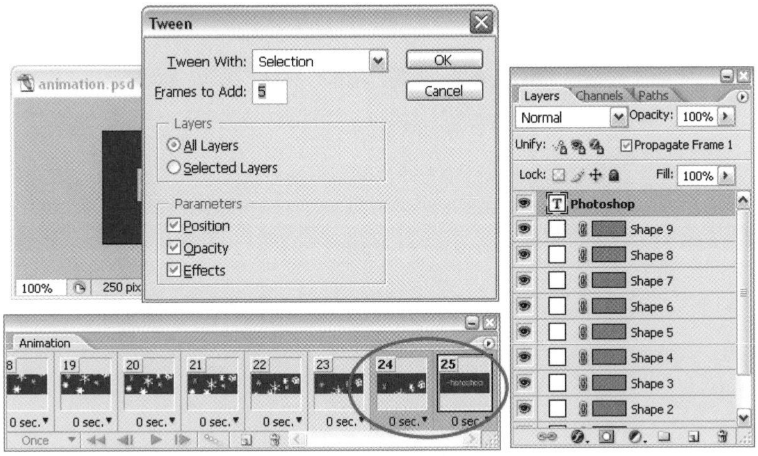

Tweening the last two frames

Notice that, in the tween we've just created, the type layer for the initial frame (24) is invisible, while the type layer for the final frame (25) is visible. Photoshop will automatically apply a fading-in effect to the frames in between these two, as shown in the example below. Check it out by selecting the newly-created frames and having a look at their text layers in the **Layers** palette—you'll see that each layer's opacity has been slightly incremented to create the effect.

Fading in the text

Test the animation by clicking on the **Play** icon at the bottom of the **Animation** palette, as shown in this example.

Playing the animation

You can specify the number of times you want the animation to play by clicking on the small triangle at the bottom-left of the **Animation** palette. This will display the **Looping Options** menu shown overleaf. You can choose to play your animation once only, in an infinite loop, or a specific number of times.

Changing the looping options

That's it—our animation's done! To use it, all I have to do is to save it as a web-optimized GIF. Then, I can add the image to my web site, and watch the pretty snowflakes fall.

The final animated GIF (just a few frames shown)

Discussion

With ImageReady, you can export your animation into the Macromedia Flash *.swf* format by selecting **File > Export > Macromedia Flash SWF**. This will bring up the **Macromedia Flash (SWF) Export** dialog box. For simple animations, the default settings are usually good to go. Click **OK** and specify where the file should be written, then click **Save**. ImageReady will create an *.swf* file of your animation, which you can embed into your web page like a regular Flash movie!

> **WARNING   A Little Less Flashy**
>
> ImageReady doesn't optimize the final *.swf* file as well as Macromedia Flash would, so it may be best to create more complex animations (ones that use larger images and run for longer periods) in Flash itself.

Summary

Now you can tackle large photo editing tasks with confidence and ease! This chapter provided you with all the tools you'll need to automate time-consuming tasks. We talked about actions, batch processing, and droplets. We also learned how to use Photoshop's automated Web Photo Gallery generator. Then we tried our hands at some animation, and discovered that Photoshop lets us create pretty cool animations, and we can use ImageReady to convert those animations to Flash movies!

It's been a chapter of great discoveries—the perfect way to end our Photoshop adventures. Now, it's up to you to expand your Photoshop horizons even further!

Index

BUILD YOUR OWN

STANDARDS
COMPLIANT
WEBSITE
USING
DREAMWEAVER 8

BY RACHEL ANDREW

A PRACTICAL STEP-BY-STEP GUIDE TO MASTERING DREAMWEAVER 8

BUILD YOUR OWN
WEB SITE
THE RIGHT WAY
USING
HTML & CSS
BY IAN LLOYD

2ND EDITION

sitepoint®

HTML UTOPIA:
DESIGNING WITHOUT TABLES USING CSS

BY RACHEL ANDREW
& DAN SHAFER

THE ULTIMATE BEGINNER'S GUIDE TO CSS

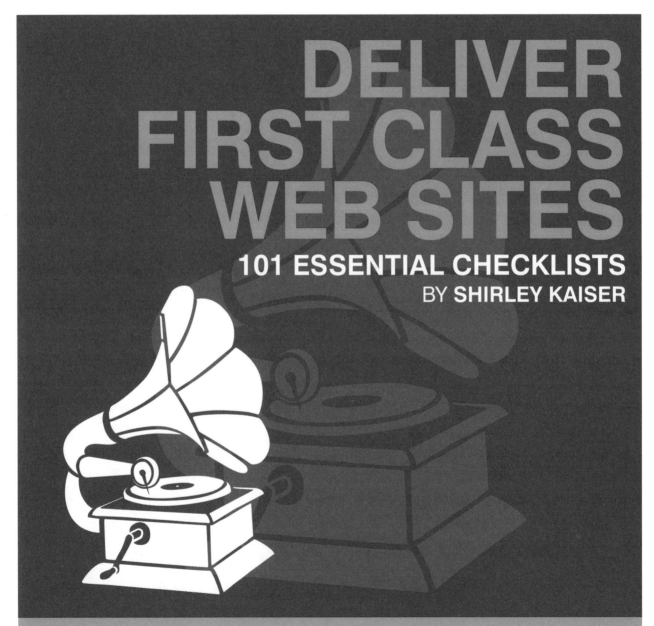

DELIVER
FIRST CLASS
WEB SITES

101 ESSENTIAL CHECKLISTS
BY SHIRLEY KAISER

101 CHECKLISTS FOR WEB DESIGN, USABILITY, SEO, AND MORE